LanCom
Language & Communication

대치동 기적의 중학영어 영단어 1800 3단계

발행일	2025년 11월 20일 1쇄 발행
지은이	더 좋은 교육연구소
발행인	손건
편집기획	김상배, 장수경
마케팅	최관호, 김재명
디자인	보스코
제작	최승용
인쇄	선경프린테크
발행처	랭컴
주소	서울시 영등포구 영등포동 4가 146-5
등록번호	312-2006-00060
도서구입문의	전화 02-2636-0895 팩스 02-2636-0896

ISBN 979-11-7142-094-0 13740

국제학교 학생들만큼 영어를 잘하게 만들어주는, 세상에 없던 대한민국 유일의 주니어용 쉐도잉 & 딕테이션 영단어 교재

대치동, 기적의 중학영어 영단어 1800

하루 20단어, 20문장씩
이미지로 연상하고 듣고 따라하면서 학습하는
가장 확실하고, 놀라운 실력향상 프로그램

AI 학습자료와 인강

세상에 없던 대한민국 유일의 주니어용 쉐도잉 & 딕테이션 영단어 교재

VOCABULARY LEVEL 3
AGE 7-15

정말, 놀라운 대치동 기적의 중학영어 3 STEP 반복 훈련법이 적용된 주니어 필수교재!

LanCom
Language & Communication

국제학교 학생들만큼 영어를 잘하게 만들어 주는, 대치동 기적의 3 STEP 학습법과 훈련법이 적용된
대치동 기적의 속진선행 영재교육 프로그램 안내

대치동 기적의 영재교육 속진선행 PROGRAM

대상 / 단계	속진선행 영재교육	수월성 선행교육	평준화 현행교육
고등 대기고 3단계 8권	초등 5, 6학년 때 완성	중학 1, 2, 3학년 때 완성	고등 1, 2, 3학년 때 완성
중학 대기중 3단계 8권	초등 3, 4학년 때 완성	초등 4, 5, 6학년 때 완성	중학 1, 2, 3학년 때 완성
초등 대기초 6단계 14권	초등 1, 2학년 때 완성	초등 1, 2, 3학년 때 완성	초등 1, 2, 3, 4, 5, 6학년 때 완성

*대치동 기적의 초등영어, 중학영어, 고등영어 시리즈는 대치동 기적의 속진선행 영재교육 PROGRAM에서 사용하는 핵심 교재입니다.

*대치동 기적의 초등영어, 중학영어, 고등영어 시리즈의 핵심 공부법은 QR 찍고 따라하기 입니다. QR 찍고 따라만 해도 기적이 일어납니다!

*대치동 기적의 초등영어, 중학영어, 고등영어의 내용은 인생에서 언젠가 한 번은 완성해야 할 피할 수 없는 영어 학습의 필수 과정입니다. 따라서 최대한 어린 시기에 빨리 완성해야 합니다. 부모가 아이의 언어학습을 미루면 결국 아이는 언어습득을 포기하게 되거나 늦은 시기에 시작한 대가를 치르게 될 뿐 이로운 점은 하나도 없습니다.

대치동 기적의 초등영어 LEVEL CHART

Book Level	대기초 영단어 1800	대기초 통문장 1800	내용
총정리 워크북			국제학교 학생들만큼 영어를 잘하게 만들어 주는 대치동 기적의 초등영어 커리큘럼은 총정리 워크북을 포함해 전체 14권 6단계로 구성되어 있습니다. 먼저 대기초 영단어 1단계와 대기초 통문장 1단계를 한 달에 끝내세요. 한 달에 2권씩 6개월 안에 6단계의 대기초 시리즈를 끝냅니다. 이후 바로 대치동 기적의 중학영어 커리큘럼을 순서대로 공부해 나가면 됩니다.
6단계			
5단계			
4단계			
3단계			
2단계			
1단계			

*대치동 기적의 초등영어는 만4세에서 만12세 사이의 학습자를 위한 교재입니다.

국제학교 학생들만큼 영어를 잘하게 만들어 주는, 대치동 기적의 3 STEP 학습법과 훈련법이 적용된
대치동 기적의 초등영어, 중학영어, 고등영어 시리즈 안내

대치동 기적의 중학영어 LEVEL CHART

Book Level	대기중 영단어 1800	대기중 통문장 1800	내용
총정리 워크북			대치동 기적의 중학영어 커리큘럼은 총정리 워크북을 포함해 전체 8권 3단계로 구성되어 있습니다. 먼저 대기중 영단어 1단계와 대기중 통문장 1단계를 한 달에 끝내세요, 한 달에 2권씩 3개월 안에 3단계의 대기중 시리즈를 끝내고 대치동 기적의 고등영어 커리큘럼을 순서대로 공부해 나가면 됩니다.
3단계			
2단계			
1단계			

*국제학교 학생들의 수준이 되기 위해서는 대기중 공부 시기에 사이먼 미국교과서 100에서 900까지를 병행해 완성해야 합니다!

*대치동 기적의 중학영어는 만7세에서 만15세 사이의 학습자를 위한 교재입니다.

대치동 기적의 고등영어 LEVEL CHART

Book Level	대기고 영단어 1800	대기고 통문장 1800	내용
총정리 워크북			대치동 기적의 고등영어 커리큘럼은 총정리 워크북을 포함해 전체 8권 3단계로 구성되어 있습니다. 먼저 대기고 영단어 1단계와 대기고 통문장 1단계를 한 달에 끝내세요, 한 달에 2권씩 3개월 안에 3단계의 대기고 시리즈를 끝내고 본격적인 수능영어 모의고사 문제 풀이를 시작하면 됩니다.
3단계			
2단계			
1단계			

*국제학교 학생들의 수준이 되기 위해서는 대기고 공부 시기에 사이먼 미국교과서 1000에서 1800까지를 병행해 완성해야 합니다!

*대치동 기적의 고등영어는 만10세에서 만18세 사이의 학습자를 위한 교재입니다.

미국 영국 캐나다 호주 독일 프랑스 이탈리아 일본 인도 학생들이 공부하는 세계 최고의 주니어 영어교육 프로그램

사이먼 미국교과서 시리즈 안내

Dr. Simon's Magic English Series LEVEL CHART

Book Level	Subject	USA Grade in School	Typical Age
1800 1700 1600	 Technology Series	**Grade 6** (Non-native Grade 8-9) 대치동 기준 중학 2, 3학년부터	
1500 1400 1300	 Social Science Series	**Grade 5** (Non-native Grade 7-8) 대치동 기준 중학 1, 2학년부터	**Age 10-12** (Non-native Age 13-15)
1200 1100 1000	 Science Series	**Grade 4** (Non-native Grade 6-7) 대치동 기준 초중 6, 1학년부터	
900 800 700	 History Series	**Grade 3** (Non-native Grade 5-6) 대치동 기준 초등 5, 6학년부터	
600 500 400	 Biography Series	**Grade 2** (Non-native Grade 4-5) 대치동 기준 초등 4, 5학년부터	**Age 7-9** (Non-native Age 10-12)
300 200 100	 Literature Series	**Grade 1** (Non-native Grade 3-4) 대치동 기준 초등 3, 4학년부터	

*CORRELATED TO USA CURRENT STATE STANDARDS

*시리즈 전체 18권을 끝내게 되면 TOEFL READING과 LISTENING 섹션의 만점과 대한민국 수능영어 절대 1등급의 영어실력 달성이 가능합니다.

VOCA 100-900		**VOCABULARY BOOK 100-900** 사이먼 미국교과서 100에서 900까지의 어휘를 총정리한 영영 사전식 단어장 겸 테스트 북
VOCA 1000-1800		**VOCABULARY BOOK 1000-1800** 사이먼 미국교과서 1000에서 1800까지의 어휘를 총정리한 영영 사전식 단어장 겸 테스트 북

첨단기술 시리즈

기술적인 문해력 향상과 디지털 시민성 개발, 창의적인 문제 해결능력과 혁신력 발전, 직업적인 진로 방향성 인식과 미래 직업 시장에 대한 이해, 윤리적인 기술의 사용과 기술의 사회적 영향에 대한 이해를 목적으로 하는 시리즈

사회과학 시리즈

사회적인 현상과 인간관계에 대한 이해, 세계 문화의 이해와 다양성 인식, 시민의식과 공동체 참여의식 향상, 현재와 미래 사회 변화에 대한 이해, 분쟁의 해결능력과 비판적 사고능력의 발달을 목적으로 하는 시리즈

과학 시리즈

탐구적인 태도와 호기심 개발, 문제 해결능력과 비판적 사고능력 발달, 과학적 사고와 관련된 기술과 지식 습득, 인간의 신체와 자연과 환경에 대한 이해와 지속 가능성 인식, 미래 직업적 가능성과 **STEM** 분야에 대한 이해를 목적으로 하는 시리즈

역사 시리즈

역사인식과 시대상황의 이해, 문화적인 다양성 인정과 세계 시민성 강화, 과거의 실수로부터 배우는 교훈과 상식 습득, 시간과 사건의 원인 · 결과 관계 이해, 역사적인 연속성 속에서 자아 정체성 구축을 목적으로 하는 시리즈

인물전기 시리즈

인류를 이끈 위대한 위인들의 소개, 영감을 주는 역사적 롤 모델의 제시, 도덕적 가치와 성찰의 중요성 인식, 인내와 끈기와 근성의 가치 습득, 역사적인 인물들이 인류사회에 끼친 사회적 영향력 이해를 목적으로 하는 시리즈

문학 시리즈

문학적 지식의 향상과 언어 기술의 개발, 인간의 경험과 감정에 대한 이해, 비판적 사고와 분석력 개발, 창의적인 사고와 상상력 발달을 목적으로 하는 시리즈

5회 반복 표제어 QR   5회 반복 예문 QR

DAY 01

30 days

AI 학습자료와 인강 youpass.co.kr

PREVIEW A 다음 단어의 뜻을 한국어로 써보세요.

□ planet ______	□ policy ______
□ pleasure ______	□ polish ______
□ plenty ______	□ political ______
□ plot ______	□ politics ______
□ plural ______	□ poll ______
□ poet ______	□ pollute ______
□ poetry ______	□ pollution ______
□ poison ______	□ popularity ______
□ polar ______	□ population ______
□ pole ______	□ portion ______

PREVIEW B 사진을 보고 알맞은 영어 단어를 **PREVIEW A**에서 찾아 써보세요.

______

______

______

______

1201 ☐☐☐

planet
[ˈplænɪt]

n 행성

= **world, globe, celestial body, orb**

\+ **planetary** **a** 행성의

Q: Have you ever thought about living on another planet?
다른 행성에서 사는 것에 대해 생각해 본 적이 있나요?

A: ....

1202 ☐☐☐

pleasure
[ˈpleʒər]

n 기쁨, 즐거움

= **delight, joy, enjoyment, satisfaction, gratification**

\+ **please** **v** 기쁘게 하다 **pleasant** **a** 즐거운 **pleased** **a** 기쁜 **pleasantly** **adv** 즐겁게

Q: Is it a pleasure to work with your new colleagues?
새 동료들과 일하는 것이 즐거운가요?

A: ....

1203 ☐☐☐

plenty
[ˈplenti]

n 많음, 풍부함 **adv** 충분히

= **abundance, ample, sufficient, copious, numerous**

\+ **plentiful** **a** 풍부한

Q: Do you have plenty of time to finish the project before deadline?
마감 기한 전에 프로젝트를 마칠 시간이 충분한가요?

A: ....

1204 ☐☐☐

plot
[plɑːt]

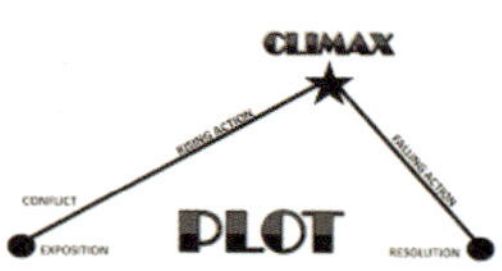

n 줄거리, 음모, 작은 땅 **v** 음모를 꾸미다

= **storyline, scheme, conspiracy, land, map, plan**

\+ **an involved plot** 복잡한 줄거리

Q: Can you explain the plot of the movie you watched last night?
어젯밤 본 영화의 줄거리를 설명해 줄 수 있나요?

A: ....

1205 ☐☐☐

plural
[ˈplʊrəl]

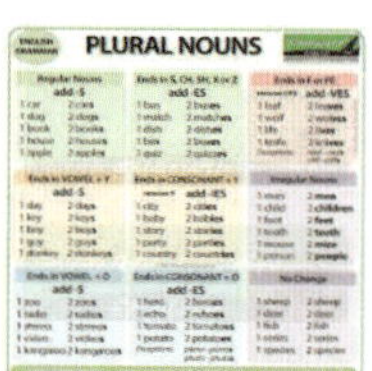

a 복수의 **n** 복수형

= **multiple, more than one, diverse**

\+ **plurality** **n** 다수

Q: Do you know the plural forms of all the irregular nouns?
모든 불규칙 명사의 복수형을 아나요?

A: ....

1206 □□□

poet
['poʊɪt]

n 시인

= writer, versifier, bard, lyricist

+ poetry n 시 poem n 시 poetic a 시적인

Q: Who is your favorite poet and why do you admire their work?
가장 좋아하는 시인은 누구이고, 그들의 작품을 왜 존경하나요?

A: ....

1207 □□□

poetry
['poʊɪtri]

Putting words
On paper to
Express in part
Thoughts from me
Right to
Your heart

n 시, 운문

= verse, poems, prose, rhymes

+ poet n 시인 poem n 시 poetic a 시적인

Q: Did you enjoy reading poetry during your literature classes?
문학 수업 시간 동안 시 읽는 것을 즐겼나요?

A: ....

1208 □□□

poison
['pɔɪzn]

n 독 v 독살하다, 해치다

= toxin, venom, bane, contaminate, corrupt

+ poisonous a 유독한

Q: Did the detectives suspect that the victim was poisoned?
형사들은 피해자가 독살되었다고 의심했나요?

A: ....

1209 □□□

polar
['poʊlər]

a 극지방의, 극의

= extreme, opposing, arctic, frigid

+ pole n 극, 기둥 polarity n 극성

Q: Have you learned about polar bears and their habitat in school?
학교에서 북극곰과 그들의 서식지에 대해 배웠나요?

A: ....

1210 □□□

pole
[poʊl]

n 막대기, (지구나 자석의) 극

= post, rod, axis, extremity, terminal

+ polar a 극지방의, 양극의

Q: Did the explorers reach the North Pole during their expedition?
탐험하는 동안 그 탐험가들이 북극에 도달했나요?

A: ....

1211 □□□

policy
[ˈpɑːləsi]

n 정책, 방침

= rule, guideline, strategy, principle, plan
+ insurance policy 보험 증권[증서]

Q: What is your company's policy on remote work and flexible hours?
당신 회사에서 원격 근무와 유연 근무 시간에 대한 정책은 무엇인가요?

A: ....

1212 □□□

polish
[ˈpɑːlɪʃ]

v 닦다, 광내다 n 광택제

= shine, refine, buff, improve
+ polished a 세련된, 윤이 나는

Q: Do you need to polish your presentation before tomorrow's meeting?
내일 회의 전에 발표를 다듬어야 하나요?

A: ....

1213 □□□

political
[pəˈlɪtɪkl]

a 정치적인

= governmental, civic, public, strategic
+ politics n 정치 politician n 정치인 politically adv 정치적으로

Q: Are you interested in discussing political issues with your friends?
친구들과 정치적인 문제에 대해 토론하는 데 관심이 있나요?

A: ....

1214 □□□

politics
[ˈpɑːlətɪks]

n 정치

= government, statecraft, public affairs, diplomacy
+ political a 정치적인 politician n 정치인

Q: Do you think politics influences the economy in many ways?
정치가 여러 면에서 경제에 영향을 미친다고 생각하나요?

A: ....

1215 □□□

poll
[poʊl]

n 여론조사, 투표 v 여론조사하다

= survey, ballot, election, tally, vote
+ carry out[conduct] a poll 여론 조사[투표/개표]를 실시[시행]하다

Q: Did the latest poll show a change in public opinion?
여론조사에서 대중의 의견 변화가 나타났나요?

A: ....

1216 □□□

pollute
[pəˈluːt]

v 오염시키다

= contaminate, corrupt, foul, defile, dirty

+ pollution n 오염 **pollutant** n 오염물질 **polluted** a 오염된

Q: How can individuals help reduce actions that pollute the environment? 개인들이 환경을 오염시키는 행동을 줄이는 데 어떻게 기여할 수 있나요?

A: ....

1217 □□□

pollution
[pəˈluːʃn]

n 오염

= contamination, impurity, environmental damage, defilement

+ pollute v 오염시키다 **pollutant** n 오염물질

Q: What are the main causes of pollution in your city nowadays?
요즘 당신 도시의 주요 오염 원인은 무엇인가요?

A: ....

1218 □□□

popularity
[ˌpɑːpjuˈlærəti]

n 인기

= fame, renown, acceptance, prevalence, vogue

+ popular a 인기 있는 **popularly** adv 대중적으로

Q: Do you think the popularity of electric cars will continue rising?
전기차의 인기가 계속 상승할 것이라고 생각하나요?

A: ....

1219 □□□

population
[ˌpɑːpjuˈleɪʃn]

n 인구, 주민

= inhabitants, residents, populace, citizenry

+ populate v 거주시키다, 채우다 **populated** a 인구가 거주하는

Q: Is the population of your hometown growing or shrinking lately?
최근에 당신 고향의 인구가 늘어나고 있나요 아니면 줄어들고 있나요?

A: ....

1220 □□□

portion
[ˈpɔːrʃn]

n 부분, 몫

= part, share, segment, serving, section

+ a substantial[significant] portion of the population 그 인구의 상당 부분

Q: Is this portion of the meal enough for two people to share comfortably?
이 식사량이 두 사람이 편안하게 나눠 먹기에 충분한가요?

A: ....

DAY 01 | DICTATION TEST

5회 반복 예문 QR

DICTATION TEST 예문 QR을 듣고 다음 빈칸에 올바른 단어를 쓰세요.

1201. Have you ever thought about living on another ______________?

1202. Is it a ______________ to work with your new colleagues?

1203. Do you have ______________ of time to finish the project before deadline?

1204. Can you explain the ______________ of the movie you watched last night?

1205. Do you know the ______________ forms of all the irregular nouns?

1206. Who is your favorite ______________ and why do you admire their work?

1207. Did you enjoy reading ______________ during your literature classes?

1208. Did the detectives suspect that the victim was ______________?

1209. Have you learned about ______________ bears and their habitat in school?

1210. Did the explorers reach the North ______________ during their expedition?

1211. What is your company's ______________ on remote work and flexible hours?

1212. Do you need to ______________ your presentation before tomorrow's meeting?

1213. Are you interested in discussing ______________ issues with your friends?

1214. Do you think ______________ influences the economy in many ways?

1215. Did the latest ______________ show a change in public opinion?

1216. How can individuals help reduce actions that ______________ the environment?

1217. What are the main causes of ______________ in your city nowadays?

1218. Do you think the ______________ of electric cars will continue rising?

1219. Is the ______________ of your hometown growing or shrinking lately?

1220. Is this ______________ of the meal enough for two people to share comfortably?

5회 반복 표제어 QR　5회 반복 예문 QR

DAY 02

30 days

PREVIEW A 다음 단어의 뜻을 한국어로 써보세요.

- ☐ **portrait** ________
- ☐ **pose** ________
- ☐ **position** ________
- ☐ **positive** ________
- ☐ **possess** ________
- ☐ **possible** ________
- ☐ **postpone** ________
- ☐ **posture** ________
- ☐ **potential** ________
- ☐ **poverty** ________
- ☐ **powder** ________
- ☐ **practical** ________
- ☐ **pray** ________
- ☐ **precious** ________
- ☐ **precise** ________
- ☐ **predator** ________
- ☐ **predict** ________
- ☐ **prefer** ________
- ☐ **pregnant** ________
- ☐ **prejudice** ________

PREVIEW B 사진을 보고 알맞은 영어 단어를 **PREVIEW A** 에서 찾아 써보세요.

________　________　________　________

1221 □□□

portrait
[ˈpɔːrtrət]

n 초상화

= painting, likeness, depiction, representation
+ self-portrait **n** 자화상

Q: Did the artist capture her true personality in this portrait?
화가가 이 초상화에 그녀의 진정한 성격을 담아냈나요?

A: ....

1222 □□□

pose
[poʊz]

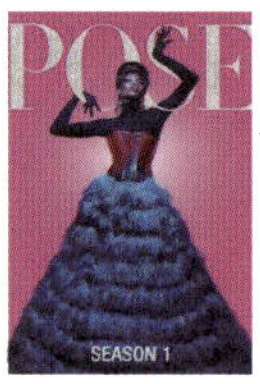

v 자세를 취하다, 제기하다 **n** 자세

= position, attitude, posture, put forth, present
+ strike a pose 포즈를 취하다

Q: Will you pose for a picture with us after the ceremony?
행사 후에 우리와 함께 사진 찍을 포즈를 취해 주실 수 있나요?

A: ....

1223 □□□

position
[pəˈzɪʃn]

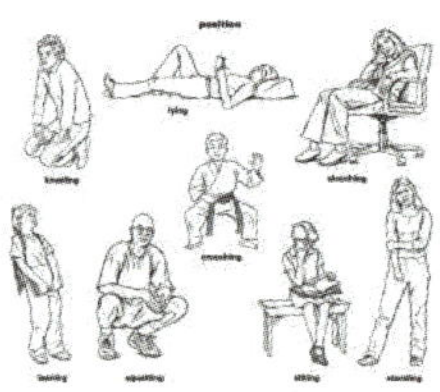

n 위치, 지위, 자세 **v** 위치시키다

= location, place, status, rank, job, stance
+ position paper (기관·정부 부서의) 성명서 **lotus position** 결가부좌, 연화좌, 책상다리

Q: Are you happy with your current position? 현재 직위에 만족하나요?

A: ....

1224 □□□

positive
[ˈpɑːzətɪv]

a 긍정적인, 확실한, 양수의

= optimistic, affirmative, constructive, certain, beneficial
+ positivity **n** 긍정성 **positively** **adv** 긍정적으로

Q: Do you stay positive during difficult times?
어려운 시기에도 긍정적인 태도를 유지하나요?

A: ....

1225 □□□

possess
[pəˈzes]

v 소유하다

= own, have, hold, acquire, control
+ possession **n** 소유, 재산 **possessor** **n** 소유자

Q: Do you possess skills helpful for this project?
이 프로젝트에 도움이 될 만한 기술을 가지고 있나요?

A: ....

1226 □□□

possible
[ˈpɑːsəbl]

a 가능한

= **feasible, achievable, potential, conceivable, likely**
\+ **possibility** **n** 가능성 **possibly** **adv** 아마도 **impossible** **a** 불가능한

Q: Is it possible to finish before the deadline?
마감 기한 전에 끝내는 것이 가능한가요?

A: ....

1227 □□□

postpone
[poʊstˈpoʊn]

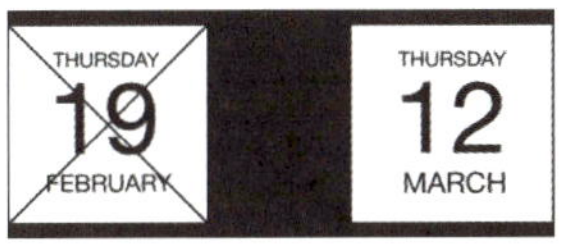

v 연기하다, 미루다

= **delay, defer, put off, suspend, reschedule**
\+ **postponement** **n** 연기

Q: Do we need to postpone the meeting until next week?
회의를 다음 주로 연기해야 할까요?

A: ....

1228 □□□

posture
[ˈpɑːstʃər]

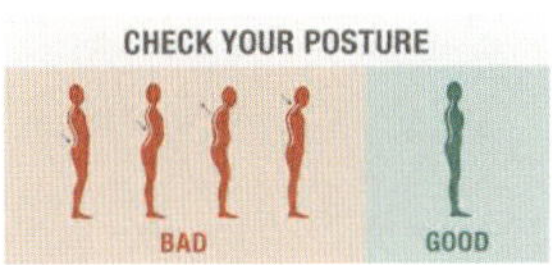

n 자세, 태도

= **stance, bearing, attitude, position, pose**
\+ **an upright posture** 꼿꼿한 자세

Q: Does good posture help reduce back pain?
좋은 자세가 허리 통증을 줄이는 데 도움이 되나요?

A: ....

1229 □□□

potential
[pəˈtenʃl]

n 잠재력 **a** 잠재적인

= **capability, possibility, promise, latent, inherent**
\+ **potentially** **adv** 잠재적으로

Q: Does this candidate have potential to lead?
이 후보자가 리더로서의 잠재력이 있나요?

A: ....

1230 □□□

poverty
[ˈpɑːvərti]

n 가난, 빈곤

= **destitution, indigence, hardship, privation, lack**
\+ **poor** **a** 가난한

Q: What can help reduce poverty in developing countries?
개발도상국의 빈곤을 줄이는 데 무엇이 도움이 될 수 있나요?

A: ....

1231 □□□

powder
[ˈpaʊdər]

n 가루, 분말 **v** 분을 바르다

= **dust, fine particles, cosmetic, apply powder**
+ **powdery** **a** 분말 같은

Q: Did you remember to add the baking powder to the cookie dough?
쿠키 반죽에 베이킹파우더 넣는 거 기억했어?

A: ....

1232 □□□

practical
[ˈpræktɪkl]

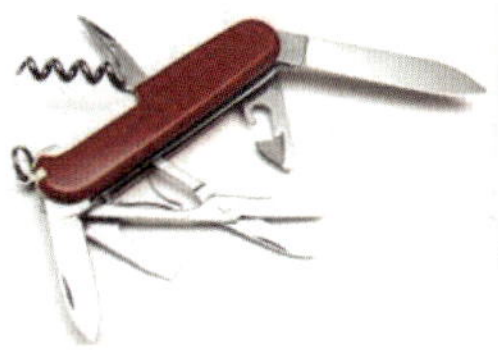

a 실용적인, 실제적인

= **pragmatic, realistic, useful, functional, sensible**
+ **practice** **n** 연습, 실행 **practitioner** **n** 개업의 **practically** **adv** 실질적으로
practice **v** 연습하다

Q: Do you think this solution is truly practical for our everyday use?
이 해결책이 우리 일상생활에 정말로 실용적이라고 생각하세요?

A: ....

1233 □□□

pray
[preɪ]

v 기도하다

= **worship, supplicate, appeal, entreat**
+ **prayer** **n** 기도

Q: Do you pray daily or just on holidays?
매일 기도하나요 아니면 휴일에만 기도하나요?

A: ....

1234 □□□

precious
[ˈpreʃəs]

a 귀중한, 소중한

= **valuable, cherished, treasured, esteemed, rare**
+ **preciousness** **n** 귀중함

Q: What's your most precious childhood memory?
가장 소중한 어린 시절의 추억은 무엇인가요?

A: ....

1235 □□□

precise
[prɪˈsaɪs]

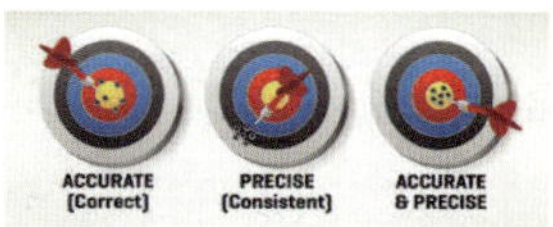

a 정확한, 정밀한

= **exact, accurate, specific, definite, meticulous**
+ **precision** **n** 정확성 **precisely** **adv** 정확히

Q: Can you give a precise time for the meeting?
회의 시간을 정확하게 알려줄 수 있나요?

A: ....

1236 □□□

predator
[ˈpredətər]

n 포식자

= **hunter, carnivore, exploiter**
+ **predatory** **a** 약탈적인

Q: Are lions the main predators in the savannah?
사자가 사바나의 주요 포식자인가요?

A: ....

1237 □□□

predict
[prɪˈdɪkt]

v 예측하다

= **forecast, foresee, foretell, prophesy, anticipate**
+ **prediction** **n** 예측 **predictable** **a** 예측 가능한 **predictably** **adv** 예측 가능하게

Q: Can you predict the weather for next week?
다음 주 날씨를 예측할 수 있나요?

A: ....

1238 □□□

prefer
[prɪˈfɜːr]

v ~을 더 좋아하다

= **favor, choose, opt for, like better**
+ **preference** **n** 선호 **preferable** **a** 더 나은, 선호되는 **preferably** **adv** 가급적

Q: Do you prefer coffee or tea in the morning?
아침에는 커피와 차 중에 무엇을 더 선호하시나요?

A: ....

1239 □□□

pregnant
[ˈpregnənt]

a 임신한

= **expecting, gravid, enceinte, expectant**
+ **pregnancy** **n** 임신

Q: Is she pregnant or was it a false alarm?
그녀가 임신한 건가요 아니면 거짓 경보였나요?

A: ....

1240 □□□

prejudice
[ˈpredʒədɪs]

n 편견, 선입관

= **bias, bigotry, discrimination, unfairness, prejudge**
+ **prejudiced** **a** 편견을 가진

Q: Do you think historical events sometimes contribute to modern-day prejudice? 역사적 사건들이 때때로 현대 편견의 원인이 된다고 생각하시나요?

A: ....

DAY 02 | DICTATION TEST

5회 반복 예문 QR

DICTATION TEST 예문 QR을 듣고 다음 빈칸에 올바른 단어를 쓰세요.

1221. Did the artist capture her true personality in this ________________?

1222. Will you ________________ for a picture with us after the ceremony?

1223. Are you happy with your current ________________?

1224. Do you stay ________________ during difficult times?

1225. Do you ________________ skills helpful for this project?

1226. Is it ________________ to finish before the deadline?

1227. Do we need to ________________ the meeting until next week?

1228. Does good ________________ help reduce back pain?

1229. Does this candidate have ________________ to lead?

1230. What can help reduce ________________ in developing countries?

1231. Did you remember to add the baking ________________ to the cookie dough?

1232. Do you think this solution is truly ________________ for our everyday use?

1233. Do you ________________ daily or just on holidays?

1234. What's your most ________________ childhood memory?

1235. Can you give a ________________ time for the meeting?

1236. Are lions the main ________________ in the savannah?

1237. Can you ________________ the weather for next week?

1238. Do you ________________ coffee or tea in the morning?

1239. Is she ________________ or was it a false alarm?

1240. Do you think historical events sometimes contribute to modern-day ________________?

5회 반복 표제어 QR　5회 반복 예문 QR

DAY 03

30 days

AI 학습자료와 인강 youpass.co.kr

PREVIEW A 다음 단어의 뜻을 한국어로 써보세요.

□ **prescribe** ________	□ **priceless** ________
□ **present** ________	□ **pride** ________
□ **presentation** ________	□ **priest** ________
□ **preserve** ________	□ **primary** ________
□ **press** ________	□ **prime** ________
□ **pressure** ________	□ **primitive** ________
□ **pretend** ________	□ **principal** ________
□ **prevent** ________	□ **principle** ________
□ **previous** ________	□ **prior** ________
□ **prey** ________	□ **priority** ________

PREVIEW B 사진을 보고 알맞은 영어 단어를 **PREVIEW A** 에서 찾아 써보세요.

____

____

____

____

1241 □□□

prescribe
[prɪˈskraɪb]

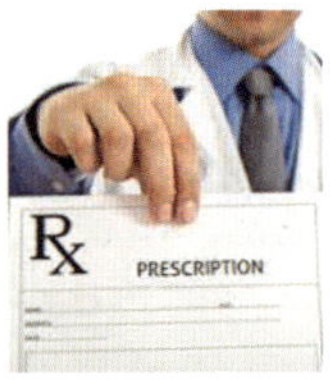

v 처방하다, 규정하다

= **order, dictate, recommend, authorize**
+ **prescription** **n** 처방, 처방전

Q: Did the doctor prescribe any medicine for your cold symptoms?
의사가 감기 증상에 대해 약을 처방했나요?

A:

1242 □□□

present
[ˈpreznt] **n** [prɪˈzent] **v**

a 현재의, 참석한 **n** 선물, 현재 **v** 발표하다, 주다, 제시하다

= **gift, current, introduce, show, offer, now**
+ **presence** **n** 존재

Q: Will you be presenting your findings at next Thursday's meeting?
다음 주 목요일 회의에서 당신의 발견을 발표할 건가요?

A:

1243 □□□

presentation
[ˌpreznˈteɪʃn]

n 발표, 제시

= **demonstration, display, performance, speech, offering**
+ **present** **v** 발표하다, 제시하다

Q: Is your presentation ready for the conference next week?
다음 주 학회 발표 준비는 되었나요?

A:

1244 □□□

preserve
[prɪˈzɜːrv]

v 보존하다, 보호하다

= **conserve, protect, save, maintain, retain**
+ **preservation** **n** 보존

Q: How can we preserve natural habitats for future generations better?
미래 세대를 위해 자연 서식지를 어떻게 더 잘 보존할 수 있을까요?

A:

1245 □□□

press
[pres]

v 누르다, 강요하다 **n** 언론, 압력

= **push, urge, insist, iron, media, force**
+ **press conference** 기자 회견(**news conference**)

Q: Did the journalists press you for more details during the interview?
기자들이 인터뷰 동안 더 많은 세부 사항을 요구했나요?

A:

1246 □□□

pressure
[ˈpreʃər]

n 압력, 압박

= stress, strain, force, influence, compel

\+ blood pressure 혈압

Q: How do you handle pressure when deadlines are very tight?
마감 기한이 매우 촉박할 때 압박감을 어떻게 다루나요?

A:

1247 □□□

pretend
[prɪˈtend]

v ~인 체하다

= feign, simulate, make believe, assume, imagine

\+ pretense[pretence] **n** 가장, 겉치레

Q: Why do you always pretend not to hear me when I ask you to do chores? 제가 집안일 시킬 때 왜 항상 못 들은 척하는 거예요?

A:

1248 □□□

prevent
[prɪˈvent]

v 막다, 예방하다

= stop, hinder, avert, avoid, preclude

\+ prevention **n** 예방 preventative[preventive] **a** 예방적인

Q: What steps can prevent accidents in the workplace effectively?
직장에서 사고를 효과적으로 예방할 수 있는 조치는 무엇인가요?

A:

1249 □□□

previous
[ˈpriːviəs]

a 이전의, 앞선

= preceding, former, earlier, prior, past

\+ previously **adv** 이전에

Q: Did you review the previous report before starting the new project?
새 프로젝트를 시작하기 전에 이전 보고서를 검토했나요?

A:

1250 □□□

prey
[preɪ]

n 먹이, 희생자 **v** 잡아먹다

= victim, quarry, hunt, feed on, exploit

\+ bird of prey (독수리 · 매 · 올빼미 등의) 맹금류

Q: What animals usually prey on rabbits in this forest area?
이 숲 지역에서 어떤 동물들이 보통 토끼를 잡아먹나요?

A:

1251 □□□

priceless
[ˈpraɪsləs]

a 매우 귀중한

= **invaluable, beyond price, inestimable**
+ **price** n 가격

Q: Is this family heirloom really priceless or just very old?
이 가보가 정말 값을 매길 수 없을 정도로 귀한가요, 아니면 그저 매우 오래된 건가요?

A: ....

1252 □□□

pride
[praɪd]

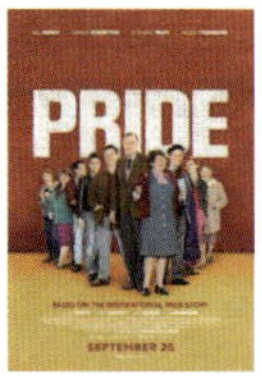

n 자부심, 자만심

= **self-esteem, dignity, arrogance, satisfaction**
+ **proud** a 자랑스러운 **proudly** adv 자랑스럽게

Q: What do you take pride in the most about your achievements?
당신의 성과 중 무엇을 가장 자랑스러워하나요?

A: ....

1253 □□□

priest
[pri:st]

n 성직자, 사제

= **clergyman, minister, cleric, divine**
+ **priesthood** n 성직

Q: Have you ever talked to a priest about your personal problems?
개인적인 문제에 대해 사제와 이야기해 본 적이 있나요?

A: ....

1254 □□□

primary
[ˈpraɪmeri]

a 주된, 기본적인

= **main, chief, principal, fundamental, initial**
+ **primarily** adv 주로, 본래

Q: What is the primary goal of this training program for new hires?
신입 사원을 위한 이 교육 프로그램의 주된 목표는 무엇인가요?

A: ....

1255 □□□

prime
[praɪm]

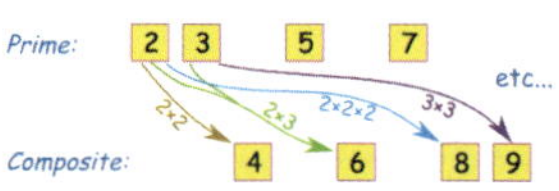

a 가장 중요한, 최고의 n 전성기

= **main, fundamental, optimal, peak, best**
+ **prime minister** 내각수상 **prime number** 소수(素數)

Q: Is this the prime location for opening a new coffee shop?
여기가 새로운 커피숍을 열기에 최적의 장소인가요?

A: ....

1256 □□□

primitive
[ˈprɪmətɪv]

a 원시적인

= ancient, basic, crude, rudimentary, undeveloped

\+ primitiveness **n** 원시성

Q: Did early humans use primitive tools made of stone and wood?
초기 인류는 돌과 나무로 만든 원시적인 도구를 사용했나요?

A: ....

1257 □□□

principal
[ˈprɪnsəpl]

a 주요한 **n** 교장, 원금

= main, chief, primary, head, director, capital

\+ principle **n** 원칙, 원리

Q: What's the principal reason you decided to pursue this career path?
이 직업 경로를 택하기로 결정한 주된 이유는 무엇인가요?

A: ....

1258 □□□

principle
[ˈprɪnsəpl]

n 원리, 원칙

= rule, law, tenet, doctrine, standard

\+ principal **n** 교장, 원금

Q: Which principle most often guides your decision-making at work?
직장에서 의사 결정을 할 때 어떤 원칙이 가장 자주 당신을 이끄나요?

A: ....

1259 □□□

prior
[ˈpraɪər]

a 이전의, 앞선

= previous, earlier, preceding, former

\+ priority **n** 우선순위 prior to **prep** ~에 앞서

Q: Did you have any prior experience before joining this company?
이 회사에 입사하기 전에 어떤 이전 경험이 있었나요?

A: ....

1260 □□□

priority
[praɪˈɔːrəti]

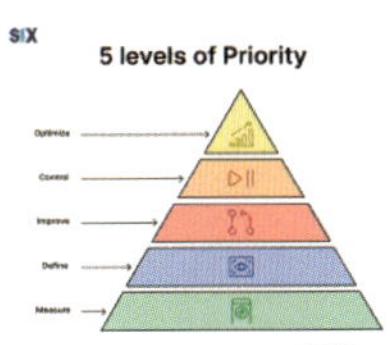

n 우선순위

= preference, urgency, precedence, primary concern

\+ prior **a** 우선하는

Q: What is your top priority when managing multiple projects simultaneously? 여러 프로젝트를 동시에 관리할 때 최우선 순위는 무엇인가요?

A: ....

DAY 03 | DICTATION TEST

5회 반복 예문 QR

DICTATION TEST 예문 QR을 듣고 다음 빈칸에 올바른 단어를 쓰세요.

1241. Did the doctor ______________ any medicine for your cold symptoms?
1242. Will you be ______________ your findings at next Thursday's meeting?
1243. Is your ______________ ready for the conference next week?
1244. How can we ______________ natural habitats for future generations better?
1245. Did the journalists ______________ you for more details during the interview?
1246. How do you handle ______________ when deadlines are very tight?
1247. Why do you always ______________ not to hear me when I ask you to do chores?
1248. What steps can ______________ accidents in the workplace effectively?
1249. Did you review the ______________ report before starting the new project?
1250. What animals usually ______________ on rabbits in this forest area?
1251. Is this family heirloom really ______________ or just very old?
1252. What do you take ______________ in the most about your achievements?
1253. Have you ever talked to a ______________ about your personal problems?
1254. What is the ______________ goal of this training program for new hires?
1255. Is this the ______________ location for opening a new coffee shop?
1256. Did early humans use ______________ tools made of stone and wood?
1257. What's the ______________ reason you decided to pursue this career path?
1258. Which ______________ most often guides your decision-making at work?
1259. Did you have any ______________ experience before joining this company?
1260. What is your top ______________ when managing multiple projects simultaneously?

5회 반복 표제어 QR   5회 반복 예문 QR

DAY 04

30 days

AI 학습자료와 인강 youpass.co.kr

PREVIEW A 다음 단어의 뜻을 한국어로 써보세요.

□ privacy ________	□ profession ________
□ private ________	□ professional ________
□ privilege ________	□ professor ________
□ probably ________	□ profit ________
□ procedure ________	□ profound ________
□ proceed ________	□ progress ________
□ process ________	□ prohibit ________
□ produce ________	□ promote ________
□ product ________	□ pronounce ________
□ productive ________	□ pronunciation ________

PREVIEW B 사진을 보고 알맞은 영어 단어를 **PREVIEW A**에서 찾아 써보세요.

____

____

____

____

1261 □□□

privacy
[ˈpraɪvəsi]

n 사생활

= **seclusion, solitude, confidentiality, secrecy**
+ **private** **a** 개인의, 사적인

Q: Is privacy more important than convenience?
사생활이 편리함보다 더 중요한가요?

A:

1262 □□□

private
[ˈpraɪvət]

a 사적인, 개인적인

= **personal, confidential, secluded, secret, individual**
+ **privacy** **n** 사생활 **privatization** **n** 민영화 **privatize** **v** 민영화하다
privately **adv** 개인적으로

Q: Is this a private event or can anyone attend?
이것은 비공개 행사인가요, 아니면 누구나 참석할 수 있나요?

A:

1263 □□□

privilege
[ˈprɪvəlɪdʒ]

n 특권, 특혜

= **right, advantage, benefit, prerogative, honor**
+ **privileged** **a** 특권을 가진

Q: Do you feel it's a privilege to work here?
여기서 일하는 것이 특권이라고 느끼나요?

A:

1264 □□□

probably
[ˈprɑːbəbli]

adv 아마도

= **likely, possibly, perhaps, presumably**
+ **probable** **a** 있을 법한 **probability** **n** 확률

Q : Do you think you'll probably finish the project this week?
이번 주에 프로젝트를 끝낼 수도 있을 것 같나요?

A:

1265 □□□

procedure
[prəˈsiːdʒər]

n 절차, 과정

= **method, process, protocol, steps, sequence**
+ **procedural** **a** 절차상의

Q: Can you explain the procedure to apply?
지원 절차를 설명해 줄 수 있나요?

A:

1266 □□□

proceed
[prə'siːd]

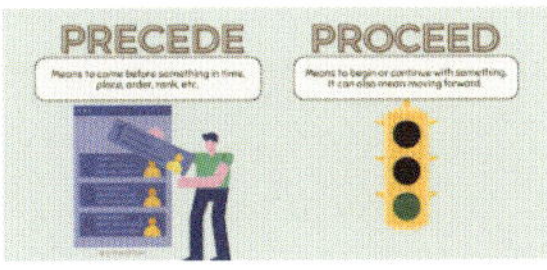

v 진행하다, 나아가다

= continue, advance, progress, go ahead
+ proceeding n 진행, 소송

Q: Should we proceed despite the recent setbacks?
최근의 차질에도 불구하고 진행해야 할까요?

A:

1267 □□□

process
['prɑːses] n ['prə'ses] v

n 과정 v 처리하다

= method, procedure, operation, handle, treat
+ processed a 가공된

Q: How long does the hiring process take?
채용 절차는 얼마나 걸리나요?

A:

1268 □□□

produce
[prə'duːs] v ['prɑːduːs] n

v 생산하다, 만들다 n 농산물

= create, make, yield, generate, result, crop
+ product n 제품 production n 생산 producer n 생산자 productive a 생산적인

Q: Can your company produce enough units to meet the sudden surge in demand? 귀사는 갑작스러운 수요 증가를 충족시킬 만큼 충분한 양을 생산할 수 있나요?

A:

1269 □□□

product
['prɑːdʌkt]

n 제품, 생산물

= item, merchandise, outcome, result, creation
+ produce v 생산하다 production n 생산

Q: Is this product popular among young people?
이 제품이 젊은 사람들 사이에서 인기가 많나요?

A:

1270 □□□

productive
[prə'dʌktɪv]

a 생산적인, 다산의

= fruitful, efficient, constructive, fertile, effective
+ productivity n 생산성 productively adv 생산적으로

Q: What makes your work environment productive?
무엇이 당신의 작업 환경을 생산적으로 만드나요?

A:

1271 □□□

profession
[prəˈfeʃn]

n 직업, 전문직

= occupation, career, vocation, calling, field

\+ professional n 전문가

Q: What inspired you to choose this profession?
이 직업을 선택하게 된 계기는 무엇인가요?

A: ....

1272 □□□

professional
[prəˈfeʃənl]

a 직업의, 전문적인 n 전문가

= expert, skilled, competent, specialized, paid

\+ profession n 직업 professionalism n 전문성 professionally adv 전문적으로

Q: Are you looking for a professional mentor?
전문 멘토를 찾고 있나요?

A: ....

1273 □□□

professor
[prəˈfesər]

n 교수

= academic, lecturer, scholar, educator

\+ professorship n 교수직

Q: Did the professor assign homework today?
교수님이 오늘 숙제를 내주셨나요?

A: ....

1274 □□□

profit
[ˈprɑːfɪt]

n 이익, 수익 v 이익을 얻다

= gain, earnings, benefit, advantage

\+ profitable a 수익성 있는 profitably adv 수익성 있게

Q: How does the company plan to increase profit?
회사는 어떻게 이익을 늘릴 계획인가요?

A: ....

1275 □□□

profound
[prəˈfaʊnd]

a 심오한, 깊은

= deep, intense, thoughtful, insightful, fundamental

\+ profundity n 심오함 profoundly adv 깊이, 대단히

Q: Did that documentary leave a profound impact on your understanding of history?
그 다큐멘터리가 역사에 대한 당신의 이해에 깊은 영향을 남겼나요?

A: ....

1276 □□□

progress
[ˈprɑːgres] n [prəˈgres] v

n 진행, 진보 v 진보하다

= advance, improvement, development, move forward, develop

+ progressive a 진보적인

Q: Can you show the project progress report?
프로젝트 진행 보고서를 보여줄 수 있나요?

A: ....

1277 □□□

prohibit
[proʊˈhɪbɪt]

v 금지하다

= forbid, ban, outlaw, prevent, disallow

+ prohibition n 금지 **prohibited** a 금지된

Q: Does the school prohibit phones during lessons?
학교에서 수업 중 휴대전화를 금지하나요?

A: ....

1278 □□□

promote
[prəˈmoʊt]

v 촉진하다, 승진시키다, 홍보하다

= advocate, advance, encourage, advertise, upgrade

+ promotion n 승진, 홍보 **promotional** a 홍보의

Q: How do you promote your products online?
온라인에서 제품을 어떻게 홍보하나요?

A: ....

1279 □□□

pronounce
[prəˈnaʊns]

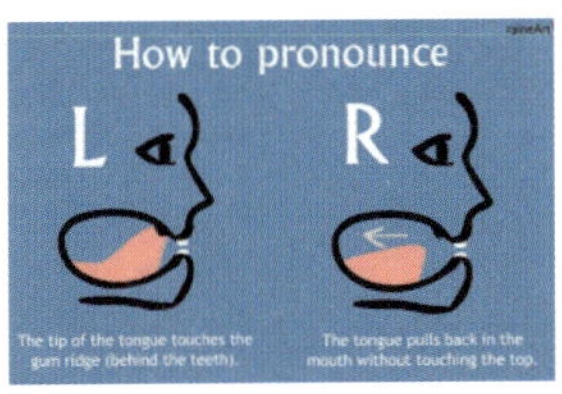

v 발음하다, 선언하다

= articulate, enunciate, declare, state

+ pronunciation n 발음 **pronounceable** a 발음할 수 있는

Q: Can you pronounce this word correctly?
이 단어를 정확하게 발음할 수 있나요?

A: ....

1280 □□□

pronunciation
[prəˌnʌnsiˈeɪʃn]

n 발음

= articulation, enunciation, accent, diction

+ pronounce v 발음하다

Q: Does daily practice improve pronunciation?
매일 연습하면 발음이 향상되나요?

A: ....

DAY 04 | DICTATION TEST

5회 반복 예문 QR

DICTATION TEST 예문 QR을 듣고 다음 빈칸에 올바른 단어를 쓰세요.

1261. Is ________________ more important than convenience?

1262. Is this a ________________ event or can anyone attend?

1263. Do you feel it's a ________________ to work here?

1264. Do you think you'll ________________ finish the project this week?

1265. Can you explain the ________________ to apply?

1266. Should we ________________ despite the recent setbacks?

1267. How long does the hiring ________________ take?

1268. Can your company ________________ enough units to meet the sudden surge in demand?

1269. Is this ________________ popular among young people?

1270. What makes your work environment ________________?

1271. What inspired you to choose this ________________?

1272. Are you looking for a ________________ mentor?

1273. Did the ________________ assign homework today?

1274. How does the company plan to increase ________________?

1275. Did that documentary leave a ________________ impact on your understanding of history?

1276. Can you show the project ________________ report?

1277. Does the school ________________ phones during lessons?

1278. How do you ________________ your products online?

1279. Can you ________________ this word correctly?

1280. Does daily practice improve ________________?

5회 반복 표제어 QR　5회 반복 예문 QR

DAY 05

30 days

AI 학습자료와 인강 youpass.co.kr

PREVIEW A 다음 단어의 뜻을 한국어로 써보세요.

- □ **proof** ______________
- □ **proper** ______________
- □ **properly** ______________
- □ **property** ______________
- □ **proportion** ______________
- □ **propose** ______________
- □ **prospect** ______________
- □ **protect** ______________
- □ **protein** ______________
- □ **protest** ______________
- □ **prove** ______________
- □ **proverb** ______________
- □ **provide** ______________
- □ **psychology** ______________
- □ **public** ______________
- □ **publication** ______________
- □ **publish** ______________
- □ **punctual** ______________
- □ **punish** ______________
- □ **pupil** ______________

PREVIEW B 사진을 보고 알맞은 영어 단어를 **PREVIEW A** 에서 찾아 써보세요.

____

____

____

____

1281 □□□

proof
[pru:f]

n 증거, 입증

= evidence, verification, confirmation, demonstration

+ prove **v** 증명하다 proven **a** 증명된

Q: Do you have proof to support your claim in the meeting?
회의에서 주장을 뒷받침할 증거가 있나요?

A: ....

1282 □□□

proper
[ˈprɑːpər]

a 적절한, 올바른

= appropriate, correct, suitable, decent, fitting

+ properness **n** 적절함 property **n** 재산, 속성 properly **adv** 적절히

Q: Isn't it proper to wear formal clothes for the company dinner?
회사 저녁 식사에 정장을 입는 것이 적절하지 않은가요?

A: ....

1283 □□□

properly
[ˈprɑːpərli]

adv 적절히, 제대로

= correctly, appropriately, suitably, accurately

+ proper **a** 적절한

Q: Did you properly install the software before using it?
사용하기 전에 소프트웨어를 제대로 설치했나요?

A: ....

1284 □□□

property
[ˈprɑːpərti]

n 재산, 부동산, 속성

= possession, estate, characteristic, attribute, quality

+ proper **a** 고유의

Q: Who owns the property next to your house?
당신 집 옆 부동산은 누가 소유하고 있나요?

A: ....

1285 □□□

proportion
[prəˈpɔːrʃn]

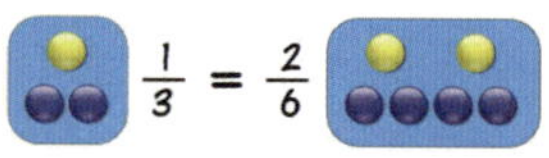

n 비율, 부분

= ratio, fraction, part, balance, scale

+ proportional **a** 비례하는 proportionally **adv** 비례하여

Q: What proportion of your income do you save monthly?
매달 수입의 어느 정도를 저축하나요?

A: ....

1286 □□□

propose
[prə'poʊz]

v 제안하다, 청혼하다

= suggest, offer, recommend, nominate, intend

+ proposal **n** 제안 **proposition** **n** 명제, 제안

Q: Are you going to propose a new idea at tomorrow's meeting?
내일 회의에서 새로운 아이디어를 제안할 건가요?

A: ....

1287 □□□

prospect
['prɑːspekt]

n 전망, 가능성 **v** 탐사하다

= outlook, potential, possibility, expectation, explore

+ prospective **a** 장래의, 유망한

Q: What are job prospects like for recent graduates in your field?
당신 분야에서 최근 졸업생들의 취업 전망은 어떤가요?

A: ....

1288 □□□

protect
[prə'tekt]

v 보호하다

= guard, shield, defend, preserve, safeguard

+ protection **n** 보호 **protector** **n** 보호자 **protective** **a** 보호하는

Q: How do you protect your personal data from hacking?
해킹으로부터 개인 데이터를 어떻게 보호하나요?

A: ....

1289 □□□

protein
['proʊtiːn]

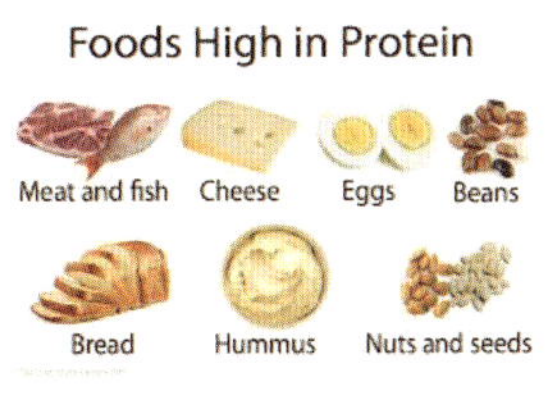

n 단백질

= nutrient, polypeptide, essential compound

+ carbohydrate **n** 탄수화물 **fat** **n** 지방 **protein nutrients** 단백질을 포함한 영양소

Q: Do you eat enough protein to build muscle during workouts?
운동 중에 근육을 만들기 위해 충분한 단백질을 섭취하나요?

A: ....

1290 □□□

protest
['proʊtest] **n** [prə'test] **v**

n 항의, 시위 **v** 항의하다

= objection, demonstration, complaint, object, complain

+ protester **n** 항의하는 사람

Q: Did people protest the new law in the city center last week?
지난주 시내에서 사람들이 새 법에 반대하는 시위를 했나요?

A: ....

1291 □□□

prove
[pru:v]

v 증명하다, ~으로 판명되다

= demonstrate, establish, verify, confirm, show
\+ proof **n** 증거 proven **a** 증명된

Q: Can you prove you finished the project before the deadline?
마감 기한 전에 프로젝트를 마쳤다는 것을 증명할 수 있나요?

A: ....

1292 □□□

proverb
[ˈprɑːvɜːrb]

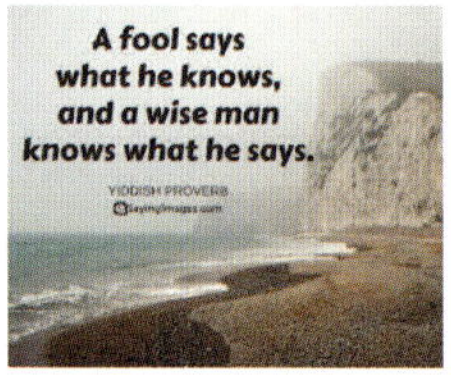

n 속담, 격언

= saying, adage, maxim, aphorism
\+ proverbial **a** 속담의

Q: What is your favorite proverb that inspires you in hard times?
힘든 시기에 당신에게 영감을 주는 가장 좋아하는 속담은 무엇인가요?

A: ....

1293 □□□

provide
[prəˈvaɪd]

v 제공하다, 공급하다

= supply, furnish, offer, give, equip
\+ provision **n** 제공, 조항 provider **n** 제공자 provided **conj** 만약 ~라면

Q: Can you provide more details about the company event next month?
다음 달 회사 행사에 대해 더 자세한 내용을 제공해 줄 수 있나요?

A: ....

1294 □□□

psychology
[saɪˈkɑːlədʒi]

n 심리학

= mental science, study of mind, behavioral science
\+ psychologist **n** 심리학자 psychological **a** 심리적인
psychologically **adv** 심리적으로

Q: Are you interested in studying psychology as a college major?
대학 전공으로 심리학을 공부하는 데 관심이 있나요?

A: ....

1295 □□□

public
[ˈpʌblɪk]

a 공공의, 대중의 **n** 대중

= communal, general, widespread, open, citizens
\+ publicity **n** 홍보, 대중의 관심 publication **n** 출판 publish **v** 출판하다
publicize **v** 홍보하다 publicly **adv** 공개적으로

Q: Is it safe to share opinions openly in public forums?
공개 포럼에서 의견을 공개적으로 공유하는 것이 안전한가요?

A: ....

1296 □□□

publication
[ˌpʌblɪˈkeɪʃn]

n 출판, 발행물

= **printing, issue, journal, book, announcement**
+ publish **v** 출판하다

Q: Did the author receive recognition for their latest publication?
작가가 최신 출판물로 인정을 받았나요?

A:

1297 □□□

publish
[ˈpʌblɪʃ]

v 출판하다, 발표하다

= **print, issue, release, disseminate, make public**
+ publication **n** 출판 **publisher** **n** 출판사

Q: When will the company publish the annual financial report?
회사는 언제 연간 재무 보고서를 발표할 건가요?

A:

1298 □□□

punctual
[ˈpʌŋktʃuəl]

a 시간을 엄수하는

= **on time, prompt, timely, exact**
+ punctuality **n** 정시성 **punctually** **adv** 정각에

Q: Are you usually punctual for meetings or do you arrive late?
회의에 보통 시간을 잘 지키나요, 아니면 늦게 도착하나요?

A:

1299 □□□

punish
[ˈpʌnɪʃ]

v 벌하다, 처벌하다

= **penalize, discipline, chastise, inflict**
+ punishment **n** 처벌 **punishable** **a** 처벌할 수 있는

Q: How does the school punish students who break rules repeatedly?
학교는 규칙을 반복적으로 어기는 학생들을 어떻게 처벌하나요?

A:

1300 □□□

pupil
[ˈpjuːpl]

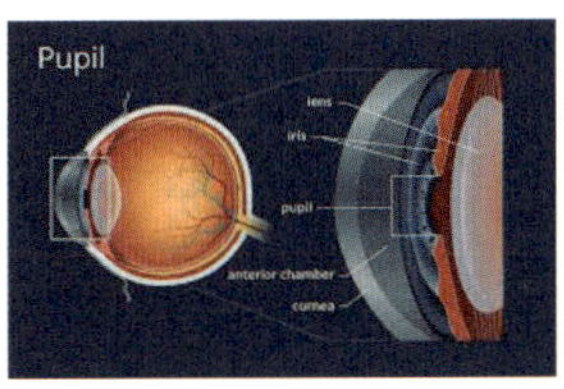

n 학생, 생도, 눈동자

= **student, learner, eye (anatomy)**
+ an inattentive pupil 주의를 기울이지 않는 학생

Q: Is the pupil expected to complete all homework on time?
학생은 모든 숙제를 제시간에 완료해야 하나요?

A:

DAY 05 | DICTATION TEST

5회 반복 예문 QR

DICTATION TEST 예문 QR을 듣고 다음 빈칸에 올바른 단어를 쓰세요.

1281. Do you have ______________ to support your claim in the meeting?

1282. Isn't it ______________ to wear formal clothes for the company dinner?

1283. Did you ______________ install the software before using it?

1284. Who owns the ______________ next to your house?

1285. What ______________ of your income do you save monthly?

1286. Are you going to ______________ a new idea at tomorrow's meeting?

1287. What are job ______________ like for recent graduates in your field?

1288. How do you ______________ your personal data from hacking?

1289. Do you eat enough ______________ to build muscle during workouts?

1290. Did people ______________ the new law in the city center last week?

1291. Can you ______________ you finished the project before the deadline?

1292. What is your favorite ______________ that inspires you in hard times?

1293. Can you ______________ more details about the company event next month?

1294. Are you interested in studying ______________ as a college major?

1295. Is it safe to share opinions openly in ______________ forums?

1296. Did the author receive recognition for their latest ______________?

1297. When will the company ______________ the annual financial report?

1298. Are you usually ______________ for meetings or do you arrive late?

1299. How does the school ______________ students who break rules repeatedly?

1300. Is the ______________ expected to complete all homework on time?

5회 반복 표제어 QR　5회 반복 예문 QR

DAY 06
30 days

AI 학습자료와 인강 youpass.co.kr

PREVIEW A 다음 단어의 뜻을 한국어로 써보세요.

□ purchase ______	□ quit ______
□ pure ______	□ quote ______
□ purify ______	□ racial ______
□ purpose ______	□ radical ______
□ pursue ______	□ rainforest ______
□ qualify ______	□ raise ______
□ quality ______	□ random ______
□ quantity ______	□ range ______
□ quarrel ______	□ rank ______
□ quarter ______	□ rapid ______

PREVIEW B 사진을 보고 알맞은 영어 단어를 **PREVIEW A**에서 찾아 써보세요.

______

______

______

______

1301 □□□

purchase
[ˈpɜːrtʃəs]

n 구매 **v** 구매하다

= **buy, acquire, procure, obtain, acquisition**
+ **purchase tax** 구매[물품]세

Q: **Did you purchase the new laptop from the store?**
새 노트북을 그 가게에서 구매했나요?

A: ……………………………………

1302 □□□

pure
[pjʊr]

a 순수한, 깨끗한

= **unadulterated, clean, genuine, absolute, chaste**
+ **purity n** 순수 **purify v** 정화하다 **purely adv** 순전히, 전적으로

Q: **Is this chocolate made from pure cocoa or mixed with others?**
이 초콜릿은 순수 코코아로 만들어졌나요, 아니면 다른 것과 섞였나요?

A: ……………………………………

1303 □□□

purify
[ˈpjʊrɪfaɪ]

v 정화하다

= **cleanse, refine, filter, sanitize, distil**
+ **purity n** 순수 **purification n** 정화 **pure a** 순수한

Q: **How long does it take to purify water with this system?**
이 시스템으로 물을 정화하는 데 얼마나 걸리나요?

A: ……………………………………

1304 □□□

purpose
[ˈpɜːrpəs]

n 목적, 의도

= **aim, goal, intention, objective, reason**
+ **purposeful a** 목적 있는 **purposeless a** 무의미한 **purposefully adv** 의도적으로

Q: **What is the main purpose of your visit to headquarters?**
본사 방문의 주된 목적은 무엇인가요?

A: ……………………………………

1305 □□□

pursue
[pərˈsuː]

v 추구하다, 뒤쫓다

= **chase, follow, seek, strive for, go after**
+ **pursuit n** 추구, 추격

Q: **Are you planning to pursue further studies after your degree?**
학위를 받은 후에 더 공부할 계획인가요?

A: ……………………………………

1306 □□□

qualify
['kwɑːlɪfaɪ]

v 자격을 얻다, 자격을 주다

= entitle, certify, train, enable, limit

+ qualification **n** 자격 **qualifier** **n** 예선전 **qualified** **a** 자격 있는

Q: Do you qualify for the scholarship based on performance?
성적에 따라 장학금을 받을 자격이 되나요?

A: ....

1307 □□□

quality
['kwɑːləti]

n 품질, 질

= standard, grade, characteristic, attribute, excellence

+ qualitative **a** 질적인

Q: How do you ensure the quality of products before shipping?
제품을 배송하기 전에 품질을 어떻게 보장하나요?

A: ....

1308 □□□

quantity
['kwɑːntəti]

n 양

= amount, volume, number, measure, portion

+ quantitative **a** 양적인

Q: What quantity of materials is needed to complete the project?
프로젝트를 완료하는 데 얼마만큼의 재료가 필요한가요?

A: ....

1309 □□□

quarrel
['kwɔːrəl]

n 싸움, 다툼 **v** 다투다

= argument, dispute, disagreement, bicker, squabble

+ an open quarrel 노골적인 말다툼 **pick a fight[quarrel]** 싸움을 걸다

Q: Did you and your friend have a quarrel over the misunderstanding?
당신과 친구가 오해 때문에 다투었나요?

A: ....

1310 □□□

quarter
['kwɔːrtər]

n 4분의 1, 분기, 지역

= fourth, district, phase, residency

+ a quarter of a mile 4분의 1마일 **a quarter to four** 4시 15분 전(3시 45분)

Q: Which quarter of the year showed highest sales in your business?
당신 사업에서 연중 어느 분기가 가장 높은 매출을 보였나요?

A: ....

1311 □□□

quit
[kwɪt]

v 그만두다, 떠나다

= stop, resign, abandon, cease, give up
\+ quitting **n** 그만두기

Q: Have you ever thought about quitting your job to start business?
사업을 시작하기 위해 직장을 그만둘 생각을 해본 적 있나요?

A: ....

1312 □□□

quote
[kwoʊt]

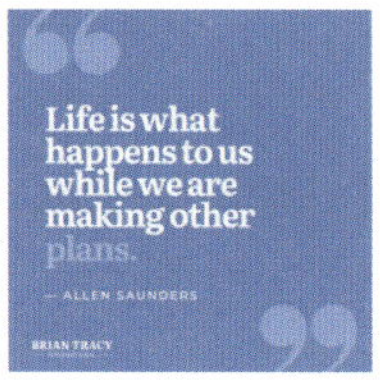

v 인용하다, 견적을 내다 **n** 인용구, 견적

= cite, excerpt, repeat, estimate, price
\+ quotation **n** 인용문

Q: Can you quote the exact line from the book that inspired you?
당신에게 영감을 준 책의 정확한 구절을 인용해 줄 수 있나요?

A: ....

1313 □□□

racial
[ˈreɪʃl]

a 인종의

= ethnic, ancestral, human classification
\+ race **n** 인종 racism **n** 인종차별 racist **n** 인종차별주의자 racially **adv** 인종적으로

Q: Is the organization committed to addressing racial discrimination?
그 조직은 인종 차별을 다루는 데 전념하고 있나요?

A: ....

1314 □□□

radical
[ˈrædɪkl]

a 근본적인, 급진적인 **n** 급진주의자

= extreme, fundamental, revolutionary, drastic, extremist
\+ radical **n** 급진주의자 radicalism **n** 급진주의 radically **adv** 근본적으로, 급진적으로

Q: Do you support any radical changes in the education system?
교육 시스템에 대한 어떤 급진적인 변화를 지지하나요?

A: ....

1315 □□□

rainforest
[ˈreɪnfɔːrɪst]

n 열대우림

= jungle, tropical forest, dense forest
\+ tropical rainforest 열대 우림

Q: Have you visited a rainforest to see its unique wildlife?
독특한 야생 동물을 보기 위해 열대우림을 방문한 적 있나요?

A: ....

1316 □□□

raise
[reɪz]

v 올리다, 키우다, 모으다 n 인상

= lift, elevate, increase, grow, nurture, collect
+ raise salaries[prices/taxes] 급여를[가격을/세금을] 인상하다

Q: Will the company raise salaries this year to keep up with inflation?
회사가 인플레이션에 맞춰 올해 급여를 인상할까요?

A: ....

1317 □□□

random
[ˈrændəm]

a 무작위의, 임의의

= arbitrary, haphazard, chance, unplanned
+ randomness n 무작위성 randomly adv 무작위로

Q: Did you just pick that number at random, or is there a reason behind it? 그 숫자를 그냥 무작위로 고른 건가요, 아니면 어떤 이유가 있나요?

A: ....

1318 □□□

range
[reɪndʒ]

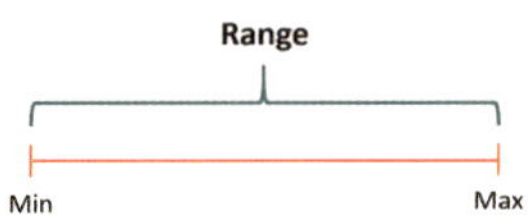

n 범위, 사거리 v 범위에 이르다

= scope, extent, variety, series, vary, stretch
+ long-range a 장거리를 가는, 장기적인 short-range a 단기적인

Q: Does this new electric car have a long driving range on a single charge? 이 새 전기차는 한 번 충전으로 주행 거리가 긴가요?

A: ....

1319 □□□

rank
[ræŋk]

n 지위, 등급 v 등급을 매기다

= position, grade, status, order, classify
+ rank and file 일반 사병들, (조직의) 일반 구성원들 taxi rank 택시 승차장(taxi stand)

Q: What is your current rank in the national tennis competition?
국가 테니스 대회에서 당신의 현재 순위는 무엇인가요?

A: ....

1320 □□□

rapid
[ˈræpɪd]

a 빠른, 신속한

= fast, quick, swift, speedy, sudden
+ rapidity n 신속함 rapidly adv 빠르게

Q: How rapid was the response from emergency services during accident? 사고 발생 시 응급 서비스의 대응은 얼마나 신속했나요?

A: ....

DAY 06 | DICTATION TEST

5회 반복 예문 QR

DICTATION TEST 예문 QR을 듣고 다음 빈칸에 올바른 단어를 쓰세요.

1301. Did you ______________ the new laptop from the store?

1302. Is this chocolate made from ______________ cocoa or mixed with others?

1303. How long does it take to ______________ water with this system?

1304. What is the main ______________ of your visit to headquarters?

1305. Are you planning to ______________ further studies after your degree?

1306. Do you ______________ for the scholarship based on performance?

1307. How do you ensure the ______________ of products before shipping?

1308. What ______________ of materials is needed to complete the project?

1309. Did you and your friend have a ______________ over the misunderstanding?

1310. Which ______________ of the year showed highest sales in your business?

1311. Have you ever thought about ______________ your job to start business?

1312. Can you ______________ the exact line from the book that inspired you?

1313. Is the organization committed to addressing ______________ discrimination?

1314. Do you support any ______________ changes in the education system?

1315. Have you visited a ______________ to see its unique wildlife?

1316. Will the company ______________ salaries this year to keep up with inflation?

1317. Did you just pick that number at ___________, or is there a reason behind it?

1318. Does this new electric car have a long driving ______________ on a single charge?

1319. What is your current ______________ in the national tennis competition?

1320. How ______________ was the response from emergency services during accident?

5회 반복 표제어 QR 5회 반복 예문 QR

DAY 07

30 days

AI 학습자료와 인강 youpass.co.kr

PREVIEW A 다음 단어의 뜻을 한국어로 써보세요.

□ rapidly ______	□ realize ______
□ rare ______	□ reap ______
□ rarely ______	□ reason ______
□ rate ______	□ reasonable ______
□ rather ______	□ recall ______
□ rational ______	□ receipt ______
□ raw ______	□ recent ______
□ react ______	□ recharge ______
□ realistic ______	□ reckless ______
□ reality ______	□ recognize ______

PREVIEW B 사진을 보고 알맞은 영어 단어를 **PREVIEW A** 에서 찾아 써보세요.

______

______

______

______

1321 □□□

rapidly
[ˈræpɪdli]

adv 빠르게, 신속히

= quickly, swiftly, speedily, promptly, fast
+ rapid **a** 빠른

Q: Did the situation change rapidly after yesterday's announcement?
어제 발표 후 상황이 급변했나요?

A: ……………………

1322 □□□

rare
[rer]

a 드문, 희귀한

= uncommon, scarce, infrequent, unusual, precious
+ rarity **n** 희귀성 **rarely** **adv** 드물게

Q: Is it rare to find a truly honest politician these days?
요즘 세상에 진정으로 정직한 정치인을 찾는 것이 드문 일인가요?

A: ……………………

1323 □□□

rarely
[ˈrerli]

adv 거의 ~않는

= seldom, infrequently, hardly ever, almost never
+ rare **a** 드문

Q: Do you rarely eat out, or do you do it quite often?
외식을 거의 하지 않나요, 아니면 꽤 자주 하나요?

A: ……………………

1324 □□□

rate
[reɪt]

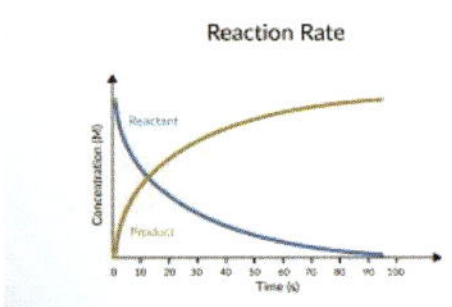

n 비율, 속도, 요금 **v** 평가하다

= speed, pace, ratio, price, evaluate, assess
+ rated **a** 등급이 매겨진

Q: What is the current exchange rate between dollar and euro?
달러와 유로 간 현재 환율은 얼마인가요?

A: ……………………

1325 □□□

rather
[ˈræðər]

adv 오히려, 다소

= instead, preferably, somewhat, quite
+ sooner rather than later 차라리 일찌감치

Q: Would you rather have coffee or tea at the morning meeting?
아침 회의에서 커피나 차 중에 어느 것을 마실 건가요?

A: ……………………

1326 □□□

rational
[ˈræʃənl]

a 합리적인, 이성적인

= **logical, reasonable, sensible, coherent, sound**
\+ **ration** **n** 배급식량, 배급량 **v** 배급하다 **rationality** **n** 합리성 **rationally** **adv** 합리적으로

Q: Is it rational to invest all your savings in one stock?
모든 저축을 한 주식에 투자하는 것이 합리적인가요?

A:

1327 □□□

raw
[rɔː]

a 날것의, 가공하지 않은

= **uncooked, unprocessed, crude, natural, unrefined**
\+ **rawness** **n** 날것의 상태

Q: Do you prefer raw vegetables or cooked ones?
생채소를 선호하나요, 아니면 익힌 채소를 선호하나요?

A:

1328 □□□

react
[riˈækt]

v 반응하다

= **respond, behave, answer, act, acknowledge**
\+ **reaction** **n** 반응 **reactant** **n** 반응물 **reactive** **a** 반응성의

Q: How did your team react to the sudden deadline change?
팀은 갑작스러운 마감 기한 변경에 어떻게 반응했나요?

A:

1329 □□□

realistic
[ˌriːəˈlɪstɪk]

a 현실적인

= **practical, sensible, achievable, authentic, true-to-life**
\+ **reality** **n** 현실 **realism** **n** 현실주의 **realistically** **adv** 현실적으로

Q: Is it realistic to expect the project to finish early?
프로젝트가 일찍 끝날 것이라고 기대하는 것이 현실적인가요?

A:

1330 □□□

reality
[riˈæləti]

n 현실

= **actuality, truth, fact, existence, real world**
\+ **real** **a** 실제의 **realistic** **a** 현실적인 **realize** **v** 깨닫다, 실현하다

Q: Does the reality match what you imagined?
현실이 당신이 상상했던 것과 일치하나요?

A:

1331 □□□

realize
[ˈriːəlaɪz]

v 깨닫다, 실현하다

= **understand, comprehend, achieve, fulfill, become aware**
+ **realization** **n** 깨달음, 실현 **realized** **a** 실현된

Q: When did you realize the plan needed major adjustments?
언제 계획에 큰 조정이 필요하다는 것을 깨달았나요?

A: ....

1332 □□□

reap
[riːp]

v 수확하다, 거두다

= **harvest, gather, obtain, acquire, collect**
+ **reap what one has sown** 자신이 뿌린 씨를 거둬들이다, 자신의 행동의 보상을 받다 (자업자득)

Q: Do you think you will reap benefits from your hard work?
당신의 노력이 결실을 맺을 것이라고 생각하나요?

A: ....

1333 □□□

reason
[ˈriːzn]

n 이유, 이성 **v** 추론하다

= **cause, justification, logic, motive, explain, think**
+ **reasonable** **a** 합리적인 **unreasonable** **a** 비합리적인 **reasonably** **adv** 합리적으로

Q: What is the main reason you changed your career path?
경력 경로를 바꾼 주된 이유는 무엇인가요?

A: ....

1334 □□□

reasonable
[ˈriːznəbl]

a 합리적인, 적당한

= **sensible, fair, logical, moderate, rational**
+ **reason** **n** 이유 **reasonableness** **n** 합리성 **reasonably** **adv** 합리적으로

Q: Is it reasonable to ask now for a deadline extension?
지금 마감 기한 연장을 요청하는 것이 합리적인가요?

A: ....

1335 □□□

recall
[rɪˈkɔːl]

v 기억해내다, 회수하다 **n** 회수

= **remember, recollect, revoke, withdraw, memory**
+ **beyond recall** (본디의 상태로) 돌이킬[되돌릴] 수 없는, 기억할 수 없는
have instant recall 즉각 기억하다

Q: Can you recall the moment when you first met your girlfriend?
여자 친구를 처음 만났을 때를 기억할 수 있나요?

A: ....

1336 □□□

receipt
[rɪˈsiːt]

n 영수증

= **proof of purchase, voucher, acknowledgment, income**

+ **receive** **v** 받다

Q: Did you receive a receipt after buying electronics?
전자기기를 구매한 후 영수증을 받았나요?

A:

1337 □□□

recent
[ˈriːsnt]

a 최근의

= **new, fresh, late, current, latest**

+ **recently** **adv** 최근에

Q: Have you read any interesting books in the recent past?
최근에 재미있는 책 읽은 거 있나요?

A:

1338 □□□

recharge
[ˌriːˈtʃɑːrdʒ]

v 재충전하다

= **replenish, restore, re-energize, renew**

+ **recharge the traffic card** 교통 카드를 충전하다

Q: How often do you take breaks to recharge energy?
에너지를 재충전하기 위해 얼마나 자주 휴식을 취하나요?

A:

1339 □□□

reckless
[ˈrekləs]

a 무모한, 부주의한

= **careless, heedless, rash, irresponsible, impetuous**

+ **recklessness** **n** 무모함 **recklessly** **adv** 무모하게

Q: Was it reckless to drive fast on the icy road?
얼음이 언 도로에서 빠르게 운전하는 것이 무모했나요?

A:

1340 □□□

recognize
[ˈrekəgnaɪz]

v 인식하다, 인정하다

= **identify, acknowledge, perceive, discern, appreciate**

+ **recognition** **n** 인식, 인정 **recognizable** **a** 인식할 수 있는

Q: Did you recognize who called from an unknown number?
모르는 번호로 전화한 사람이 누구인지 알아보았나요?

A:

DAY 07 | DICTATION TEST

5회 반복 예문 QR

DICTATION TEST 예문 QR을 듣고 다음 빈칸에 올바른 단어를 쓰세요.

1321. Did the situation change ______________ after yesterday's announcement?

1322. Is it ______________ to find a truly honest politician these days?

1323. Do you ______________ eat out, or do you do it quite often?

1324. What is the current exchange ______________ between dollar and euro?

1325. Would you ______________ have coffee or tea at the morning meeting?

1326. Is it ______________ to invest all your savings in one stock?

1327. Do you prefer ______________ vegetables or cooked ones?

1328. How did your team ______________ to the sudden deadline change?

1329. Is it ______________ to expect the project to finish early?

1330. Does the ______________ match what you imagined?

1331. When did you ______________ the plan needed major adjustments?

1332. Do you think you will ______________ benefits from your hard work?

1333. What is the main ______________ you changed your career path?

1334. Is it ______________ to ask now for a deadline extension?

1335. Can you ______________ the moment when you first met your girlfriend?

1336. Did you receive a ______________ after buying electronics?

1337. Have you read any interesting books in the ______________ past?

1338. How often do you take breaks to ______________ energy?

1339. Was it ______________ to drive fast on the icy road?

1340. Did you ______________ who called from an unknown number?

5회 반복 표제어 QR 5회 반복 예문 QR

DAY 08
30 days

PREVIEW A 다음 단어의 뜻을 한국어로 써보세요.

□ recommend ________	□ reform ________
□ recover ________	□ refresh ________
□ recreate ________	□ refund ________
□ recruit ________	□ refuse ________
□ recycle ________	□ regard ________
□ reduce ________	□ region ________
□ refer ________	□ register ________
□ reference ________	□ regret ________
□ refine ________	□ regular ________
□ reflect ________	□ regulate ________

PREVIEW B 사진을 보고 알맞은 영어 단어를 **PREVIEW A**에서 찾아 써보세요.

____

____

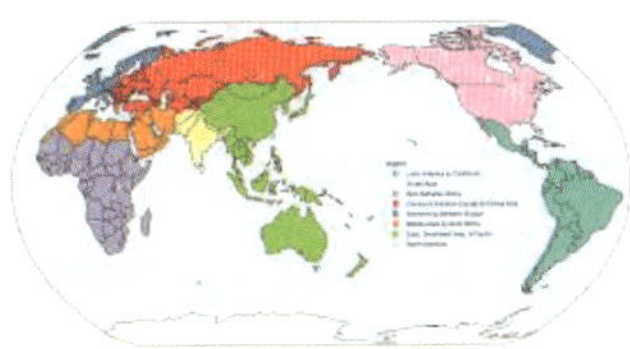
____

____

DAY 01 DAY 02 DAY 03 DAY 04 DAY 05 DAY 06 DAY 07 DAY 08 DAY 09 DAY 10 DAY 11 DAY 12 DAY 13 DAY 14 DAY 15 DAY 16 DAY 17 DAY 18 DAY 19 DAY 20 DAY 21 DAY 22 DAY 23 DAY 24 DAY 25 DAY 26 DAY 27 DAY 28 DAY 29 DAY 30

1341 □□□

recommend
[ˌrekəˈmend]

v 추천하다

= suggest, advise, endorse, commend, advocate
+ recommendation **n** 추천

Q: Can you recommend a restaurant near the city center?
시내 중심가 근처에 식당 추천해 줄 수 있나요?

A: ....

1342 □□□

recover
[rɪˈkʌvər]

v 회복하다, 되찾다

= regain, retrieve, heal, recuperate, find
+ recovery **n** 회복 **recoverable** **a** 회복 가능한

Q: How long will it take to recover after surgery?
수술 후 회복하는 데 얼마나 걸릴까요?

A: ....

1343 □□□

recreate
[ˌriːkriˈeɪt]

v 재창조하다, 재현하다

= reproduce, re-enact, invent again, refresh, relax
+ recreation **n** 재창조, 오락 **recreational** **a** 오락의

Q: Can we recreate the exact conditions of the experiment in a new lab? 새로운 실험실에서 실험의 정확한 조건을 재현할 수 있을까요?

A: ....

1344 □□□

recruit
[rɪˈkruːt]

v 모집하다 **n** 신병, 신입사원

= enlist, hire, enroll, enlistee, new member
+ recruitment **n** 모집

Q: Is your company planning to recruit employees this quarter?
귀사는 이번 분기에 직원을 채용할 계획인가요?

A: ....

1345 □□□

recycle
[ˌriːˈsaɪkl]

v 재활용하다

= reuse, reprocess, reclaim, convert
+ recycling **n** 재활용

Q: Do you recycle plastic and paper separately each week?
매주 플라스틱과 종이를 분리해서 재활용하나요?

A: ....

1346 □□□

reduce
[rɪˈduːs]

v 줄이다, 감소시키다

= lessen, decrease, diminish, lower, curtail
+ reduction n 감소 **reduced a** 감소된

Q: What steps can we take to reduce energy in the school?
학교에서 에너지를 줄이기 위해 어떤 조치를 취할 수 있을까요?

A: ....

1347 □□□

refer
[rɪˈfɜːr]

v 참조하다, 언급하다

= mention, allude, consult, direct, relate
+ reference n 참고, 참조 **referential a** 참조적인

Q: Could you refer me to a plumber for repair?
수리를 위해 배관공을 소개해 줄 수 있나요?

A: ....

1348 □□□

reference
[ˈrefrəns]

n 참조, 참고, 추천서

= mention, citation, source, referral, consult
+ refer v 참조하다

Q: Did you include references from your last job?
지난 직장에서의 추천서들을 포함했나요?

A: ....

1349 □□□

refine
[rɪˈfaɪn]

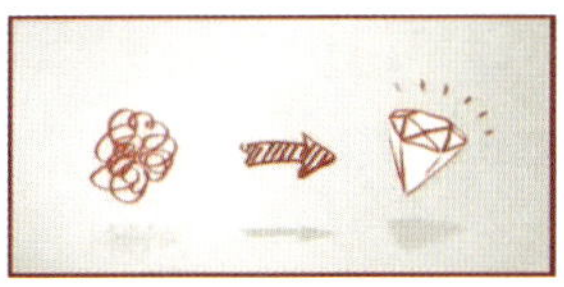

v 정제하다, 개선하다

= purify, perfect, improve, polish, process
+ refinement n 정제, 개선 **refined a** 정제된, 세련된

Q: How do you plan to refine your presentation before the meeting?
회의 전에 발표를 어떻게 다듬을 계획인가요?

A: ....

1350 □□□

reflect
[rɪˈflekt]

v 반사하다, 반영하다, 숙고하다

= mirror, echo, ponder, consider, indicate, show
+ reflection n 반사, 심사숙고 **reflective a** 반사적인, 사색적인

Q: Does this painting accurately reflect the artist's mood at the time?
이 그림이 그 당시 화가의 기분을 정확히 반영하고 있나요?

A: ....

1351 □□□

reform
[rɪˈfɔːrm]

n 개혁 **v** 개혁하다

= improve, restructure, amend, revise, change

+ reformer **n** 개혁가

Q: Are there plans to reform policies about benefits?
혜택에 대한 정책을 개혁할 계획이 있나요?

A: ……………………………………

1352 □□□

refresh
[rɪˈfreʃ]

v 상쾌하게 하다, 새로 고침하다

= revive, invigorate, freshen, renew, update

+ refreshment **n** 새롭게 함, 다과 **refreshing** **a** 상쾌한 **refreshed** **a** 상쾌해진

Q: Do you refresh your browser when the site loads slowly?
사이트가 느리게 로드될 때 브라우저를 새로 고치나요?

A: ……………………………………

1353 □□□

refund
[ˈriːfʌnd] **n** [rɪˈfʌnd] **v**

n 환불 **v** 환불하다

= reimbursement, repayment, return money

+ receive a full refund 전액을 환불 받다

Q: Can I get a refund if the product lacks quality?
제품 품질이 떨어지면 환불받을 수 있나요?

A: ……………………………………

1354 □□□

refuse
[rɪˈfjuːz] **v** [ˈrefjuːs] **n**

v 거절하다

= reject, decline, deny, turn down, garbage

+ refusal **n** 거절

Q: Is there any reason why you refused to attend the meeting?
당신이 회의 참석을 거절한 이유가 따로 있나요?

A: ……………………………………

1355 □□□

regard
[rɪˈgɑːrd]

v 여기다, 간주하다 **n** 고려, 관심

= consider, view, esteem, respect, attention

+ regardless **adv** 개의치 않고 **regardless of** ~와 상관없이

Q: Do you still regard him as a close friend despite the recent disagreement? 최근 의견 불일치에도 불구하고 당신은 여전히 그를 가까운 친구로 여기나요?

A: ……………………………………

1356 □□□

region
[ˈriːdʒən]

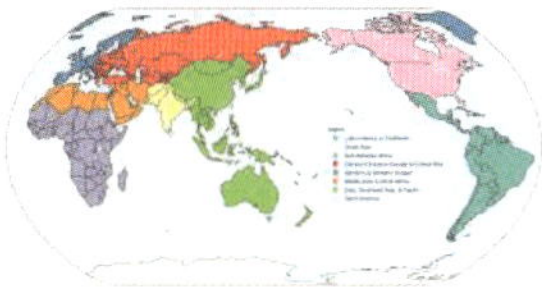

n 지역, 지방

= area, territory, district, zone, domain

+ regional **a** 지역적인 **regionally** **adv** 지역적으로

Q: Which region will see the most growth?
어떤 지역이 가장 큰 성장을 보일까요?

A: ....

1357 □□□

register
[ˈredʒɪstər]

v 등록하다 **n** 등록부, 출석부

= enroll, record, sign up, list, record, registry

+ registration **n** 등록

Q: Have you already registered for the conference?
회의에 이미 등록했나요?

A: ....

1358 □□□

regret
[rɪˈgret]

n 후회, 유감 **v** 후회하다

= remorse, sorrow, lament, mourn, feel bad about

+ regrettable **a** 유감스러운 **regrettably** **adv** 유감스럽게도

Q: Do you regret not taking that offer last year?
작년에 그 제안을 받아들이지 않았던 것을 후회하나요?

A: ....

1359 □□□

regular
[ˈregjələr]

a 규칙적인, 평범한

= customary, usual, normal, routine, consistent

+ regularity **n** 규칙성 **regularly** **adv** 정기적으로 **irregular** **a** 불규칙한

Q: Are you a regular visitor to the gym?
헬스장에 정기적으로 가는 사람인가요?

A: ....

1360 □□□

regulate
[ˈregjuleɪt]

v 규제하다, 조절하다

= control, govern, supervise, adjust, standardize

+ regulation **n** 규제, 규칙 **regulator** **n** 규제 기관 **regulatory** **a** 규제하는

Q: How does the government regulate factory emissions?
정부는 공장 배출물을 어떻게 규제하나요?

A: ....

DAY 08 | DICTATION TEST

5회 반복 예문 QR

DICTATION TEST 예문 QR을 듣고 다음 빈칸에 올바른 단어를 쓰세요.

1341. Can you ______________ a restaurant near the city center?

1342. How long will it take to ______________ after surgery?

1343. Can we ______________ the exact conditions of the experiment in a new lab?

1344. Is your company planning to ______________ employees this quarter?

1345. Do you ______________ plastic and paper separately each week?

1346. What steps can we take to ______________ energy in the school?

1347. Could you ______________ me to a plumber for repair?

1348. Did you include ______________ from your last job?

1349. How do you plan to ______________ your presentation before the meeting?

1350. Does this painting accurately ______________ the artist's mood at the time?

1351. Are there plans to ______________ policies about benefits?

1352. Do you ______________ your browser when the site loads slowly?

1353. Can I get a ______________ if the product lacks quality?

1354. Is there any reason why you ______________ to attend the meeting?

1355. Do you still ______________ him as a close friend despite the recent disagreement?

1356. Which ______________ will see the most growth?

1357. Have you already ______________ for the conference?

1358. Do you ______________ not taking that offer last year?

1359. Are you a ______________ visitor to the gym?

1360. How does the government ______________ factory emissions?

5회 반복 표제어 QR　　5회 반복 예문 QR

DAY 09

30 days

AI 학습자료와 인강 youpass.co.kr

PREVIEW A 다음 단어의 뜻을 한국어로 써보세요.

□ reinforce ________	□ religion ________
□ reject ________	□ religious ________
□ relate ________	□ rely ________
□ related ________	□ remain ________
□ relationship ________	□ remark ________
□ relative ________	□ remarkable ________
□ release ________	□ remember ________
□ relevant ________	□ remind ________
□ relief ________	□ remote ________
□ relieve ________	□ remove ________

PREVIEW B 사진을 보고 알맞은 영어 단어를 **PREVIEW A** 에서 찾아 써보세요.

____

____

____

____

1361 □□□

reinforce
[ˌriːɪnˈfɔːrs]

v 강화하다, 보강하다

= strengthen, support, bolster, fortify, enhance
+ reinforcement **n** 강화, 보강

Q: How can we reinforce teamwork to boost productivity?
생산성을 높이기 위해 팀워크를 어떻게 강화할 수 있을까요?

A: ....

1362 □□□

reject
[rɪˈdʒekt]

v 거절하다, 거부하다

= refuse, decline, dismiss, discard, renounce
+ rejection **n** 거절

Q: Did the manager reject your proposal yesterday?
어제 관리자가 당신의 제안을 거절했나요?

A: ....

1363 □□□

relate
[rɪˈleɪt]

v 관련시키다, 이야기하다

= connect, associate, tell, recount, empathize
+ relation **n** 관계 **relationship** **n** 관계 **related** **a** 관련된 **relative** **a** 상대적인

Q: Can you relate this example to the main topic?
이 예시를 주요 주제와 연관 지을 수 있나요?

A: ....

1364 □□□

related
[rɪˈleɪtɪd]

a 관련된

= connected, associated, linked, kindred, relevant
+ relation **n** 관계 **relationship** **n** 관계

Q: Are these documents related to the contract?
이 문서들이 계약과 관련이 있나요?

A: ....

1365 □□□

relationship
[rɪˈleɪʃnʃɪp]

n 관계

= connection, bond, ties, rapport, affair
+ relate **v** 관련시키다

Q: How would you describe your relationship with your partner?
파트너와의 관계를 어떻게 묘사하시겠어요?

A: ....

1366 □□□

relative
[ˈrelətɪv]

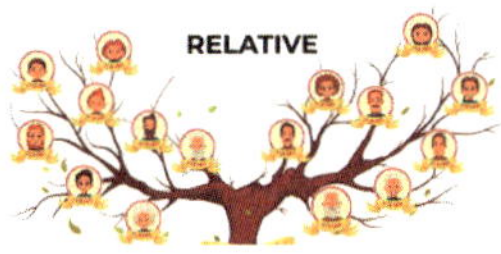

a 상대적인 **n** 친척

= comparative, dependent, related, kin, family member
+ relativity n 상대성 **relatively adv** 상대적으로

Q: Do you have any relatives living near your house?
당신의 집 근처에 사는 친척들이 있나요?

A: ....

1367 □□□

release
[rɪˈliːs]

v 풀어주다, 발매하다 **n** 출시, 해방

= set free, unleash, publish, launch, issue, discharge
+ press release (기관 · 정당 · 정부 부처의) 대언론 공식 발표[성명]

Q: When will the company release the latest version?
회사가 최신 버전을 언제 출시할 예정인가요?

A: ....

1368 □□□

relevant
[ˈreləvənt]

a 관련된, 적절한

= pertinent, applicable, germane, significant, related
+ relevance n 관련성 **relevantly adv** 관련하여

Q: Is this information relevant to the situation?
이 정보가 상황에 관련이 있나요?

A: ....

1369 □□□

relief
[rɪˈliːf]

n 안도, 구호품

= comfort, solace, aid, alleviation, assistance
+ relieve v 경감시키다

Q: Do you think taking a break will bring you some relief?
휴식을 취하면 좀 안도감이 생길 것 같은가요?

A: ....

1370 □□□

relieve
[rɪˈliːv]

v 완화시키다, 안도하게 하다

= ease, alleviate, lessen, soothe, help, assist
+ relief n 안도, 경감

Q: What do you do to relieve stress after work?
퇴근 후 스트레스를 풀기 위해 무엇을 하나요?

A: ....

1371 □□□

religion
[rɪˈlɪdʒən]

n 종교

= **faith, belief, creed, spirituality, worship**
+ **religious** **a** 종교적인

Q: How does religion influence culture in your country?
당신 나라에서는 종교가 문화에 어떻게 영향을 미치나요?

A: ....

1372 □□□

religious
[rɪˈlɪdʒəs]

a 종교적인

= **spiritual, devout, pious, sacred, faithful**
+ **religion** **n** 종교 **religiously** **adv** 종교적으로

Q: Are you active in any religious groups?
어떤 종교 단체에서 활동하고 있나요?

A: ....

1373 □□□

rely
[rɪˈlaɪ]

v 의존하다, 신뢰하다

= **depend, count on, trust, confide in**
+ **reliance** **n** 의존 **reliable** **a** 신뢰할 수 있는 **reliably** **adv** 신뢰할 수 있게

Q: Can we rely on this data for decisions?
결정을 위해 이 데이터에 의존할 수 있나요?

A: ....

1374 □□□

remain
[rɪˈmeɪn]

v 남아있다, ~인 채로 있다

= **stay, linger, persist, continue, leftover**
+ **remainder** **n** 나머지

Q: How many participants remain for the workshop?
워크숍에 몇 명의 참가자가 남아 있나요?

A: ....

1375 □□□

remark
[rɪˈmɑːrk]

n 언급, 발언 **v** 언급하다

= **comment, observation, statement, say, note**
+ **remarkable** **a** 놀라운 **remarkably** **adv** 놀랍게도

Q: Did the client make any remark about the product?
고객이 제품에 대해 어떤 언급이라도 했나요?

A: ....

1376 □□□

remarkable
[rɪˈmɑːrkəbl]

a 놀랄 만한, 주목할 만한

= extraordinary, noteworthy, amazing, impressive, significant
+ remark **n** 언급 remarkably **adv** 놀랍게도

Q: What's the most remarkable thing your team achieved?
당신 팀이 이룬 가장 놀라운 성과는 무엇인가요?

A: ....

1377 □□□

remember
[rɪˈmembər]

v 기억하다

= recall, recollect, retain, keep in mind
+ remembrance **n** 기억, 추모

Q: Do you remember our first meeting at the party?
파티에서 우리의 첫 만남을 기억하나요?

A: ....

1378 □□□

remind
[rɪˈmaɪnd]

v 상기시키다, 생각나게 하다

= prompt, nudge, help someone remember, jog someone's memory
+ reminder **n** 상기시키는 것

Q: Can you remind me to send the email?
이메일 보내는 것을 상기시켜 줄 수 있나요?

A: ....

1379 □□□

remote
[rɪˈmoʊt]

a 먼, 외딴, 원격의

= distant, faraway, isolated, secluded, unlikely
+ remoteness **n** 멀리 떨어져 있음 remotely **adv** 멀리서, 원격으로

Q: Are you okay working from a remote location?
원격지에서 일하는 것이 괜찮으신가요?

A: ....

1380 □□□

remove
[rɪˈmuːv]

v 제거하다, 없애다

= take away, eliminate, extract, detach, dismiss
+ removal **n** 제거 removable **a** 제거 가능한

Q: When will IT remove the old software?
부서에서 언제 오래된 소프트웨어를 제거할까요?

A: ....

DAY 09 | DICTATION TEST

5회 반복 예문 QR

DICTATION TEST 예문 QR을 듣고 다음 빈칸에 올바른 단어를 쓰세요.

1361. How can we ______________ teamwork to boost productivity?

1362. Did the manager ______________ your proposal yesterday?

1363. Can you ______________ this example to the main topic?

1364. Are these documents ______________ to the contract?

1365. How would you describe your ______________ with your partner?

1366. Do you have any ______________ living near your house?

1367. When will the company ______________ the latest version?

1368. Is this information ______________ to the situation?

1369. Do you think taking a break will bring you some ______________?

1370. What do you do to ______________ stress after work?

1371. How does ______________ influence culture in your country?

1372. Are you active in any ______________ groups?

1373. Can we ______________ on this data for decisions?

1374. How many participants ______________ for the workshop?

1375. Did the client make any ______________ about the product?

1376. What's the most ______________ thing your team achieved?

1377. Do you ______________ our first meeting at the party?

1378. Can you ______________ me to send the email?

1379. Are you okay working from a ______________ location?

1380. When will IT ______________ the old software?

5회 반복 표제어 QR 5회 반복 예문 QR

DAY 10

30 days

AI 학습자료와 인강 youpass.co.kr

PREVIEW A 다음 단어의 뜻을 한국어로 써보세요.

□ renew ____________	□ reputation ____________
□ repair ____________	□ request ____________
□ repeat ____________	□ require ____________
□ repeatedly ____________	□ rescue ____________
□ replace ____________	□ research ____________
□ reply ____________	□ resemble ____________
□ represent ____________	□ resent ____________
□ representative ____________	□ reserve ____________
□ reproduce ____________	□ resident ____________
□ republic ____________	□ resign ____________

PREVIEW B 사진을 보고 알맞은 영어 단어를 PREVIEW A에서 찾아 써보세요.

____

____

____

____

1381 □□□

renew
[rɪˈnuː]

v 갱신하다, 재개하다

= restore, resume, renovate, extend, replenish
+ renewal n 갱신 renewable a 재생 가능한

Q: How often do coral reefs renew after bleaching?
산호초는 백화 현상 후에 얼마나 자주 재생되나요?

A:

1382 □□□

repair
[rɪˈper]

v 수리하다 n 수리

= mend, fix, restore, renovate, mending, restoration
+ repairable a 수리 가능한

Q: Can you repair the printer before the meeting?
회의 전에 프린터를 수리해 줄 수 있나요?

A:

1383 □□□

repeat
[rɪˈpiːt]

v 반복하다 n 반복

= reiterate, reproduce, duplicate, echo, recurrence
+ repetition n 반복 repeated a 반복된 repeatedly adv 반복적으로

Q: Could you repeat the main points again?
주요 요점들을 다시 반복해 주시겠어요?

A:

1384 □□□

repeatedly
[rɪˈpiːtɪdli]

adv 반복해서, 되풀이하여

= often, frequently, again and again, continually
+ repeat v 반복하다 repeated a 반복된

Q: Why did the system crash repeatedly?
시스템이 왜 반복적으로 다운되었나요?

A:

1385 □□□

replace
[rɪˈpleɪs]

v 대체하다, 교체하다

= substitute, supersede, exchange, put back
+ replacement n 교체 replaceable a 교체 가능한

Q: When will they replace the old computers?
그들은 언제 오래된 컴퓨터를 교체할 건가요?

A:

1386 □□□

reply
[rɪˈplaɪ]

n 답변 v 답변하다

= answer, respond, retort, response, acknowledgement

\+ a tart reply 톡 쏘는 듯한 대답 a curt reply 퉁명스러운 대답 a pert reply 당돌한 대답

Q: Did you get a reply from the client?
고객에게서 답장을 받았나요?

A:

1387 □□□

represent
[ˌreprɪˈzent]

v 대표하다, 나타내다

= stand for, symbolize, depict, act for, illustrate

\+ representation n 대표, 표현 representative n 대표자 a 대표하는

Q: Who will represent our department?
우리 부서를 누가 대표할 건가요?

A:

1388 □□□

representative
[ˌreprɪˈzentətɪv]

n 대표자 a 대표하는

= typical, characteristic, delegate, spokesperson, example

\+ representation n 대표 represent v 대표하다

Q: Do you think this painting is truly representative of his early artistic style? 이 그림이 그의 초기 예술적 스타일을 진정으로 대표한다고 생각하시나요?

A:

1389 □□□

reproduce
[ˌriːprəˈduːs]

v 번식하다, 복제하다

= procreate, copy, duplicate, replicate, generate

\+ reproduction n 번식, 복제 reproductive a 생식의, 번식의

Q: Can scientists successfully reproduce the results of the experiment in different labs? 과학자들이 다른 실험실에서도 그 실험 결과를 성공적으로 재현할 수 있을까요?

A:

1390 □□□

republic
[rɪˈpʌblɪk]

n 공화국

= commonwealth, democratic state, self-governing state

\+ republican a 공화국의

Q: Have you visited the Republic of Korea?
대한민국을 방문해 본 적 있나요?

A:

1391 □□□

reputation
[ˌrepjuˈteɪʃn]

n 명성, 평판

= standing, renown, prestige, character, name
+ reputable **a** 평판 좋은
Q: How does the company keep its reputation?
회사는 어떻게 명성을 유지하나요?
A: ......

1392 □□□

request
[rɪˈkwest]

n 요청 **v** 요청하다

= ask, appeal, demand, query, petition
+ as requested 부탁받은 대로
Q: Did you send a request for resources?
자원 요청을 보냈나요?
A: ......

1393 □□□

require
[rɪˈkwaɪər]

v 필요로 하다, 요구하다

= need, demand, necessitate, oblige, stipulate
+ requirement **n** 요구사항, 필요조건 **required** **a** 필수적인
Q: Does the job require coding skills?
그 일은 코딩 기술을 필요로 하나요?
A: ......

1394 □□□

rescue
[ˈreskjuː]

n 구조 **v** 구조하다

= save, retrieve, free, liberate, salvation
+ a search and rescue team 수색 구조팀
Q: How fast did the rescue team arrive?
구조팀이 얼마나 빨리 도착했나요?
A: ......

1395 □□□

research
[ˈriːsɜːrtʃ] [rɪˈsɜːrtʃ]

n 연구, 조사 **v** 연구하다

= study, investigation, exploration, examine, inquire
+ researcher **n** 연구원 **researched** **a** 연구된
Q: Do you think the company will invest more in research and development next year? 내년에 회사가 연구 개발에 더 많이 투자할 것이라고 생각하시나요?
A: ......

1396 □□□

resemble
[rɪˈzembl]

v ~와 닮다

= **look like, be similar to, take after, bear a likeness**
+ **resemblance** **n** 유사성

Q: Does your office resemble the old one?
당신의 사무실이 예전 사무실과 닮았나요?

A: ....

1397 □□□

resent
[rɪˈzent]

v 분개하다, 불쾌하게 여기다

= **begrudge, feel bitter about, take offense at**
+ **resentment** **n** 분개, 원한 **resentful** **a** 분개하는

Q: Do you resent changes to your plan?
당신의 계획 변경에 불만을 품고 있나요?

A: ....

1398 □□□

reserve
[rɪˈzɜːrv]

v 예약하다, 비축하다 **n** 비축물, 보호 구역

= **book, set aside, store, retain, supply, shy**
+ **reservation** **n** 예약 **reserved** **a** 예약된, 내성적인

Q: Did you reserve a room for the meeting?
회의를 위해 방을 예약했나요?

A: ....

1399 □□□

resident
[ˈrezɪdənt]

n 주민, 거주자

= **inhabitant, dweller, citizen, occupant, local**
+ **residence** **n** 거주, 주거 **residential** **a** 주거의

Q: Are you a permanent resident of this city, or are you just visiting?
이 도시의 영주권자인가요, 아니면 그저 방문 중인가요?

A: ....

1400 □□□

resign
[rɪˈzaɪn]

v 사임하다, 체념하다

= **quit, step down, relinquish, surrender, submit**
+ **resignation** **n** 사직, 체념

Q: Did your colleague resign after restructuring?
동료가 구조 조정 후에 사임했나요?

A: ....

DAY 10 | DICTATION TEST

5회 반복 예문 QR

DICTATION TEST 예문 QR을 듣고 다음 빈칸에 올바른 단어를 쓰세요.

1381. How often do coral reefs ______________ after bleaching?

1382. Can you ______________ the printer before the meeting?

1383. Could you ______________ the main points again?

1384. Why did the system crash ______________?

1385. When will they ______________ the old computers?

1386. Did you get a ______________ from the client?

1387. Who will ______________ our department?

1388. Do you think this painting is truly ______________ of his early artistic style?

1389. Can scientists successfully ______________ the results of the experiment in different labs?

1390. Have you visited the ______________ of Korea?

1391. How does the company keep its ______________?

1392. Did you send a ______________ for resources?

1393. Does the job ______________ coding skills?

1394. How fast did the ______________ team arrive?

1395. Do you think the company will invest more in ______________ and development next year?

1396. Does your office ______________ the old one?

1397. Do you ______________ changes to your plan?

1398. Did you ______________ a room for the meeting?

1399. Are you a permanent ______________ of this city, or are you just visiting?

1400. Did your colleague ______________ after restructuring?

5회 반복 표제어 QR　5회 반복 예문 QR

DAY 11

30 days

AI 학습자료와 인강 youpass.co.kr

PREVIEW A 다음 단어의 뜻을 한국어로 써보세요.

- ☐ **resist** ______
- ☐ **resolution** ______
- ☐ **resolve** ______
- ☐ **resource** ______
- ☐ **respect** ______
- ☐ **respectable** ______
- ☐ **respectful** ______
- ☐ **respective** ______
- ☐ **respond** ______
- ☐ **response** ______
- ☐ **responsible** ______
- ☐ **restore** ______
- ☐ **restrict** ______
- ☐ **retire** ______
- ☐ **reveal** ______
- ☐ **reverse** ______
- ☐ **revise** ______
- ☐ **revive** ______
- ☐ **revolution** ______
- ☐ **reward** ______

PREVIEW B 사진을 보고 알맞은 영어 단어를 **PREVIEW A** 에서 찾아 써보세요.

______

______

______

______

1401 □□□

resist
[rɪˈzɪst]

v 저항하다, 견디다

= **oppose, withstand, defy, fight, hold out**
\+ **resistance** **n** 저항 **resistant** **a** 저항하는 **resistible** **a** 저항할 수 있는

Q: How do you resist distractions while working on tasks?
업무를 할 때 방해 요소를 어떻게 이겨내나요?

A: ……………………

1402 □□□

resolution
[ˌrezəˈluːʃn]

n 해결, 결의, 해상도

= **decision, determination, solution, proposal, clarity**
\+ **resolve** **v** 해결하다, 결심하다 **resolute** **a** 단호한

Q: Have you made a resolution to improve work-life balance?
워라밸 개선을 위한 결심을 했나요?

A: ……………………

1403 □□□

resolve
[rɪˈzɑːlv]

v 해결하다, 결심하다 **n** 결심

= **solve, settle, decide, determine, fix**
\+ **resolution** **n** 결심, 해결 **resolved** **a** 결심한

Q: Could you resolve the issue before the Friday deadline?
금요일 마감 기한 전에 문제를 해결할 수 있나요?

A: ……………………

1404 □□□

resource
[ˈriːsɔːrs] [rɪˈsɔːrs]

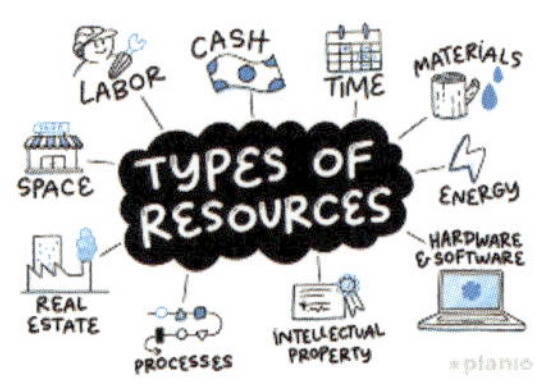

n 자원, 수단

= **asset, supply, means, source, capability**
\+ **resourceful** **a** 수완이 좋은

Q: Can you share a resource for learning advanced programming?
고급 프로그래밍 학습을 위한 자료를 공유해 줄 수 있나요?

A: ……………………

1405 □□□

respect
[rɪˈspekt]

n 존경, 측면 **v** 존경하다

= **admire, honor, esteem, regard, consideration**
\+ **respectable** **a** 존경할 만한 **respectful** **a** 공손한 **respective** **a** 각각의
respectfully **adv** 공손하게 **respectively** **adv** 각각

Q: How do you show respect to colleagues in your company?
당신의 회사에서는 동료들에게 어떻게 존경을 표현하나요?

A: ……………………

1406 □□□

respectable
[rɪˈspektəbl]

a 존경할 만한, 훌륭한

= reputable, honorable, decent, worthy, admirable

+ respect n 존경 **respectability n** 존경받을 만함 **respectably adv** 존경받을 만하게

Q: Do you think this candidate has a respectable background?
이 후보자가 존경할 만한 배경을 가지고 있다고 생각하나요?

A: ……

1407 □□□

respectful
[rɪˈspektfl]

a 존경심을 표하는, 공손한

= polite, courteous, deferential, reverent

+ respect n 존경 **respectfully adv** 공손하게

Q: Are employees expected to stay respectful during talks?
직원들은 대화 중에 예의를 지켜야 하나요?

A: ……

1408 □□□

respective
[rɪˈspektɪv]

a 각자의, 개별적인

= individual, separate, particular, distinct

+ respectively adv 각각

Q: Will the students be assigned to their respective classrooms based on their grades? 학생들은 성적에 따라 각자의 교실에 배정될까요?

A: ……

1409 □□□

respond
[rɪˈspɑːnd]

v 응답하다, 반응하다

= reply, answer, react, acknowledge, reciprocate

+ response n 응답 **responsibility n** 책임 **responsive a** 반응하는 **responsible a** 책임 있는

Q: How quickly do you respond to customer inquiries?
고객 문의에 얼마나 빨리 응답하나요?

A: ……

1410 □□□

response
[rɪˈspɑːns]

n 응답, 반응

= answer, reply, reaction, feedback, acknowledgment

+ respond v 응답하다 **responsive a** 반응하는

Q: What was the customer's response after you explained it?
설명한 후 고객의 반응은 어땠나요?

A: ……

1411 □□□

responsible
[rɪˈspɑːnsəbl]

a 책임감 있는, ~의 원인이 되는

= accountable, liable, in charge, trustworthy, reliable

+ responsibility n 책임 **responsibly** adv 책임감 있게 **irresponsible** a 무책임한

Q: Who is responsible for the company's social media?
회사 소셜 미디어 담당자는 누구인가요?

A: ....

1412 □□□

restore
[rɪˈstɔːr]

v 복구하다, 회복하다

= repair, revive, return, reinstate, bring back

+ restoration n 복원, 회복 **restorative** a 회복시키는

Q: Can we restore the old photographs to their original condition?
오래된 사진들을 원래 상태로 복원할 수 있을까요?

A: ....

1413 □□□

restrict
[rɪˈstrɪkt]

v 제한하다, 규제하다

= limit, confine, restrain, curb, control

+ restriction n 제한 **restricted** a 제한된

Q: Does the company restrict file access to staff?
회사가 직원들에게 파일 접근을 제한하나요?

A: ....

1414 □□□

retire
[rɪˈtaɪər]

v 은퇴하다, 퇴직하다

= withdraw, resign, step down, go to bed, pull back

+ retirement n 은퇴 **retired** a 은퇴한

Q: At what age do employees usually retire here?
여기서 직원들은 보통 몇 살에 은퇴하나요?

A: ....

1415 □□□

reveal
[rɪˈviːl]

v 드러내다, 밝히다

= disclose, expose, unveil, show, uncover

+ revelation n 폭로, 계시

Q: Will you reveal the new strategy at the next meeting?
다음 회의에서 새로운 전략을 공개할 건가요?

A: ....

1416 □□□

reverse
[rɪˈvɜːrs]

v 뒤집다, 역전시키다 n 역, 반대

= opposite, inverted, turn around, revoke, backward

+ reverse engineering 역설계, 분해 공학(다른 회사의 상품을 분해하여 그 생산 방식을 알아낸 뒤 복제하는 것)

Q: Can we reverse the effects of climate change if we act now?
지금 행동하면 기후 변화의 영향을 되돌릴 수 있을까요?

A: ……………………

1417 □□□

revise
[rɪˈvaɪz]

v 수정하다, 개정하다

= amend, alter, edit, update, modify

+ revision n 수정, 개정 **revised** a 수정된

Q: Did the editor ask you to revise the article?
편집자가 기사를 수정해 달라고 요청했나요?

A: ……………………

1418 □□□

revive
[rɪˈvaɪv]

v 소생시키다, 회복시키다

= restore, rejuvenate, revitalize, bring back, reactivate

+ revival n 부활

Q: What plans exist to revive the old product line?
오래된 제품 라인을 되살릴 어떤 계획이 있나요?

A: ……………………

1419 □□□

revolution
[ˌrevəˈluːʃn]

n 혁명, 회전

= rebellion, uprising, drastic change, rotation, upheaval

+ revolutionary a 혁명적인 **revolve** v 돌다, 회전하다

Q: How did the digital revolution change business?
디지털 혁명이 비즈니스를 어떻게 변화시켰나요?

A: ……………………

1420 □□□

reward
[rɪˈwɔːrd]

n 보상 v 보상하다

= prize, award, bonus, recompense, compensate

+ rewarding a 보람 있는

Q: What reward does the company offer for great performance?
회사는 뛰어난 성과에 대해 어떤 보상을 제공하나요?

A: ……………………

DAY 11 | DICTATION TEST

5회 반복 예문 QR

DICTATION TEST 예문 QR을 듣고 다음 빈칸에 올바른 단어를 쓰세요.

1401. How do you ______________ distractions while working on tasks?

1402. Have you made a ______________ to improve work-life balance?

1403. Could you ______________ the issue before the Friday deadline?

1404. Can you share a ______________ for learning advanced programming?

1405. How do you show ______________ to colleagues in your company?

1406. Do you think this candidate has a ______________ background?

1407. Are employees expected to stay ______________ during talks?

1408. Will the students be assigned to their ______________ classrooms based on their grades?

1409. How quickly do you ______________ to customer inquiries?

1410. What was the customer's ______________ after you explained it?

1411. Who is ______________ for the company's social media?

1412. Can we ______________ the old photographs to their original condition?

1413. Does the company ______________ file access to staff?

1414. At what age do employees usually ______________ here?

1415. Will you ______________ the new strategy at the next meeting?

1416. Can we ______________ the effects of climate change if we act now?

1417. Did the editor ask you to ______________ the article?

1418. What plans exist to ______________ the old product line?

1419. How did the digital ______________ change business?

1420. What ______________ does the company offer for great performance?

5회 반복 표제어 QR   5회 반복 예문 QR

DAY 12

30 days

AI 학습자료와 인강 youpass.co.kr

PREVIEW A 다음 단어의 뜻을 한국어로 써보세요.

- ☐ rhythm
- ☐ rid
- ☐ riddle
- ☐ risk
- ☐ ritual
- ☐ rob
- ☐ root
- ☐ rotate
- ☐ route
- ☐ routine
- ☐ row
- ☐ royal
- ☐ rub
- ☐ rubber
- ☐ rude
- ☐ ruin
- ☐ rural
- ☐ rush
- ☐ rusty
- ☐ sacred

PREVIEW B 사진을 보고 알맞은 영어 단어를 **PREVIEW A**에서 찾아 써보세요.

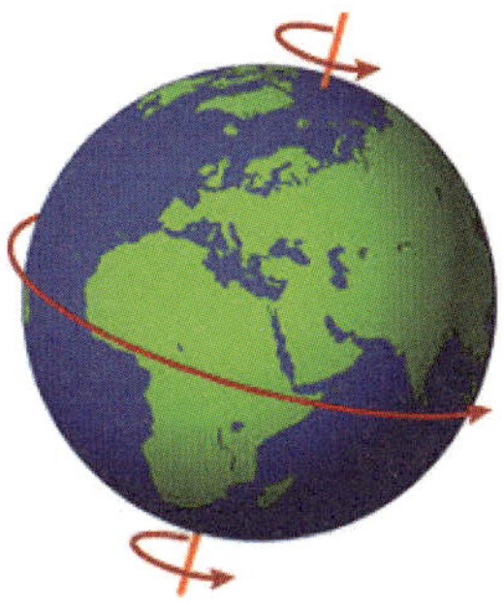

1421 □□□

rhythm
[ˈrɪðəm]

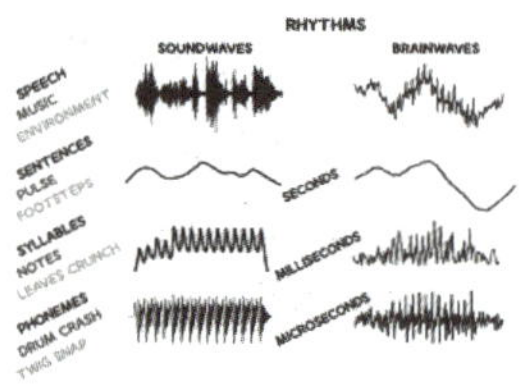

n 리듬, 율동

= beat, tempo, cadence, flow, pattern

+ rhythmic **a** 리듬감 있는 **rhythmically** **adv** 리듬감 있게

Q: Can you keep rhythm during dance practice this evening?
오늘 저녁 댄스 연습 때 리듬을 맞출 수 있나요?

A: ....

1422 □□□

rid
[rɪd]

v 제거하다, 없애다

= free, eliminate, clear, get rid of

+ get rid of 면하다, 제거하다, 끝내다

Q: How can we get rid of unnecessary files on our computer?
컴퓨터에서 불필요한 파일을 어떻게 없앨 수 있을까요?

A: ....

1423 □□□

riddle
[ˈrɪdl]

n 수수께끼

= puzzle, enigma, mystery, conundrum

+ guess a riddle 수수께끼를 알아맞히다 **find out a riddle** 수수께끼의 답을 풀다

Q: Have you tried solving a riddle that seemed impossible?
불가능해 보이는 수수께끼를 풀어본 적 있나요?

A: ....

1424 □□□

risk
[rɪsk]

n 위험 **v** 위험을 무릅쓰다

= danger, hazard, peril, gamble, venture

+ risky **a** 위험한

Q: Are you willing to take the risk of investing in a startup?
스타트업에 투자하는 위험을 감수할 의향이 있나요?

A: ....

1425 □□□

ritual
[ˈrɪtʃuəl]

n 의식, 의례 **a** 의례적인

= ceremony, rite, custom, routine, tradition

+ ritualistic **a** 의식적인 **ritually** **adv** 의례적으로

Q: Do you have a morning ritual that helps you stay focused?
집중하는 데 도움이 되는 아침 의식이 있나요?

A: ....

1426 □□□

rob
[rɑːb]

v 강탈하다, 훔치다

= steal, plunder, raid, pilfer

+ robbery **n** 강도질 **robber** **n** 강도

Q: Did anyone try to rob the store during last weekend's shift?
지난 주말 근무 중에 누가 가게를 털려고 했나요?

A: ....

1427 □□□

root
[ruːt] [rʊt]

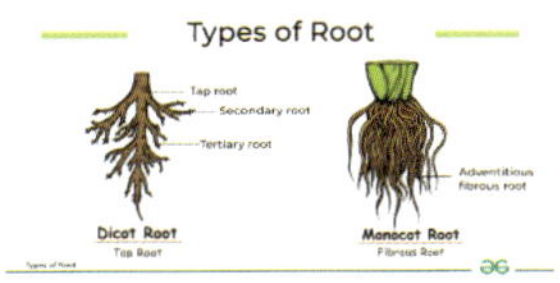

n 뿌리, 근원 **v** 뿌리내리다

= origin, source, base, foundation, extract, establish

+ rooted **a** 뿌리박은

Q: What is the root cause of delays in the last project?
지난 프로젝트 지연의 근본 원인은 무엇인가요?

A: ....

1428 □□□

rotate
[ˈroʊteɪt]

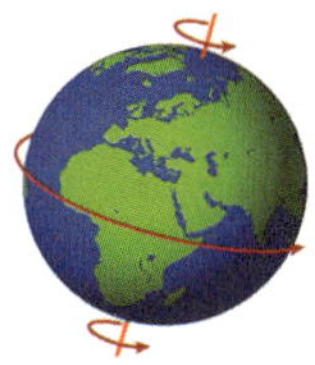

v 회전하다, 교대하다

= turn, spin, revolve, alternate, pivot

+ rotation **n** 회전 **rotational** **a** 회전하는

Q: How often do you rotate your car's tires for even wear?
타이어가 고르게 마모되도록 얼마나 자주 자동차 타이어를 교체하나요?

A: ....

1429 □□□

route
[ruːt] [raʊt]

n 경로, 노선

= path, course, way, road, itinerary

+ bus route 버스 노선

Q: Which route do you take to avoid traffic on your commute?
출퇴근 시 교통 체증을 피하기 위해 어떤 경로를 이용하나요?

A: ....

1430 □□□

routine
[ruːˈtiːn]

n 일상, 판에 박힌 일 **a** 일상적인

= custom, habit, procedure, regular, ordinary

+ routinely **adv** 일상적으로

Q: Have you developed a workout routine you stick to daily?
매일 꾸준히 지키는 운동 루틴을 만들었나요?

A: ....

1431 □□□

row
[roʊ] n v [raʊ] n

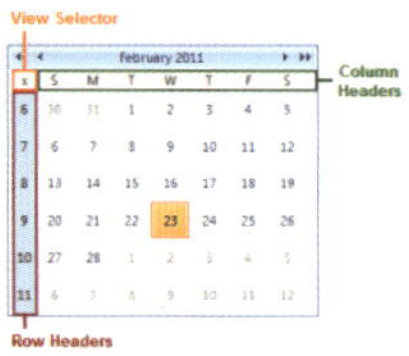

n 줄, 열, 말다툼, 말싸움 v 노를 젓다

= line, series, argument, paddle, scull

+ in a row (여러 번을) 잇달아[연이어], (며칠 · 몇 달 · 몇 년 등을) 계속해서[연이어]

Q: Did you manage to get a good seat in the front row for the concert?
콘서트 맨 앞줄에 좋은 자리를 잡으셨나요?

A: ....

1432 □□□

royal
[ˈrɔɪəl]

a 왕실의, 왕의

= regal, majestic, kingly, queenly, imperial

+ royalty n 왕족, 왕권 royally adv 왕처럼

Q: Are you interested in visiting royal palaces on vacation?
휴가 때 왕궁을 방문하는 것에 관심이 있나요?

A: ....

1433 □□□

rub
[rʌb]

v 문지르다, 비비다

= chafe, massage, scrub, wipe, polish

+ rub-down n 문질러서 닦기[윤내기], 마사지(massage)

Q: Can you rub ointment on my arm where the bite itches?
물린 곳 가려운 팔에 연고 좀 발라줄 수 있나요?

A: ....

1434 □□□

rubber
[ˈrʌbər]

n 고무

= elastic, synthetic, eraser

+ rubbery a 고무 같은

Q: Do you know where to buy quality rubber bands?
고품질 고무 밴드를 어디서 사는지 아나요?

A: ....

1435 □□□

rude
[ruːd]

a 무례한, 거친

= impolite, impudent, coarse, uncivil, offensive

+ rudeness n 무례함 rudely adv 무례하게

Q: Do you think it's rude to talk on the phone loudly in a quiet public space? 조용한 공공장소에서 전화 통화를 시끄럽게 하는 것이 무례하다고 생각하시나요?

A: ....

1436 □□□

ruin
[ˈruːɪn]

n 폐허, 파멸 **v** 망치다, 파멸시키다

= **destroy, devastate, wreck, collapse, decay, remnants**

+ **ruined** **a** 황폐한

Q: Did heavy rain ruin the outdoor event last Saturday?
지난 토요일 폭우가 야외 행사를 망쳤나요?

A: ....

1437 □□□

rural
[ˈrʊrəl]

a 시골의

= **country, rustic, pastoral, agrarian**

+ **rurality** **n** 시골스러움

Q: Do you prefer living in rural areas or busy cities?
시골 지역에 사는 것과 번화한 도시에 사는 것 중 어느 것을 선호하나요?

A: ....

1438 □□□

rush
[rʌʃ]

v 돌진하다, 서두르다 **n** 돌진, 혼잡

= **hurry, hasten, dash, surge, speed**

+ **rush hour (**출퇴근) 혼잡 시간대**,** 러시아워 **gold rush** 골드러시(새로 발견된 금광으로 사람들이 몰려드는 것**)**

Q: Why are you in such a rush today? Do you have something important to do? 오늘 왜 그렇게 급해 보여? 무슨 중요한 일이라도 있어?

A: ....

1439 □□□

rusty
[ˈrʌsti]

a 녹슨, 녹슬어 가는

= **corroded, oxidized, stale, out of practice**

+ **rust** **n** 녹

Q: Is your bike rusty from not being used this winter?
올겨울 사용하지 않아서 자전거가 녹슬었나요?

A: ....

1440 □□□

sacred
[ˈseɪkrɪd]

a 신성한

= **holy, divine, hallowed, blessed, revered**

+ **sacredness** **n** 신성함

Q: Are there sacred places tourists must visit in your country?
당신의 나라에 관광객들이 꼭 방문해야 할 신성한 장소가 있나요?

A: ....

DAY 12 | DICTATION TEST

5회 반복 예문 QR

DICTATION TEST 예문 QR을 듣고 다음 빈칸에 올바른 단어를 쓰세요.

1421. Can you keep ______________ during dance practice this evening?

1422. How can we get ______________ of unnecessary files on our computer?

1423. Have you tried solving a ______________ that seemed impossible?

1424. Are you willing to take the ______________ of investing in a startup?

1425. Do you have a morning ______________ that helps you stay focused?

1426. Did anyone try to ______________ the store during last weekend's shift?

1427. What is the ______________ cause of delays in the last project?

1428. How often do you ______________ your car's tires for even wear?

1429. Which ______________ do you take to avoid traffic on your commute?

1430. Have you developed a workout ______________ you stick to daily?

1431. Did you manage to get a good seat in the front ______________ for the concert?

1432. Are you interested in visiting ______________ palaces on vacation?

1433. Can you ______________ ointment on my arm where the bite itches?

1434. Do you know where to buy quality ______________ bands?

1435. Do you think it's ______________ to talk on the phone loudly in a quiet public space?

1436. Did heavy rain ______________ the outdoor event last Saturday?

1437. Do you prefer living in ______________ areas or busy cities?

1438. Why are you in such a ______________ today? Do you have something important to do?

1439. Is your bike ______________ from not being used this winter?

1440. Are there ______________ places tourists must visit in your country?

5회 반복 표제어 QR　5회 반복 예문 QR

DAY 13

30 days

PREVIEW A 다음 단어의 뜻을 한국어로 써보세요.

- ☐ sacrifice ______
- ☐ safety ______
- ☐ sail ______
- ☐ satellite ______
- ☐ satisfaction ______
- ☐ satisfied ______
- ☐ satisfy ______
- ☐ saving ______
- ☐ saw ______
- ☐ saying ______
- ☐ scale ______
- ☐ scatter ______
- ☐ schedule ______
- ☐ scholar ______
- ☐ scientific ______
- ☐ scold ______
- ☐ scratch ______
- ☐ scream ______
- ☐ screen ______
- ☐ script ______

PREVIEW B 사진을 보고 알맞은 영어 단어를 **PREVIEW A** 에서 찾아 써보세요.

______

______

______

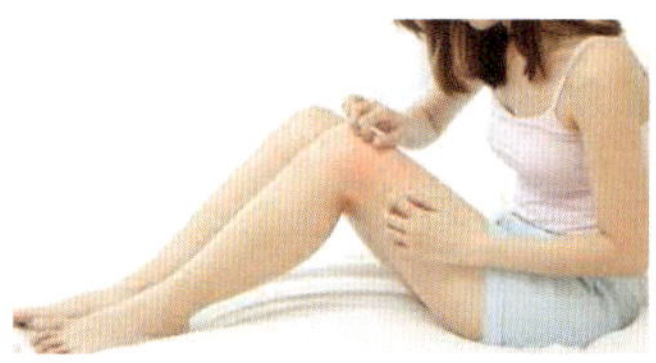
______

1441 □□□

sacrifice
[ˈsækrɪfaɪs]

n 희생, 제물 **v** 희생하다

= **offering, surrender, give up, forgo, martyrdom**
+ **self-sacrifice** **n** 자기희생 **a human sacrifice** 인신 희생(人身犧牲)

Q: Have you had to sacrifice personal time for a big project?
큰 프로젝트를 위해 개인 시간을 희생해야 했나요?

A: ______________________________

1442 □□□

safety
[ˈseɪfti]

n 안전

= **security, protection, safekeeping, well-being**
+ **safe** **a** 안전한 **safely** **adv** 안전하게

Q: What safety measures prevent accidents at your workplace?
직장에서 사고를 예방하기 위한 안전 조치는 무엇인가요?

A: ______________________________

1443 □□□

sail
[seɪl]

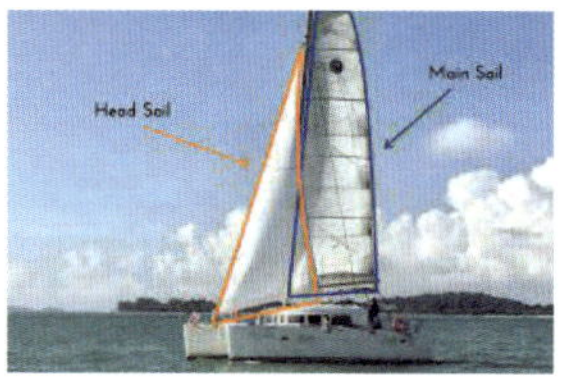

n 돛, 항해 **v** 항해하다

= **navigate, cruise, voyage, canvas, mast**
+ **sailor** **n** 선원

Q: When do you plan to sail on the cruise this summer?
이번 여름에 언제 크루즈를 타고 항해할 계획인가요?

A: ______________________________

1444 □□□

satellite
[ˈsætəlaɪt]

n 위성

= **orbiter, moon, dependent, subordinate**
+ **satellite dish** 위성 방송 수신 안테나 **satellite imagery** 인공위성이 보내오는 사진

Q: Can you explain how satellites improve remote communication?
위성이 원격 통신을 어떻게 향상시키는지 설명해 줄 수 있나요?

A: ______________________________

1445 □□□

satisfaction
[ˌsætɪsˈfækʃn]

n 만족

= **contentment, fulfillment, gratification, pleasure**
+ **satisfy** **v** 만족시키다 **satisfied** **a** 만족한 **satisfying** **a** 만족스러운, **satisfactory** **a** 만족스러운

Q: How do you measure customer satisfaction after your services?
서비스 후에 고객 만족도를 어떻게 측정하나요?

A: ______________________________

1446 □□□

satisfied
[ˈsætɪsfaɪd]

a 만족한

= content, pleased, happy, fulfilled, complacent
+ satisfaction n 만족 satisfy v 만족시키다

Q: Are you satisfied with the quality of your last order?
지난번 주문 품질에 만족하시나요?

A:

1447 □□□

satisfy
[ˈsætɪsfaɪ]

v 만족시키다

= please, fulfill, meet, appease, suffice
+ satisfaction n 만족 satisfying a 만족스러운

Q: Does a quick snack satisfy your hunger until dinner?
간단한 간식으로 저녁까지 배고픔이 해결되나요?

A:

1448 □□□

saving
[ˈseɪvɪŋ]

n 절약, 저축, 구원

= economy, thrift, rescue, salvation, accumulation
+ savings n 저축액 save v 구하다, 저축하다

Q: Do you have tips for saving money while enjoying life?
삶을 즐기면서 돈을 절약하는 팁이 있나요?

A:

1449 □□□

saw
[sɔː]

n 톱 v 톱질하다

= perceive (past of see), cut, tool, observe, understand
+ see-saw n 시소(teeter-totter)

Q: Hey, do you remember where you might have put the saw after we finished trimming the bushes yesterday? 이봐, 어제 우리가 덤불들을 다듬고 나서 톱을 어디에 두었는지 기억나?

A:

1450 □□□

saying
[ˈseɪɪŋ]

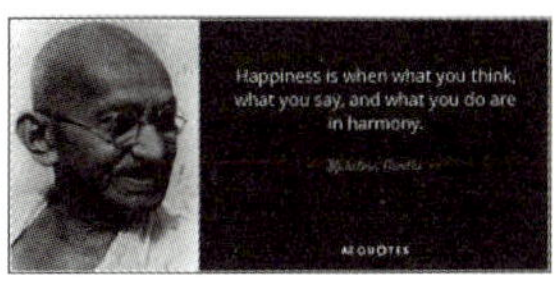

n 속담, 격언

= proverb, adage, maxim, aphorism, expression
+ say v 말하다

Q: Have you heard the saying "Time is money" and agree?
"시간은 돈이다"라는 말을 들어봤고 동의하나요?

A:

1451 □□□

scale
[skeɪl]

n 저울, 규모, 축척, 비늘 **v** 오르다

= **balance, measure, degree, proportion, climb, ascend**

+ **scalable** **a** 확장 가능한

Q: What's the scale of the new project compared to last year?
새 프로젝트의 규모는 작년에 비해 어떤가요?

A: ......

1452 □□□

scatter
[ˈskætər]

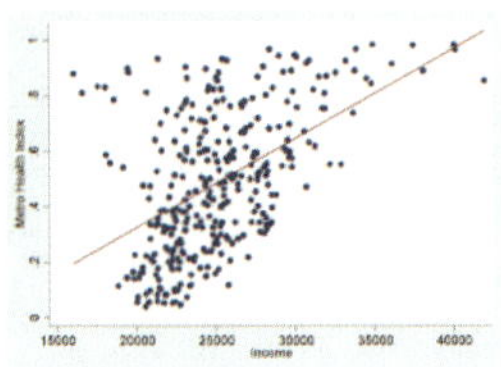

v 흩뿌리다, 흩어지게 하다

= **disperse, spread, sprinkle, strew, disseminate**

+ **scatter diagram** 산포도(散布度), 점도표(**scattergram**)

Q: Why do people scatter belongings instead of staying organized?
사람들은 왜 물건을 정리하지 않고 흩뿌려 놓을까요?

A: ......

1453 □□□

schedule
[ˈskedʒuːl] [ˈʃedʒuːl]

n 일정, 스케줄 **v** 일정을 잡다

= **timetable, agenda, program, plan, arrange**

+ **a heavy schedule** 빡빡한 일정 **a hectic schedule** 빡빡한 일정
a killing schedule 사람을 녹초가 되게 하는 스케줄

Q: Can you help schedule a meeting with the client on Tuesday?
화요일에 고객과의 회의 일정을 잡는 것을 도와줄 수 있나요?

A: ......

1454 □□□

scholar
[ˈskɑːlər]

n 학자

= **academic, intellectual, savant, researcher**

+ **scholarship** **n** 장학금, 학문 **scholarly** **a** 학문적인

Q: Are you familiar with any famous scholar in science?
과학 분야에서 유명한 학자를 알고 있나요?

A: ......

1455 □□□

scientific
[ˌsaɪənˈtɪfɪk]

a 과학적인

= **empirical, methodical, systematic, analytical**

+ **science** **n** 과학 **scientist** **n** 과학자 **scientifically** **adv** 과학적으로

Q: What scientific discoveries changed the way we think about health?
어떤 과학적 발견이 우리의 건강에 대한 이해를 바꾸었나요?

A: ......

1456 □□□

scold
[skoʊld]

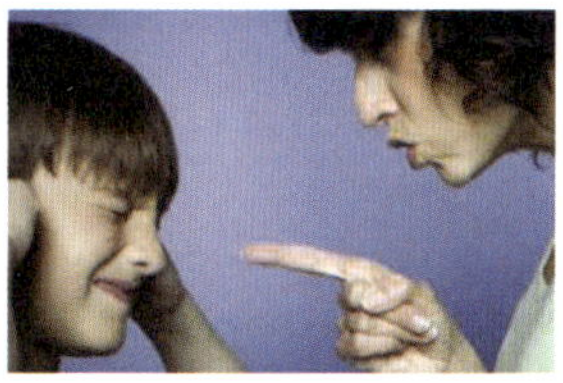

v 꾸짖다, 야단치다

= reprimand, rebuke, chide, admonish, tell off
+ scolding **n** 꾸중
Q: Did your teacher scold you for being late often?
선생님이 자주 늦는다고 꾸짖었나요?
A:

1457 □□□

scratch
[skrætʃ]

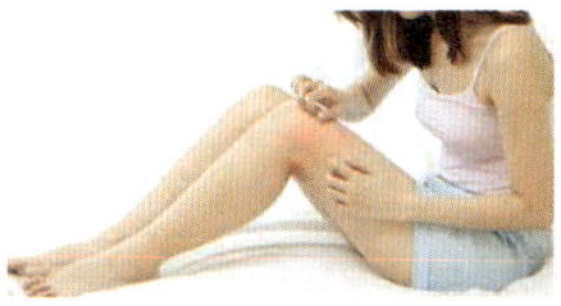

v 긁다, 할퀴다 **n** 긁힌 자국

= scrape, rub, mark, itch, start from nothing
+ from scratch 아무런 사전 준비[지식] 없이, 맨 처음부터
Q: How do you stop your cat from scratching furniture?
고양이가 가구를 긁는 것을 어떻게 막나요?
A:

1458 □□□

scream
[skriːm]

n 비명 **v** 비명을 지르다

= shriek, yell, cry out, shout, howl
+ an ear-piercing scream 귀청을 찢는 듯한 비명소리
Q: Why did the audience scream during that movie scene?
관객들이 그 영화 장면에서 왜 비명을 질렀나요?
A:

1459 □□□

screen
[skriːn]

n 화면, 스크린 **v** 가리다, 상영하다

= display, monitor, filter, shield, examine, sift
+ a computer screen 컴퓨터 화면 a cinema[movie] screen 영화(관) 스크린
Q: Can you adjust your computer screen brightness?
컴퓨터 화면 밝기를 조절할 수 있나요?
A:

1460 □□□

script
[skrɪpt]

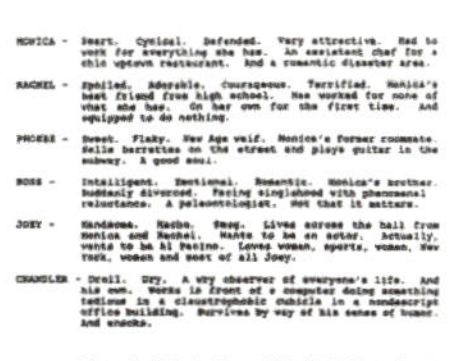

n 대본, 원고

= text, manuscript, screenplay, handwriting, transcribe
+ scripted **a** 대본 있는
Q: Did you write the company's promo video script yourself?
회사 홍보 영상 대본을 직접 썼나요?
A:

DAY 13 | DICTATION TEST

5회 반복 예문 QR

DICTATION TEST 예문 QR을 듣고 다음 빈칸에 올바른 단어를 쓰세요.

1441. Have you had to ______________ personal time for a big project?

1442. What ______________ measures prevent accidents at your workplace?

1443. When do you plan to ______________ on the cruise this summer?

1444. Can you explain how ______________ improve remote communication?

1445. How do you measure customer ______________ after your services?

1446. Are you ______________ with the quality of your last order?

1447. Does a quick snack ______________ your hunger until dinner?

1448. Do you have tips for ______________ money while enjoying life?

1449. Hey, do you remember where you might have put the ______________ after we finished trimming the bushes yesterday?

1450. Have you heard the ______________ "Time is money" and agree?

1451. What's the ______________ of the new project compared to last year?

1452. Why do people ______________ belongings instead of staying organized?

1453. Can you help ______________ a meeting with the client on Tuesday?

1454. Are you familiar with any famous ______________ in science?

1455. What ______________ discoveries changed the way we think about health?

1456. Did your teacher ______________ you for being late often?

1457. How do you stop your cat from ______________ furniture?

1458. Why did the audience ______________ during that movie scene?

1459. Can you adjust your computer ______________ brightness?

1460. Did you write the company's promo video ______________ yourself?

5회 반복 표제어 QR　5회 반복 예문 QR

DAY 14
30 days

PREVIEW A 다음 단어의 뜻을 한국어로 써보세요.

- □ seal ____________
- □ secretary ____________
- □ section ____________
- □ secure ____________
- □ security ____________
- □ seed ____________
- □ seek ____________
- □ seize ____________
- □ seldom ____________
- □ select ____________
- □ selective ____________
- □ selfish ____________
- □ senior ____________
- □ sense ____________
- □ sensible ____________
- □ sensitive ____________
- □ separate ____________
- □ sequence ____________
- □ series ____________
- □ servant ____________

PREVIEW B 사진을 보고 알맞은 영어 단어를 **PREVIEW A** 에서 찾아 써보세요.

____

____

____

____

1461 □□□

seal
[siːl]

n 물개, 도장, 봉인 v 봉인하다

= fasten, close, secure, finalize, animal, stamp
\+ before sealing the envelope 봉투를 봉하기 전에

Q: Did you seal the envelope before mailing the invitation?
초대장을 부치기 전에 봉투를 봉했나요?

A: ....

1462 □□□

secretary
[ˈsekrəteri]

n 비서, 장관

= assistant, aide, minister, clerk
\+ secretariat n 비서실 administrative assistant 행정 비서
personal assistant 개인 비서 executive assistant 임원 비서

Q: Is the new secretary scheduling appointments for next week?
새 비서가 다음 주 약속을 잡고 있나요?

A: ....

1463 □□□

section
[ˈsekʃn]

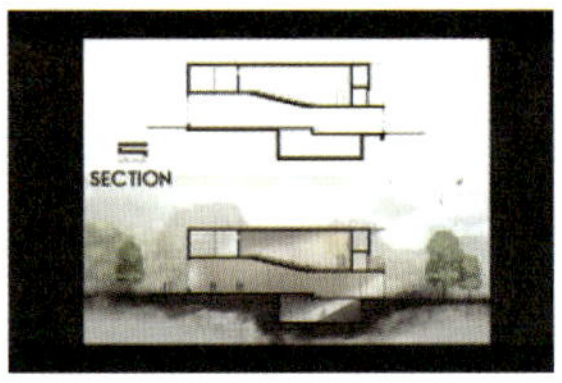

n 부분, 구역, 절단

= part, segment, portion, division, area
\+ cross section 횡단면, 단면도, (전체의 모습을 보여주는 대표적인) 단면

Q: Which report section was most useful or interesting?
어떤 보고서 부분이 가장 유용하거나 흥미로웠나요?

A: ....

1464 □□□

secure
[sɪˈkjʊr]

a 안전한, 확실한 v 안전하게 하다, 확보하다

= safe, protected, firm, stable, obtain, fasten
\+ security n 안전, 보안 securely adv 안전하게

Q: How do you secure your home when leaving for vacation?
휴가 갈 때 집을 어떻게 안전하게 하나요?

A: ....

1465 □□□

security
[sɪˈkjʊrəti]

n 보안, 안전

= safety, protection, safeguard, guarantee, assurance
\+ secure a 안전한

Q: What security system protects your building at night?
밤에 어떤 보안 시스템이 당신의 건물을 보호하나요?

A: ....

1466 □□□

seed
[siːd]

n 씨앗 **v** 씨를 뿌리다

= kernel, germ, origin, beginning, plant, sow
+ seed money 종자돈(seed capital)

Q: Did you plant the seed in a sunny spot to grow well?
씨앗을 햇볕이 잘 드는 곳에 심어서 잘 자라게 했나요?

A: ....

1467 □□□

seek
[siːk]

v 찾다, 추구하다

= search for, pursue, try to find, look for
+ seeker **n** 탐구자

Q: Are you planning to seek advice about your career?
직업에 대한 조언을 구할 계획인가요?

A: ....

1468 □□□

seize
[siːz]

v 붙잡다, 압수하다

= grab, grasp, capture, confiscate, apprehend
+ seizure **n** 압수, 발작

Q: Why didn't they seize the chance to expand quickly?
그들은 왜 빠르게 확장할 기회를 잡지 않았나요?

A: ....

1469 □□□

seldom
[ˈseldəm]

adv 거의 ~않는

= rarely, infrequently, hardly ever, not often
+ not seldom 이따금, 흔히

Q: Do you seldom check email, or was my message missed?
이메일을 거의 확인하지 않나요, 아니면 제 메시지를 놓쳤나요?

A: ....

1470 □□□

select
[sɪˈlekt]

v 선택하다, 선발하다 **a** 선별된

= choose, pick, elect, opt, chosen, exclusive
+ selection **n** 선택 selective **a** 선택적인

Q: How did you select the final candidates for the scholarship?
장학금을 위한 최종 후보자를 어떻게 선정했나요?

A: ....

1471 □□□

selective

[sɪˈlektɪv]

a 선택적인, 까다로운

= choosy, discerning, particular, careful

+ selection **n** 선택 selectivity **n** 선택성 selectively **adv** 선택적으로

Q: Are you selective when choosing books to read?

책을 고를 때 까다로운 편인가요?

A: ....

1472 □□□

selfish

[ˈselfɪʃ]

a 이기적인

= self-centered, egoistic, self-serving, greedy

+ selfishness **n** 이기심 selfishly **adv** 이기적으로

Q: Is it selfish to take a break when your team needs help?

팀이 도움이 필요할 때 휴식을 취하는 것이 이기적인가요?

A: ....

1473 □□□

senior

[ˈsiːniər]

a 연상의, 선배의 **n** 선배, 고학년

= older, elder, superior, veteran, higher-ranking

+ seniority **n** 선임

Q: Do you think the company should offer more benefits to its senior employees? 회사가 고참 직원들에게 더 많은 혜택을 제공해야 한다고 생각하시나요?

A: ....

1474 □□□

sense

[sens]

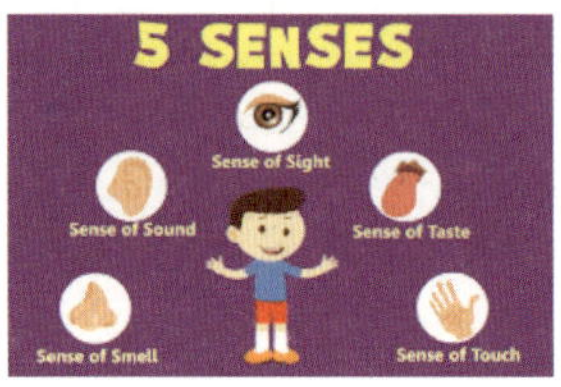

n 감각, 의미, 분별력 **v** 감지하다

= feeling, perception, meaning, intuition, detect, understand

+ sensitivity **n** 민감성 sensible **a** 합리적인 sensitive **a** 민감한 sensory **a** 감각의

Q: Does it make sense to put the main points of our presentation on separate slides? 우리 발표의 주요 요점을 각각 다른 슬라이드에 넣는 것이 합리적일까요?

A: ....

1475 □□□

sensible

[ˈsensəbl]

a 현명한, 분별 있는

= practical, reasonable, logical, wise, prudent

+ sense **n** 감각 sensibility **n** 감각, 분별력 sensibly **adv** 현명하게

Q: Is it sensible to cancel the trip because of the weather? 날씨 때문에 여행을 취소하는 것이 현명할까요?

A: ....

1476 □□□

sensitive
[ˈsensətɪv]

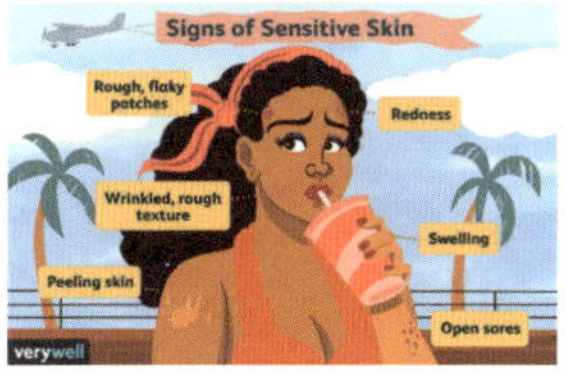

a 민감한, 감성적인

= delicate, emotional, susceptible, tender, reactive

+ sensitivity n 민감성 **sensitively** adv 민감하게

Q: Are you sensitive to criticism or take feedback calmly?
비판에 민감한 편인가요, 아니면 피드백을 침착하게 받아들이나요?

A: ....

1477 □□□

separate
[ˈsepərət] a [ˈsepəreɪt] v

v 분리하다, 헤어지다 a 분리된

= divide, detach, disconnect, distinct, individual, apart

+ separation n 분리 **separately** adv 개별적으로

Q: How do you separate work from personal time when working remotely? 원격으로 일과 개인 시간을 어떻게 분리하나요?

A: ....

1478 □□□

sequence
[ˈsiːkwəns]

n 순서, 연속

= order, succession, series, arrangement, follow

+ sequential a 순차적인 **sequentially** adv 순차적으로

Q: Did you understand the sequence of events?
사건의 순서를 이해했나요?

A: ....

1479 □□□

series
[ˈsɪriːz]

n 연속, 시리즈

= sequence, succession, set, string, chain

+ Fibonacci series 피보나치 수열(**1, 1, 2, 3, 5, 8, 13 ...**처럼 **1**로 시작하고, 앞 두 수의 합이 그 다음 수로 이뤄진 수열) **a series of mishaps** 일련의 작은 불행들

Q: Have you started watching the new drama series?
새로운 드라마 시리즈 시청을 시작했나요?

A: ....

1480 □□□

servant
[ˈsɜːrvənt]

n 하인, 종

= attendant, domestic, helper, employee

+ serve v 봉사하다

Q: Do you believe technology should be our servant, not our master?
당신은 기술이 우리의 주인이 아니라 우리의 종[하인] 이 되어야 한다고 생각하시나요?

A: ....

DAY 14 | DICTATION TEST

5회 반복 예문 QR

DICTATION TEST 예문 QR을 듣고 다음 빈칸에 올바른 단어를 쓰세요.

1461. Did you ______________ the envelope before mailing the invitation?

1462. Is the new ______________ scheduling appointments for next week?

1463. Which report ______________ was most useful or interesting?

1464. How do you ______________ your home when leaving for vacation?

1465. What ______________ system protects your building at night?

1466. Did you plant the ______________ in a sunny spot to grow well?

1467. Are you planning to ______________ advice about your career?

1468. Why didn't they ______________ the chance to expand quickly?

1469. Do you ______________ check email, or was my message missed?

1470. How did you ______________ the final candidates for the scholarship?

1471. Are you ______________ when choosing books to read?

1472. Is it ______________ to take a break when your team needs help?

1473. Do you think the company should offer more benefits to its ______________ employees?

1474. Does it make ______________ to put the main points of our presentation on separate slides?

1475. Is it ______________ to cancel the trip because of the weather?

1476. Are you ______________ to criticism or take feedback calmly?

1477. How do you ______________ work from personal time when working remotely?

1478. Did you understand the ______________ of events?

1479. Have you started watching the new drama ______________?

1480. Do you believe technology should be our ______________, not our master?

5회 반복 표제어 QR　5회 반복 예문 QR

DAY 15

30 days

AI 학습자료와 인강 youpass.co.kr

PREVIEW A 다음 단어의 뜻을 한국어로 써보세요.

□ serve	______	□ shave	______
□ session	______	□ shelter	______
□ setting	______	□ shift	______
□ settle	______	□ shock	______
□ several	______	□ shoot	______
□ severe	______	□ shore	______
□ sew	______	□ shortage	______
□ shallow	______	□ shot	______
□ shame	______	□ shut	______
□ share	______	□ sigh	______

PREVIEW B 사진을 보고 알맞은 영어 단어를 PREVIEW A 에서 찾아 써보세요.

______

______

______

______

1481 ☐☐☐

serve
[sɜːrv]

v 봉사하다, 제공하다, 근무하다

= assist, provide, offer, function, cater, deliver

+ service n 서비스 **server n** 봉사자, 서버

Q: Did they serve dinner at the party last night?
어젯밤 파티에서 저녁 식사를 제공했나요?

A: ……………………

1482 ☐☐☐

session
[ˈseʃn]

n 회의, 시간, 기간

= meeting, gathering, period, sitting, assembly

+ a photo[recording/training] session 사진 촬영 시간[녹음 기간/훈련 기간]

Q: When does the next training session start for new students?
신입생들을 위한 다음 교육 시간은 언제 시작되나요?

A: ……………………

1483 ☐☐☐

setting
[ˈsetɪŋ]

n 배경, 환경, 설정

= environment, backdrop, context, location, adjustment

+ set v 놓다, 설정하다

Q: Do you prefer the setting of this novel?
이 소설의 배경이 마음에 드나요?

A: ……………………

1484 ☐☐☐

settle
[ˈsetl]

v 정착하다, 해결하다, 진정시키다

= resolve, decide, establish, reside, calm, pay

+ settlement n 정착, 합의 **settled a** 정착된, 안정된

Q: Have you settled into your new apartment comfortably?
새 아파트에 편안하게 정착했나요?

A: ……………………

1485 ☐☐☐

several
[ˈsevrəl]

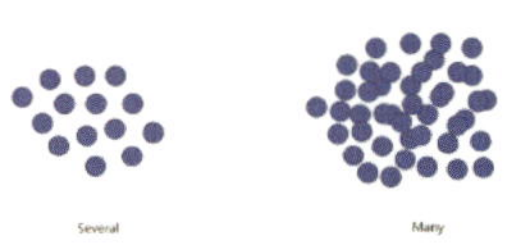

a 몇몇의

= a few, various, diverse, numerous

+ several months later 몇 달[개월] 뒤에

Q: Did you meet several new people at the recent conference?
최근 회의에서 여러 명의 새로운 사람들을 만났나요?

A: ……………………

1486 □□□

severe
[sɪˈvɪr]

a 심각한, 엄격한

= **harsh, strict, intense, serious, critical**

+ **severity** **n** 심각성 **severely** **adv** 심하게

Q: Was the storm damage as severe as predicted?
폭풍 피해가 예상만큼 심각했나요?

A: ....

1487 □□□

sew
[soʊ]

v 바느질하다

= **stitch, mend, repair, join**

+ **sewing** **n** 바느질

Q: Can you sew this button back onto my shirt today?
오늘 이 단추를 제 셔츠에 다시 달아줄 수 있나요?

A: ....

1488 □□□

shallow
[ˈʃæloʊ]

a 얕은, 얄팍한

= **superficial, flimsy, facile, lacking depth, trivial**

+ **shallowness** **n** 얕음

Q: Is this river shallow enough for kids to play safely?
이 강이 아이들이 안전하게 놀기에 충분히 얕은가요?

A: ....

1489 □□□

shame
[ʃeɪm]

n 수치심, 부끄러움 **v** 창피하게 하다

= **humiliation, disgrace, embarrassment, regret, dishonor**

+ **shameful** **a** 수치스러운 **shameless** **a** 뻔뻔스러운 **shamefully** **adv** 수치스럽게

Q: Did you feel a sense of shame after you realized you had accidentally offended your friend? 친구에게 실수로 불쾌감을 주었다는 것을 깨달은 후에 죄책감을 느꼈나요?

A: ....

1490 □□□

share
[ʃer]

n 몫, 주식 **v** 공유하다, 나누다

= **portion, part, division, contribute, participate, divide**

+ **market share** 시장 점유율

Q: Will you share your presentation slides after the meeting?
회의 후에 발표 자료를 공유해 줄 건가요?

A: ....

1491 □□□

shave
[ʃeɪv]

v 면도하다, (아슬아슬하게 위험 등을) 피하다

= trim, cut, scrape, remove hair, close call
+ have a shave 면도를 하다

Q: Did you forget to shave again before the interview?
면접 전에 또 면도하는 것을 잊었나요?

A: ....

1492 □□□

shelter
[ˈʃeltər]

n 피난처, 보호소 **v** 보호하다

= refuge, sanctuary, protection, cover, housing
+ a bus shelter (지붕이 달린) 버스 정류소 **an animal shelter** 동물 보호소
an air-raid shelter 방공호

Q: Is there nearby shelter available for emergency storms?
비상 폭풍을 위한 근처 대피소가 있나요?

A: ....

1493 □□□

shift
[ʃɪft]

n 변화, 교대 근무 **v** 바꾸다, 이동하다

= change, alter, move, transfer, switch, turn
+ paradigm shift 인식 체계[패러다임]의 대전환

Q: What time does your work shift start tomorrow?
내일 당신의 근무 교대 시간은 몇 시에 시작하나요?

A: ....

1494 □□□

shock
[ʃɑːk]

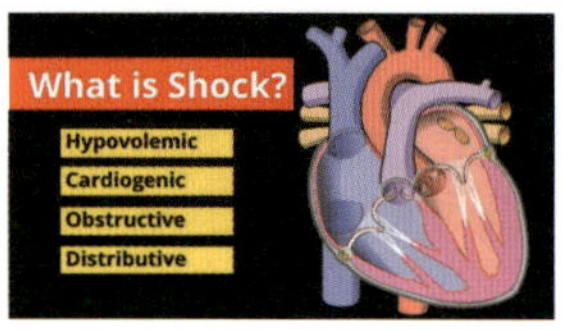

n 충격 **v** 충격을 주다

= surprise, jolt, trauma, stun, electrify
+ shocking a 충격적인 **shocked a** 충격 받은 **shockingly adv** 충격적으로

Q: Were you shocked by the unexpected news from her?
그녀에게서 온 예상치 못한 소식에 충격 받았나요?

A: ....

1495 □□□

shoot
[ʃuːt]

v 쏘다, 촬영하다 **n** 촬영

= fire, discharge, launch, sprout, photograph, rapidly move
+ shot n 총격, 발사

Q: Did you shoot that photo during your Iceland vacation?
그 사진을 아이슬란드 휴가 중에 찍었나요?

A: ....

1496 □□□

shore
[ʃɔːr]

n 해안, 강변

= coast, beach, bank, land beside water
+ a rocky[sandy] shore 바위[모래] 해변

Q: Have you camped on the shore of a lake in autumn?
가을에 호숫가에서 캠핑해 본 적 있나요?

A: ....

1497 □□□

shortage
[ˈʃɔːrtɪdʒ]

n 부족, 결핍

= scarcity, deficit, lack, deficiency, dearth
+ short **a** 짧은, 부족한

Q: Is there a shortage of supplies after the flood?
홍수 후에 생필품 부족이 있나요?

A: ....

1498 □□□

shot
[ʃɑːt]

n 발사, 사진, 주사

= attempt, try, photograph, injection, bullet, chance
+ shoot **v** 쏘다

Q: Did you get your flu shot at the clinic?
병원에서 독감 주사를 맞았나요?

A: ....

1499 □□□

shut
[ʃʌt]

v 닫다, 닫히다 **a** 닫힌

= close, seal, fasten, enclose, prohibit
+ shut down 문을 닫다, (기계가) 멈추다[정지하다] shut up 입을 다물다[닥치다]

Q: Did you remember to shut all the windows before leaving the house?
집을 나서기 전에 창문 다 닫는 걸 기억했나요?

A: ....

1500 □□□

sigh
[saɪ]

n 한숨 **v** 한숨 쉬다

= mourn, lament, breathe heavily, longing, exhalation
+ a deep sigh 깊은 한숨 소리 a weary sigh 피곤한 한숨
a resigned sigh 체념한 듯한 한숨

Q: Did you hear her sigh after getting her test results?
그녀가 시험 결과를 받은 후 한숨 쉬는 것을 들었나요?

A: ....

DAY 15 | DICTATION TEST

5회 반복 예문 QR

DICTATION TEST 예문 QR을 듣고 다음 빈칸에 올바른 단어를 쓰세요.

1481. Did they _______________ dinner at the party last night?

1482. When does the next training _______________ start for new students?

1483. Do you prefer the _______________ of this novel?

1484. Have you _______________ into your new apartment comfortably?

1485. Did you meet _______________ new people at the recent conference?

1486. Was the storm damage as _______________ as predicted?

1487. Can you _______________ this button back onto my shirt today?

1488. Is this river _______________ enough for kids to play safely?

1489. Did you feel a sense of _______________ after you realized you had accidentally offended your friend?

1490. Will you _______________ your presentation slides after the meeting?

1491. Did you forget to _______________ again before the interview?

1492. Is there nearby _______________ available for emergency storms?

1493. What time does your work _______________ start tomorrow?

1494. Were you _______________ by the unexpected news from her?

1495. Did you _______________ that photo during your Iceland vacation?

1496. Have you camped on the _______________ of a lake in autumn?

1497. Is there a _______________ of supplies after the flood?

1498. Did you get your flu _______________ at the clinic?

1499. Did you remember to _______________ all the windows before leaving the house?

1500. Did you hear her _______________ after getting her test results?

5회 반복 표제어 QR 5회 반복 예문 QR

DAY 16
30 days

AI 학습자료와 인강 youpass.co.kr

PREVIEW A 다음 단어의 뜻을 한국어로 써보세요.

- ☐ sight ________
- ☐ sightseeing ________
- ☐ signal ________
- ☐ signature ________
- ☐ significant ________
- ☐ silence ________
- ☐ silly ________
- ☐ similar ________
- ☐ similarity ________
- ☐ simplify ________
- ☐ simultaneously ________
- ☐ since ________
- ☐ sincere ________
- ☐ sink ________
- ☐ site ________
- ☐ situation ________
- ☐ skillful ________
- ☐ slave ________
- ☐ slice ________
- ☐ slight ________

PREVIEW B 사진을 보고 알맞은 영어 단어를 **PREVIEW A** 에서 찾아 써보세요.

____

____

____

____

1501 □□□

sight
[saɪt]

n 시력, 시야, 광경

= vision, view, spectacle, scene, aim, see

+ sightseeing n 관광

Q: Is the Eiffel Tower a must-see sight for tourists visiting Paris?
에펠탑은 파리를 방문하는 관광객들에게 꼭 봐야 할 명소인가요?

A: ……………………………………

1502 □□□

sightseeing
[ˈsaɪtˌsiːɪŋ]

n 관광

= touring, exploring, visiting, tourism

+ sight n 경치

Q: Have you gone sightseeing in any famous city recently?
최근에 유명한 도시로 관광을 하러 간 적이 있나요?

A: ……………………………………

1503 □□□

signal
[ˈsɪgnəl]

n 신호 v 신호하다

= sign, indication, gesture, warning, transmit, communicate

+ a danger[warning/distress] signal 위험[경고/재난] 신호

Q: Does your phone lose signal when you enter the underground station? 지하철역에 들어갈 때 휴대폰 신호가 끊기나요?

A: ……………………………………

1504 □□□

signature
[ˈsɪgnətʃər]

n 서명

= autograph, mark, sign off on, distinct characteristic

+ sign v 서명하다

Q: Did you forget to add your signature at the bottom?
아래쪽에 서명을 추가하는 것을 잊었나요?

A: ……………………………………

1505 □□□

significant
[sɪgˈnɪfɪkənt]

a 중요한, 의미심장한

= important, notable, meaningful, substantial, crucial

+ significance n 중요성 significantly adv 상당히, 중요하게

Q: Was there any significant change in your health after the trip?
여행 후에 건강에 어떤 중요한 변화가 있었나요?

A: ……………………………………

1506 □□□

silence
[ˈsaɪləns]

n 침묵, 고요 v 침묵시키다

= **quiet, stillness, hush, quieten, suppress**
+ **silent** a 조용한 **silently** adv 조용히

Q: Did the teacher ask for silence before starting the test?
선생님이 시험 시작 전에 조용히 하라고 요청했나요?

A: ....

1507 □□□

silly
[ˈsɪli]

a 어리석은, 바보 같은

= **foolish, absurd, ridiculous, nonsensical, trivial**
+ **silliness** n 어리석음

Q: Don't you think it was silly to panic over that?
그것 때문에 당황했던 것이 어리석었다고 생각하지 않나요?

A: ....

1508 □□□

similar
[ˈsɪmələr]

a 비슷한

= **alike, comparable, analogous, resembling, parallel**
+ **similarity** n 유사성 **similarly** adv 비슷하게

Q: Are your new shoes similar to the old ones?
새 신발이 옛날 신발과 비슷한가요?

A: ....

1509 □□□

similarity
[ˌsɪməˈlærəti]

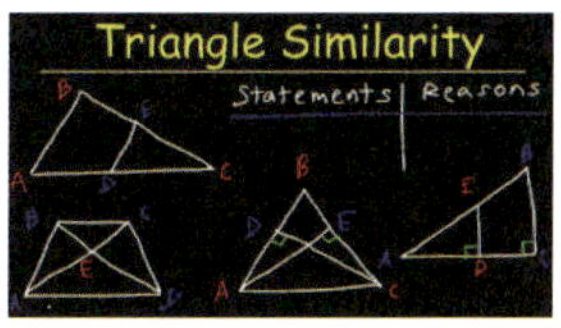

n 유사성, 비슷함

= **resemblance, likeness, analogy, correspondence**
+ **similar** a 유사한

Q: Did you notice any similarity between these two cases?
이 두 사건 사이에 어떤 유사점을 발견했나요?

A: ....

1510 □□□

simplify
[ˈsɪmplɪfaɪ]

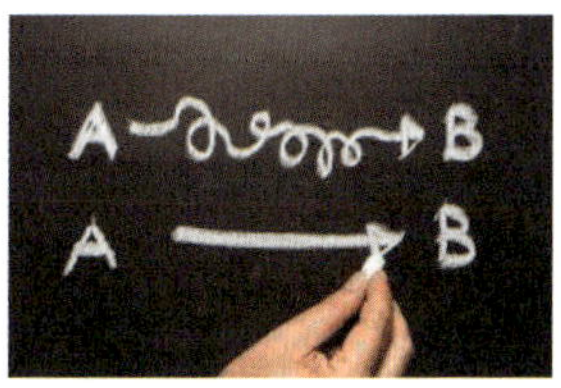

v 단순화하다

= **streamline, clarify, ease, reduce, facilitate**
+ **simplification** n 단순화 **simple** a 간단한

Q: Can you simplify this explanation for younger students?
어린 학생들을 위해 이 설명을 간단하게 해줄 수 있나요?

A: ....

1511 □□□

simultaneously
[ˌsaɪmlˈteɪniəsli]

adv 동시에

= concurrently, at once, at the same time, in parallel
+ simultaneous **a** 동시에 일어나는

Q: Were you able to work and attend class simultaneously?
일과 수업을 동시에 할 수 있었나요?

A: ....

1512 □□□

since
[sɪns]

prep ~이래로 **conj** ~한 이후로, ~이므로, ~때문에

= because, as, from the time that
+ ever since ~이후로 줄곧[계속]

Q: Have you felt better since taking the new medicine?
새 약을 먹은 후로 기분이 나아졌나요?

A: ....

1513 □□□

sincere
[sɪnˈsɪr]

a 진심 어린, 성실한

= genuine, heartfelt, honest, earnest, true
+ sincerity **n** 진실성 **sincerely** **adv** 진심으로

Q: Was his apology really sincere or forced?
그의 사과가 정말 진심이었나요, 아니면 억지였나요?

A: ....

1514 □□□

sink
[sɪŋk]

v 가라앉다, 침몰시키다 **n** 싱크대

= submerge, descend, decline, drop, basin
+ sink or swim 자력으로 살아남느냐 아니면 완전히 망하느냐

Q: Did the boat sink after hitting the rock?
배가 바위에 부딪힌 후 침몰했나요?

A: ....

1515 □□□

site
[saɪt]

n 장소, 부지, 유적지

= location, place, spot, venue, website
+ construction site 건설현장(building site)

Q: Have you recently visited the construction site?
최근에 건설 현장을 방문했나요?

A: ....

1516 □□□

situation
[ˌsɪtʃuˈeɪʃn]

n 상황, 처지

= **circumstance, condition, state, position, scenario**
+ **situated** **a** 위치한

Q: Is the situation under control after the meeting?
회의 후에 상황이 통제되고 있나요?

A: ....

1517 □□□

skillful
[ˈskɪlfl]

a 숙련된, 능숙한

= **expert, proficient, adept, talented, capable**
+ **skill** **n** 기술 **skillfully** **adv** 능숙하게

Q: Is she as skillful at painting as at music?
그녀는 음악만큼 그림에도 능숙한가요?

A: ....

1518 □□□

slave
[sleɪv]

n 노예

= **bondman, serf, drudge, subservient, toil**
+ **slavery** **n** 노예 제도

Q: Have you read stories about a slave gaining freedom?
노예가 자유를 얻는 이야기에 대해 읽어본 적 있나요?

A: ....

1519 □□□

slice
[slaɪs]

n 얇게 썬 조각 **v** 얇게 썰다

= **portion, piece, cut, section, carve**
+ **a slice of melon** 멜론 한 쪽

Q: Did you eat the last pizza slice without asking?
묻지도 않고 마지막 피자 조각을 먹었나요?

A: ....

1520 □□□

slight
[slaɪt]

a 약간의, 사소한

= **small, minor, negligible, delicate, insult, dismiss**
+ **slightly** **adv** 약간

Q: Did you notice the slight color difference between these shirts?
이 셔츠들 사이에 약간의 색상 차이를 발견했나요?

A: ....

DAY 16 | DICTATION TEST

5회 반복 예문 QR

DICTATION TEST 예문 QR을 듣고 다음 빈칸에 올바른 단어를 쓰세요.

1501. Is the Eiffel Tower a must-see ______________ for tourists visiting Paris?

1502. Have you gone ______________ in any famous city recently?

1503. Does your phone lose ______________ when you enter the underground station?

1504. Did you forget to add your ______________ at the bottom?

1505. Was there any ______________ change in your health after the trip?

1506. Did the teacher ask for ______________ before starting the test?

1507. Don't you think it was ______________ to panic over that?

1508. Are your new shoes ______________ to the old ones?

1509. Did you notice any ______________ between these two cases?

1510. Can you ______________ this explanation for younger students?

1511. Were you able to work and attend class ______________?

1512. Have you felt better ______________ taking the new medicine?

1513. Was his apology really ______________ or forced?

1514. Did the boat ______________ after hitting the rock?

1515. Have you recently visited the construction ______________?

1516. Is the ______________ under control after the meeting?

1517. Is she as ______________ at painting as at music?

1518. Have you read stories about a ______________ gaining freedom?

1519. Did you eat the last pizza ______________ without asking?

1520. Did you notice the ______________ color difference between these shirts?

5회 반복 표제어 QR　5회 반복 예문 QR

DAY 17

30 days

AI 학습자료와 인강 youpass.co.kr

PREVIEW A 다음 단어의 뜻을 한국어로 써보세요.

- ☐ slightly ________
- ☐ slip ________
- ☐ slope ________
- ☐ smoke ________
- ☐ smooth ________
- ☐ sneeze ________
- ☐ snore ________
- ☐ social ________
- ☐ soil ________
- ☐ soldier ________
- ☐ solid ________
- ☐ solution ________
- ☐ somehow ________
- ☐ somewhat ________
- ☐ somewhere ________
- ☐ sore ________
- ☐ sort ________
- ☐ soul ________
- ☐ source ________
- ☐ southern ________

PREVIEW B 사진을 보고 알맞은 영어 단어를 PREVIEW A에서 찾아 써보세요.

____

____

____

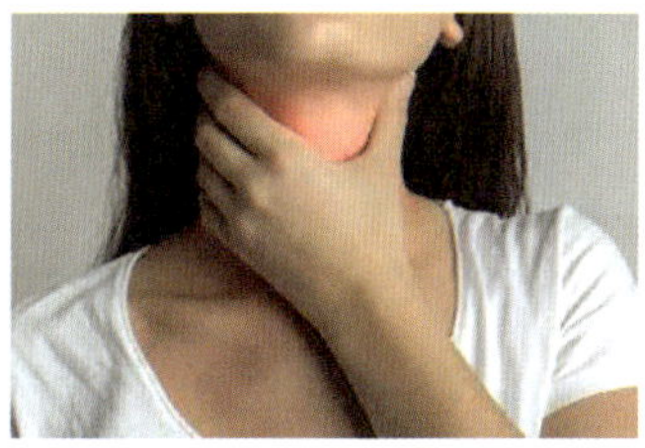
____

1521 □□□

slightly
['slaɪtli]

adv 약간, 조금

= a little, somewhat, marginally, a bit
+ slight **a** 약간의, 가벼운

Q: Did the weather get slightly warmer this morning than yesterday?
오늘 아침 날씨가 어제보다 약간 더 따뜻해졌나요?

A:

1522 □□□

slip
[slɪp]

v 미끄러지다, 실수하다 **n** 미끄러짐, 실수

= slide, fall, err, lapse, mistake, escape
+ slippery **a** 미끄러운

Q: Did you see her slip on the wet floor near the kitchen?
부엌 근처 젖은 바닥에서 그녀가 미끄러지는 것을 보았나요?

A:

1523 □□□

slope
[sloʊp]

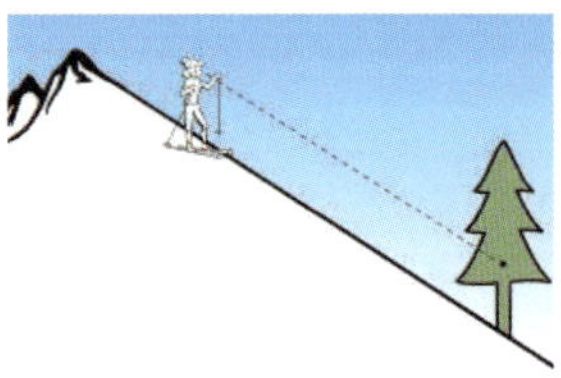

n 경사, 비탈 **v** 경사지다

= incline, gradient, slant, hill, pitch
+ a gentle[steep] slope 완만한[가파른] 경사

Q: Is this slope too steep for biking down safely?
이 경사가 자전거를 타고 안전하게 내려가기에는 너무 가파른가요?

A:

1524 □□□

smoke
[smoʊk]

n 연기 **v** 담배를 피우다

= fumes, vapor, exhaust, puff, ignite
+ smoker **n** 흡연자 smoky **a** 연기 나는

Q: Do you ever smoke cigarettes, or have you never tried?
담배를 피우시나요, 아니면 한 번도 피워본 적 없으신가요?

A:

1525 □□□

smooth
[smu:ð]

a 매끄러운, 순조로운 **v** 매끄럽게 하다

= even, flat, polished, calm, effortless, ease
+ smoothness **n** 매끄러움 smoothly **adv** 매끄럽게

Q: Is the surface of this table smooth enough to draw on?
이 테이블 표면이 그림을 그릴 만큼 충분히 매끄러운가요?

A:

1526 □□□

sneeze
[sni:z]

n 재채기 **v** 재채기하다

= **sternutation, expulsion of air**

+ **sneeze guard** (뷔페식당·제과점 등의) 플라스틱[유리]제의 보호물 ((음식 등의 오염 방지를 위해 설치))

Q: Did he just sneeze, or was that a cough?
그가 방금 재채기를 한 건가요, 아니면 기침이었나요?

A: ....

1527 □□□

snore
[snɔ:r]

n 코골이 **v** 코를 골다

= **breathe heavily (in sleep), noisy breathing**

+ **a terrible snore** 심한 코골기

Q: Does your brother still snore loudly when he sleeps?
당신의 남동생은 아직도 잘 때 크게 코를 고나요?

A: ....

1528 □□□

social
[ˈsoʊʃl]

a 사회적인, 사교적인

= **communal, public, societal, friendly, outgoing**

+ **society** **n** 사회 **socialism** **n** 사회주의 **socialist** **n** 사회주의자
socialize **v** 사회화하다 **socially** **adv** 사회적으로

Q: Are you going to the social event after class today?
오늘 수업 후에 사교 행사에 갈 건가요?

A: ....

1529 □□□

soil
[sɔɪl]

n 흙, 토양 **v** 더럽히다

= **earth, ground, dirt, land, dirty, stain**

+ **poor[dry/acid/sandy/fertile] soil** 척박한[건조한/산성/모래가 많은/비옥한] 토양

Q: Does this type of plant grow best in sandy soil or clay soil?
이런 종류의 식물은 모래흙에서 가장 잘 자라나요, 아니면 진흙에서 가장 잘 자라나요?

A: ....

1530 □□□

soldier
[ˈsoʊldʒər]

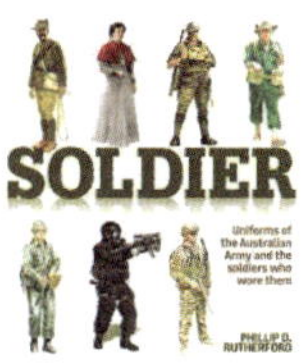

n 군인

= **warrior, fighter, serviceman, combatant**

+ **soldiering** **n** 군인 생활

Q: Did the wounded soldier receive immediate medical attention on the battlefield? 부상당한 병사는 전장에서 즉각적인 치료를 받았나요?

A: ....

1531 □□□

solid
[ˈsɑːlɪd]

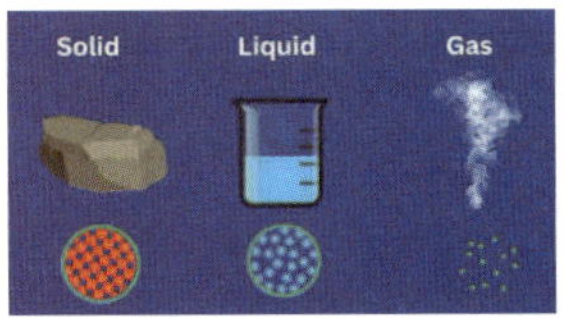

a 고체의, 단단한, 견고한 n 고체

= firm, hard, sturdy, strong, dependable, cohesive
+ solidity n 견고함 solidify v 굳히다 solidly adv 단단히

Q: Is this rock solid enough to support the weight safely?
이 바위가 무게를 안전하게 지탱할 만큼 충분히 단단한가요?

A:

1532 □□□

solution
[səˈluːʃn]

n 해결책, 용액

= answer, resolution, remedy, mixture, liquid
+ solve v 해결하다

Q: Have you found any good solution to that tricky math problem?
그 까다로운 수학 문제에 대한 좋은 해결책을 찾았나요?

A:

1533 □□□

somehow
[ˈsʌmhaʊ]

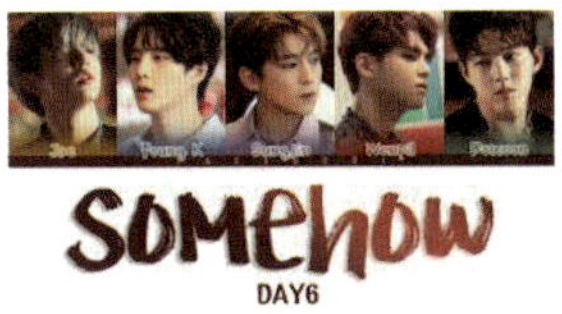

adv 어떻게든, 어쩐지

= by some means, in some way, for some reason
+ somehow or other 어떻게 해서든, 그런대로, 웬일인지

Q: Did you somehow forget your wallet again this morning?
어쩌다 보니 오늘 아침에도 지갑을 분실한 건가요?

A:

1534 □□□

somewhat
[ˈsʌmwʌt]

adv 어느 정도, 다소

= rather, slightly, to some extent, a little
+ more than somewhat 몹시, 대단히

Q: Did you find his reaction somewhat surprising or just normal?
그의 반응이 다소 놀라웠나요, 아니면 그냥 평범했나요?

A:

1535 □□□

somewhere
[ˈsʌmwer]

adv 어딘가에

= someplace, in some place, to some place
+ land up somehow or somewhere 어쩌다 어딘가에 다다르다

Q: Did you leave your phone somewhere around here last night?
어젯밤에 휴대폰을 이 근처 어딘가에 두었나요?

A:

1536 □□□

sore
[sɔːr]

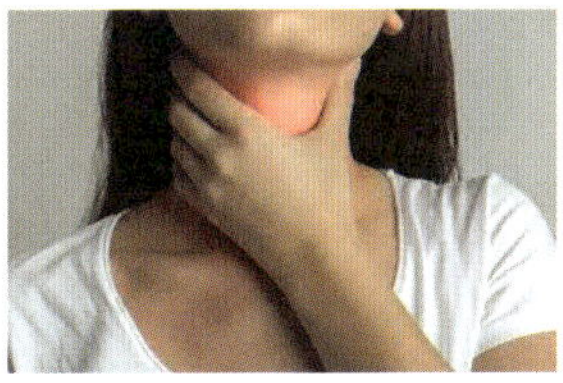

a 아픈, 쑤시는

= painful, aching, tender, sensitive, inflamed, offended
+ soreness n 아픔 sorely adv 몹시

Q: Are your muscles still sore from the hike over the weekend?
주말 하이킹 때문에 아직 근육이 아픈가요?

A: ....

1537 □□□

sort
[sɔːrt]

n 종류, 분류 v 분류하다

= type, kind, category, classify, arrange
+ sort something out ~을 정리하다, ~을 처리하다

Q: Can you sort these papers by date before we leave today?
오늘 퇴근하기 전에 이 서류들을 날짜별로 분류해 줄 수 있나요?

A: ....

1538 □□□

soul
[soʊl]

n 영혼, 정신

= spirit, psyche, essence, core, person
+ Seoul n 서울 soulful a 영혼이 담긴

Q: Do you believe every living thing has a soul of its own?
모든 생명체에 고유의 영혼이 있다고 믿나요?

A: ....

1539 □□□

source
[sɔːrs]

n 원천, 근원

= origin, fountainhead, cause, supply, derivation
+ open-source a 컴퓨터 오픈 소스(소프트웨어의 소스 프로그램이 공개되어 있는 것)

Q: Did you check the original source of that information?
그 정보의 원본 출처를 확인했나요?

A: ....

1540 □□□

southern
[ˈsʌðərn]

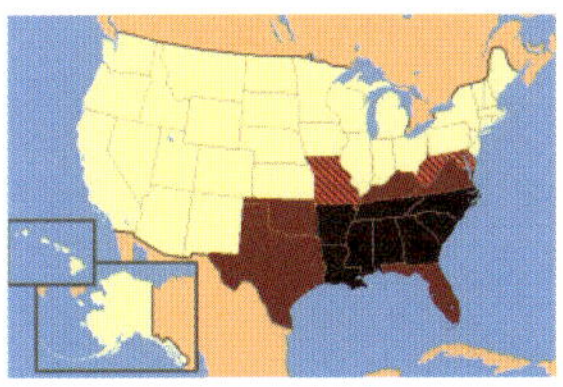

a 남쪽의

= southerly, austral, meridional
+ south n 남쪽

Q: Have you ever traveled to any southern cities?
남부 도시들로 여행 가본 적 있나요?

A: ....

DAY 17 | DICTATION TEST

5회 반복 예문 QR

DICTATION TEST 예문 QR을 듣고 다음 빈칸에 올바른 단어를 쓰세요.

1521. Did the weather get ________________ warmer this morning than yesterday?

1522. Did you see her ________________ on the wet floor near the kitchen?

1523. Is this ________________ too steep for biking down safely?

1524. Do you ever ________________ cigarettes, or have you never tried?

1525. Is the surface of this table ________________ enough to draw on?

1526. Did he just ________________, or was that a cough?

1527. Does your brother still ________________ loudly when he sleeps?

1528. Are you going to the ________________ event after class today?

1529. Does this type of plant grow best in sandy ________________ or clay soil?

1530. Did the wounded ________________ receive immediate medical attention on the battlefield?

1531. Is this rock ________________ enough to support the weight safely?

1532. Have you found any good ________________ to that tricky math problem?

1533. Did you ________________ forget your wallet again this morning?

1534. Did you find his reaction ________________ surprising or just normal?

1535. Did you leave your phone ________________ around here last night?

1536. Are your muscles still ________________ from the hike over the weekend?

1537. Can you ________________ these papers by date before we leave today?

1538. Do you believe every living thing has a ________________ of its own?

1539. Did you check the original ________________ of that information?

1540. Have you ever traveled to any ________________ cities?

5회 반복 표제어 QR　5회 반복 예문 QR

DAY 18

30 days

AI 학습자료와 인강 youpass.co.kr

PREVIEW A 다음 단어의 뜻을 한국어로 써보세요.

- ☐ **sow** ____________
- ☐ **spare** ____________
- ☐ **sparkle** ____________
- ☐ **specialize** ____________
- ☐ **species** ____________
- ☐ **specific** ____________
- ☐ **spill** ____________
- ☐ **spin** ____________
- ☐ **spine** ____________
- ☐ **spirit** ____________
- ☐ **splendid** ____________
- ☐ **split** ____________
- ☐ **spoil** ____________
- ☐ **spontaneously** ____________
- ☐ **spot** ____________
- ☐ **spray** ____________
- ☐ **spread** ____________
- ☐ **square** ____________
- ☐ **squeeze** ____________
- ☐ **stable** ____________

PREVIEW B 사진을 보고 알맞은 영어 단어를 PREVIEW A 에서 찾아 써보세요.

____

____

____

____

1541 □□□

sow
[soʊ]

v (씨를) 뿌리다

= plant, scatter, disseminate, propagate
+ sowing **n** 파종

Q: Do farmers usually sow wheat seeds in the autumn for a spring harvest? 농부들은 보통 봄 수확을 위해 가을에 밀 씨앗을 뿌리나요?

A: ....

1542 □□□

spare
[sper]

a 여분의, 한가한 **v** 아끼다, 할애하다

= extra, reserve, additional, free, yield, save
+ a spare key[tyre] 여분의 열쇠[예비 타이어]

Q: Can you spare a few minutes to help me with this task?
이 일을 돕기 위해 몇 분 할애해 줄 수 있나요?

A: ....

1543 □□□

sparkle
[ˈspɑːrkl]

n 불꽃, 반짝임 **v** 반짝이다

= glitter, gleam, shimmer, twinkle, brilliance
+ the sparkle of a diamond 다이아몬드의 광채

Q: Did her eyes sparkle when she saw the surprise gift?
그녀가 깜짝 선물을 봤을 때 눈이 반짝였나요?

A: ....

1544 □□□

specialize
[ˈspeʃəlaɪz]

v 전문으로 하다

= concentrate, focus, major in, particularize
+ specialty[speciality] **n** 전문 **specialization** **n** 전문화 **specialist** **n** 전문가 **special** **a** 특별한

Q: Does your clinic specialize in sports injuries?
당신이 일하는 클리닉은 스포츠 부상을 전문으로 하나요?

A: ....

1545 □□□

species
[ˈspiːʃiːz]

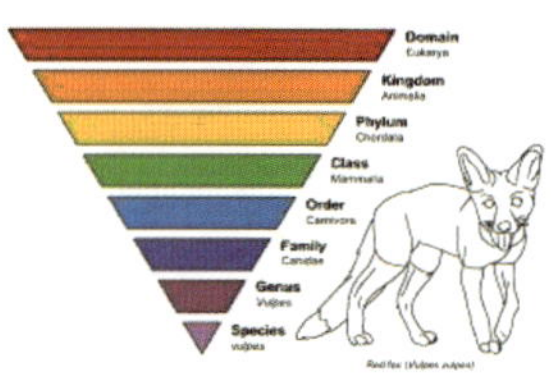

n (생물의) 종

= type, kind, variety, classification
+ a species of bird 새의 한 종류

Q: Have you seen this bird species in our park before?
이 조류 종을 우리 공원에서 전에 본 적 있나요?

A: ....

1546 □□□

specific
[spəˈsɪfɪk]

a 특정한, 구체적인

= particular, precise, definite, exact, distinct

+ specificity **n** 특수성 **specifically** **adv** 구체적으로

Q: Can you give a specific reason for missing the meeting?
회의에 불참한 구체적인 이유를 말해줄 수 있나요?

A: ....

1547 □□□

spill
[spɪl]

v 엎지르다, 흘리다 **n** 엎질러진 것

= overflow, scatter, shed, drop, leakage

+ spill the beans (비밀을) 무심코 말해 버리다

Q: Did you spill coffee all over your notes again today?
오늘 또 노트에 커피를 다 쏟았나요?

A: ....

1548 □□□

spin
[spɪn]

v 회전하다, 실을 잣다 **n** 회전

= rotate, revolve, whirl, turn, tell, narrative

+ spinner **n** 방적공, 회전하는 것

Q: Can you spin this top faster than I just did now?
제가 방금 돌린 것보다 이 팽이를 더 빨리 돌릴 수 있나요?

A: ....

1549 □□□

spine
[spaɪn]

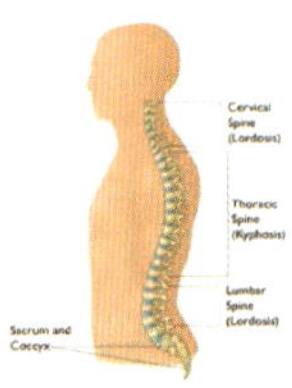

n 척추, 등뼈

= backbone, courage, ridge, thorn

+ spinal **a** 척추의

Q: Did she hurt her spine while lifting that heavy box?
그녀가 그 무거운 상자를 들다가 척추를 다쳤나요?

A: ....

1550 □□□

spirit
[ˈspɪrɪt]

n 정신, 영혼, 기분

= soul, essence, mood, morale, courage, enthusiasm

+ spiritual **a** 정신적인 **spirited** **a** 활기찬 **spiritually** **adv** 정신적으로

Q: Is the team's spirit still strong after the loss?
패배 후에도 팀의 정신력은 여전히 강한가요?

A: ....

1551 □□□

splendid
[ˈsplendɪd]

a 훌륭한, 멋진

= **magnificent, superb, grand, brilliant, excellent**
+ **splendor** **n** 장엄함 **splendidly** **adv** 훌륭하게

Q: Wasn't the sunset at the beach absolutely splendid tonight?
오늘 밤 해변의 일몰이 정말 장관이었죠?

A: ....

1552 □□□

split
[splɪt]

v 쪼개다, 분할하다 **n** 분할, 틈

= **divide, separate, cleave, rupture, disagreement**
+ **Let's split!** 어서 뜨자!

Q: Did you split the bill evenly with your friends at dinner?
저녁 식사에서 친구들과 계산을 공평하게 나눴나요?

A: ....

1553 □□□

spoil
[spɔɪl]

v 망치다, 상하다, 버릇없이 기르다

= **ruin, decay, rot, damage, indulge, pamper**
+ **spoiled[spoilt]** **a** 망가진, 버릇없는

Q: Did the heat spoil all the fresh food in the fridge?
더위가 냉장고 안의 신선한 음식을 모두 상하게 했나요?

A: ....

1554 □□□

spontaneously
[spɑːnˈteɪniəsli]

adv 자발적으로, 자연스럽게

= **impulsively, on the spur of the moment, naturally, impromptu**
+ **spontaneous** **a** 자발적인 **spontaneity** **n** 자발성

Q: Did he really start singing spontaneously at the party?
그가 파티에서 정말로 즉흥적으로 노래하기 시작했나요?

A: ....

1555 □□□

spot
[spɑːt]

n 점, 장소, 얼룩 **v** 발견하다

= **place, location, mark, stain, recognize, see**
+ **hot spot** 분쟁 지대, 활기 넘치는[신나는] 곳

Q: Did you spot any familiar faces at the event this evening?
오늘 저녁 행사에서 아는 얼굴을 발견했나요?

A: ....

1556 □□□

spray
[spreɪ]

n 스프레이, 분무기 v 뿌리다

= mist, aerosol, sprinkle, squirt, atomize

\+ spray gun 페인트 분무기

Q: Did you spray perfume before leaving the house?
집을 나서기 전에 향수를 뿌렸나요?

A:

1557 □□□

spread
[spred]

v 퍼지다, 펼치다 n 확산

= distribute, extend, diffuse, scatter, range, expanse

\+ bedspread n 침대보(bedcover, spread)

Q: Did the rumor spread quickly around the school?
소문이 학교에 빠르게 퍼졌나요?

A:

1558 □□□

square
[skwer]

Square

n 정사각형, 광장 a 정사각형의, 제곱의

= plaza, block, perfect, equitable, conventional, multiply by itself

\+ a carpet four meters square 4제곱미터짜리 카펫

Q: Did you draw that square with a ruler or by hand?
그 사각형을 자로 그렸나요 아니면 손으로 그렸나요?

A:

1559 □□□

squeeze
[skwiːz]

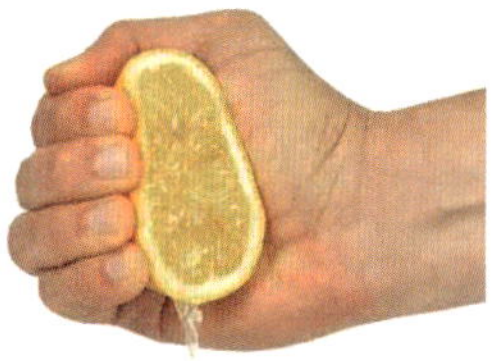

v 짜다, 꽉 쥐다 n 짜냄

= press, compress, pinch, wring, extract

\+ squeeze a tube of toothpaste 치약 통을 짜다

Q: Can you squeeze some more juice from those oranges?
그 오렌지들에서 주스를 좀 더 짤 수 있나요?

A:

1560 □□□

stable
[ˈsteɪbl]

a 안정된 n 마구간

= steady, firm, consistent, secure, constant

\+ stability n 안정성 stabilize v 안정시키다 stably adv 안정적으로

Q: Is your internet connection stable enough for video calls?
인터넷 연결이 화상 통화를 하기에 충분히 안정적인가요?

A:

DAY 18 | DICTATION TEST

5회 반복 예문 QR

DICTATION TEST 예문 QR을 듣고 다음 빈칸에 올바른 단어를 쓰세요.

1541. Do farmers usually ______________ wheat seeds in the autumn for a spring harvest?

1542. Can you ______________ a few minutes to help me with this task?

1543. Did her eyes ______________ when she saw the surprise gift?

1544. Does your clinic ______________ in sports injuries?

1545. Have you seen this bird ______________ in our park before?

1546. Can you give a ______________ reason for missing the meeting?

1547. Did you ______________ coffee all over your notes again today?

1548. Can you ______________ this top faster than I just did now?

1549. Did she hurt her ______________ while lifting that heavy box?

1550. Is the team's ______________ still strong after the loss?

1551. Wasn't the sunset at the beach absolutely ______________ tonight?

1552. Did you ______________ the bill evenly with your friends at dinner?

1553. Did the heat ______________ all the fresh food in the fridge?

1554. Did he really start singing ______________ at the party?

1555. Did you ______________ any familiar faces at the event this evening?

1556. Did you ______________ perfume before leaving the house?

1557. Did the rumor ______________ quickly around the school?

1558. Did you draw that ______________ with a ruler or by hand?

1559. Can you ______________ some more juice from those oranges?

1560. Is your internet connection ______________ enough for video calls?

5회 반복 표제어 QR 5회 반복 예문 QR

DAY 19

30 days

AI 학습자료와 인강 youpass.co.kr

PREVIEW A 다음 단어의 뜻을 한국어로 써보세요.

- ☐ **staff** ______________
- ☐ **stain** ______________
- ☐ **stamp** ______________
- ☐ **standard** ______________
- ☐ **stare** ______________
- ☐ **state** ______________
- ☐ **statement** ______________
- ☐ **station** ______________
- ☐ **statue** ______________
- ☐ **status** ______________
- ☐ **steady** ______________
- ☐ **steal** ______________
- ☐ **steel** ______________
- ☐ **steep** ______________
- ☐ **stem** ______________
- ☐ **stereotype** ______________
- ☐ **stick** ______________
- ☐ **sticky** ______________
- ☐ **stiff** ______________
- ☐ **stimulate** ______________

PREVIEW B 사진을 보고 알맞은 영어 단어를 **PREVIEW A** 에서 찾아 써보세요.

____

____

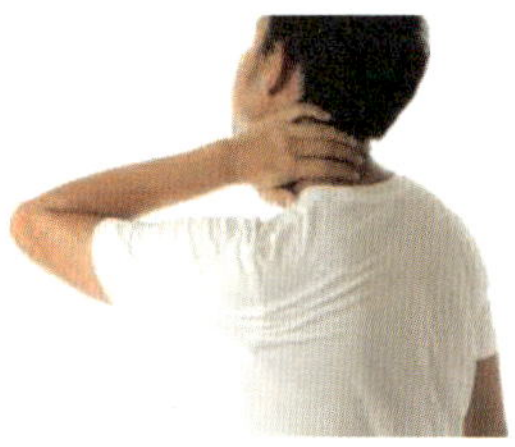
____

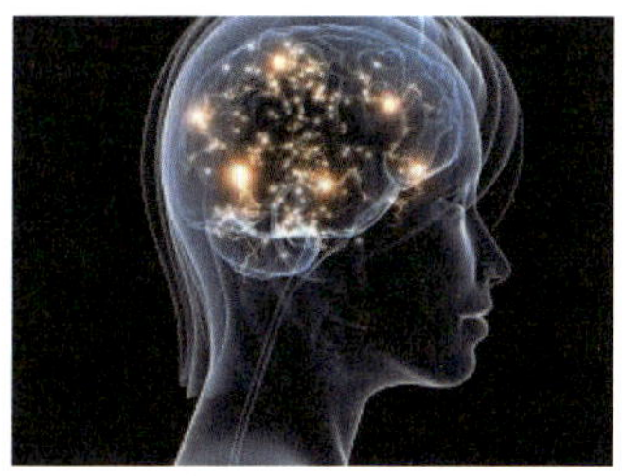
____

1561 □□□

staff
[stæf]

n 직원, 막대기

= personnel, employees, team, stick, support
+ medical staff 의료 직원

Q: How many staff members work in your department?
당신 부서에는 직원 몇 명이 일하나요?

A: ....

1562 □□□

stain
[steɪn]

n 얼룩, 오점 **v** 얼룩지게 하다

= mark, blotch, blemish, tarnish, discolor, disgrace
+ stained **a** 얼룩진

Q: Did you manage to remove the stain from your shirt?
셔츠에 묻은 얼룩을 지웠나요?

A: ....

1563 □□□

stamp
[stæmp]

n 우표, 도장 **v** 발을 구르다, 도장을 찍다

= imprint, mark, press, seal, footfall, postage stamp
+ rubber stamp 고무도장(서류에 날짜 • 기관명 등을 찍는 데 씀)

Q: Can you show me the stamp you used on the envelope?
봉투에 사용한 우표를 보여줄 수 있나요?

A: ....

1564 □□□

standard
[ˈstændərd]

n 기준, 표준 **a** 표준의

= norm, benchmark, criterion, typical, accepted, quality
+ standardization **n** 표준화 **standardize** **v** 표준화하다 **standardized** **a** 표준화된

Q: What standard do you follow for quality control?
품질 관리를 위해 어떤 기준을 따르나요?

A: ....

1565 □□□

stare
[ster]

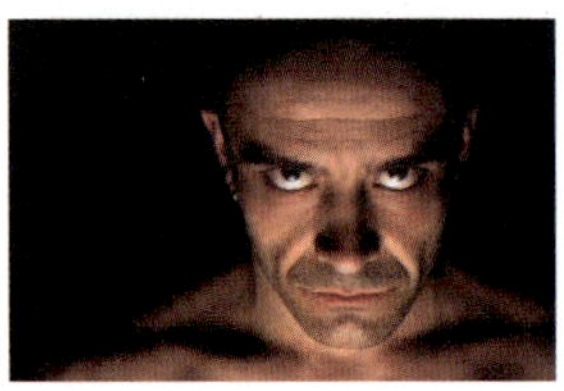

v 응시하다, 빤히 쳐다보다

= gaze, gape, glare, look intently
+ a moronic stare 멍청한 시선 **an inimical stare** 적대적인 시선

Q: Did the child just stare blankly at the screen for a long time?
아이가 오랫동안 화면을 멍하니 쳐다보기만 했나요?

A: ....

1566 □□□

state
[steɪt]

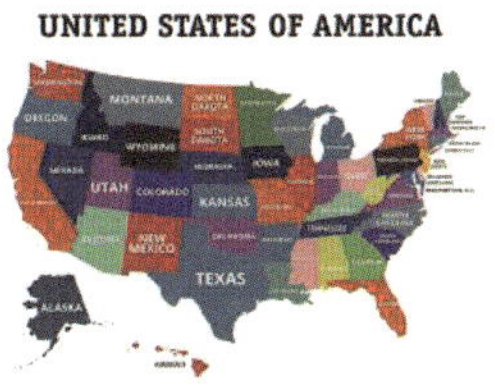

n 상태, 주(州), 국가 v 말하다, 진술하다

= condition, status, nation, country, declare, articulate
+ statement n 성명, 진술 status n 상태

Q: Can you state your opinion clearly during the meeting?
회의 중에 당신의 의견을 명확하게 말할 수 있나요?
A:

1567 □□□

statement
[ˈsteɪtmənt]

n 진술, 성명서

= declaration, assertion, announcement, account, thesis
+ state v 진술하다

Q: Did you hear the company's official statement about the merger?
합병에 대한 회사 공식 성명을 들었나요?
A:

1568 □□□

station
[ˈsteɪʃn]

n 역, 정거장, 방송국 v 배치하다

= stop, terminal, base, post, headquarters, position
+ stationary a 움직이지 않는, 정지된, 변하지 않는, 비유동적인

Q: Which station should I get off to reach the museum?
박물관에 가려면 어느 역에서 내려야 하나요?
A:

1569 □□□

statue
[ˈstætʃuː]

n 조각상

= sculpture, figure, monument, effigy
+ Statue of Liberty (미국 뉴욕 항 입구에 있는) 자유의 여신상

Q: Have you ever seen the statue in the city square?
시내 광장에 있는 동상을 본 적 있나요?
A:

1570 □□□

status
[ˈstætəs] [ˈsteɪtəs]

n 지위, 상태

= rank, standing, position, condition, prestige
+ status of booking (항공권에 명시되어 있는 이용구간의) 예약상황

Q: What is the current status of your application for the university program? 대학교 프로그램 지원 현황이 어떻게 되나요?
A:

1571 □□□

steady
[ˈstedi]

a 꾸준한, 안정된 v 안정시키다

= stable, constant, unwavering, firm, stabilize
+ steadiness n 꾸준함, 안정 steadily adv 꾸준히, 안정적으로

Q: Is the stock market showing a steady increase?
주식 시장이 꾸준히 상승하고 있나요?

A:

1572 □□□

steal
[sti:l]

v 훔치다

= pilfer, swipe, snatch, thieve, furtive
+ steal the show (어떤 상황에서 사람들의) 관심[인기]을 독차지하다

Q: Do you think someone tried to steal your bike last night?
어젯밤에 누군가 당신의 자전거를 훔치려 했다고 생각하나요?

A:

1573 □□□

steel
[sti:l]

n 강철

= metal, iron alloy, resolve, strengthen, harden
+ stainless steel 스테인리스강(鋼)

Q: How is steel made stronger for construction purposes?
건설 목적으로 강철을 어떻게 더 강하게 만드나요?

A:

1574 □□□

steep
[sti:p]

a 가파른, 급격한

= sharp, abrupt, sheer, excessive, soak, immerse
+ steepness n 경사도 steeply adv 가파르게

Q: Is the hill near your house too steep to climb easily?
당신 집 근처 언덕이 너무 가팔라서 쉽게 오르기 어렵나요?

A:

1575 □□□

stem
[stem]

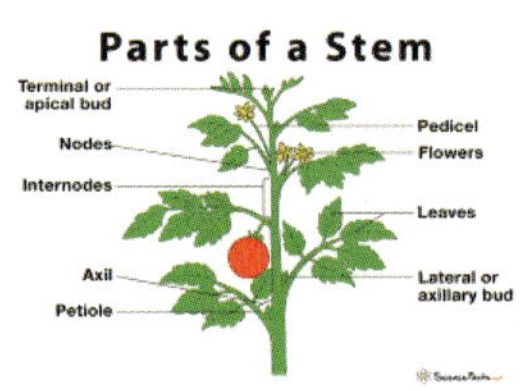

n 줄기, 어간 v 유래하다, 막다

= origin, root, stalk, branch, arise from, stop
+ stem cell 줄기 세포

Q: Can you identify the stem of this plant species?
이 식물 종의 줄기를 식별할 수 있나요?

A:

1576 □□□

stereotype
[ˈsteriətaɪp] [ˈstɪəriətaɪp]

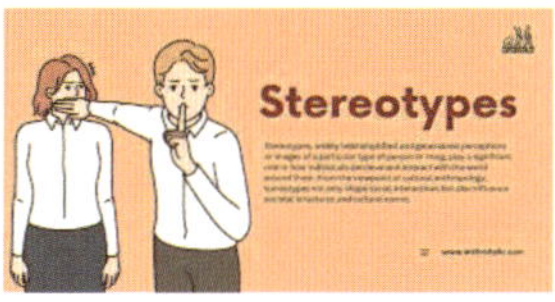

n 고정관념 **v** 고정관념을 형성하다

= cliché, archetype, preconceived notion, categorize
+ stereotypical **a** 전형적인

Q: Do you think the media sometimes reinforces harmful stereotypes about certain groups of people?
미디어가 때때로 특정 집단에 대한 해로운 고정관념을 강화한다고 생각하시나요?

A: ....

1577 □□□

stick
[stɪk]

n 막대기 **v** 달라붙다, 찌르다

= adhere, cling, poke, push, branch, pole
+ sticky **a** 끈적이는

Q: Will the glue stick hold the pieces together firmly?
이 고체풀이 조각들을 단단히 붙여줄까요?

A: ....

1578 □□□

sticky
[ˈstɪki]

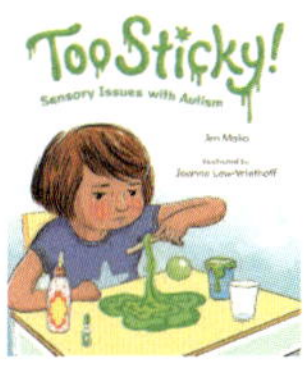

a 끈적이는, 다루기 힘든

= adhesive, gooey, tacky, difficult, awkward
+ stickiness **n** 끈적임

Q: How do you clean sticky residue from kitchen surfaces?
주방 표면의 끈적한 잔여물을 어떻게 청소하나요?

A: ....

1579 □□□

stiff
[stɪf]

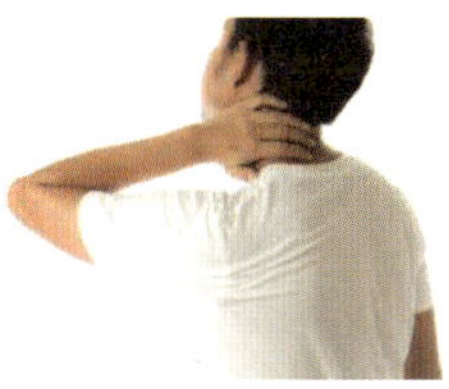

a 뻣뻣한, 굳은, 힘든

= rigid, firm, inflexible, difficult, formal
+ stiffness **n** 뻣뻣함 **stiffly** **adv** 뻣뻣하게

Q: Does your neck feel stiff after sleeping in an awkward position?
어색한 자세로 자고 나서 목이 뻐근한 건가요?

A: ....

1580 □□□

stimulate
[ˈstɪmjuleɪt]

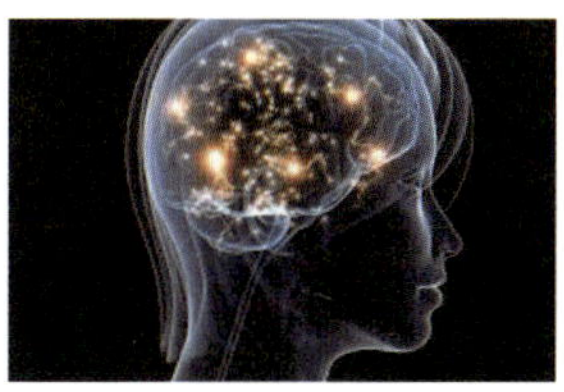

v 자극하다, 활성화하다

= arouse, activate, encourage, invigorate, prompt
+ stimulation **n** 자극 **stimulus** **n** 자극제 **stimulating** **a** 자극적인

Q: How does exercise stimulate brain function and memory?
운동이 뇌 기능과 기억력을 어떻게 자극하나요?

A: ....

DAY 19 | DICTATION TEST

5회 반복 예문 QR

DICTATION TEST 예문 QR을 듣고 다음 빈칸에 올바른 단어를 쓰세요.

1561. How many ______________ members work in your department?

1562. Did you manage to remove the ______________ from your shirt?

1563. Can you show me the ______________ you used on the envelope?

1564. What ______________ do you follow for quality control?

1565. Did the child just ______________ blankly at the screen for a long time?

1566. Can you ______________ your opinion clearly during the meeting?

1567. Did you hear the company's official ______________ about the merger?

1568. Which ______________ should I get off to reach the museum?

1569. Have you ever seen the ______________ in the city square?

1570. What is the current ______________ of your application for the university program?

1571. Is the stock market showing a ______________ increase?

1572. Do you think someone tried to ______________ your bike last night?

1573. How is steel made stronger for construction purposes?

1574. Is the hill near your house too ______________ to climb easily?

1575. Can you identify the ______________ of this plant species?

1576. Do you think the media sometimes reinforces harmful ______________ about certain groups of people?

1577. Will the glue ______________ hold the pieces together firmly?

1578. How do you clean ______________ residue from kitchen surfaces?

1579. Does your neck feel ______________ after sleeping in an awkward position?

1580. How does exercise ______________ brain function and memory?

5회 반복 표제어 QR   5회 반복 예문 QR

DAY 20

30 days

AI 학습자료와 인강 youpass.co.kr

PREVIEW A 다음 단어의 뜻을 한국어로 써보세요.

- ☐ sting ______
- ☐ stir ______
- ☐ stock ______
- ☐ stomachache ______
- ☐ stove ______
- ☐ straighten ______
- ☐ stranger ______
- ☐ strategy ______
- ☐ stream ______
- ☐ strength ______
- ☐ stress ______
- ☐ stretch ______
- ☐ strict ______
- ☐ strike ______
- ☐ string ______
- ☐ strip ______
- ☐ stripe ______
- ☐ stroke ______
- ☐ structure ______
- ☐ struggle ______

PREVIEW B 사진을 보고 알맞은 영어 단어를 **PREVIEW A**에서 찾아 써보세요.

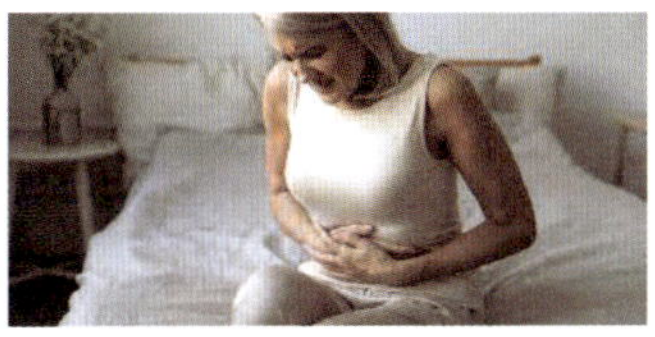
______

______

______

______

1581 □□□

sting
[stɪŋ]

n 찌름, 따가움 **v** 찌르다, 따끔거리다

= prick, bite, sharp pain, smart, infuriate
+ sting like a bee 벌처럼 쏘다[때리다]

Q: Does a bee sting hurt more than a wasp sting?
벌에 쏘인 것이 말벌에 쏘인 것보다 더 아픈가요?

A: ....

1582 □□□

stir
[stɜːr]

v 휘젓다, 뒤섞다 **n** 동요, 저음

= mix, agitate, arouse, excite, commotion
+ stir something up (강한 감정을) 불러일으키다, (논쟁 · 문제 등을) 일으키다[유발/유도하다]

Q: How long should I stir the sauce to get the right consistency?
적절한 농도를 얻으려면 소스를 얼마나 오래 저어야 하나요?

A: ....

1583 □□□

stock
[stɑːk]

n 재고, 주식 **v** 비축하다

= inventory, supply, shares, lineage, store, reserve
+ well-stocked a 재고가 풍부한 **stock market** 증권 거래업, 주식 시장, 증권 거래소

Q: Is the store well-stocked with fresh vegetables?
그 가게는 신선한 채소가 잘 비치되어 있나요?

A: ....

1584 □□□

stomachache
[ˈstʌmək͵eɪk]

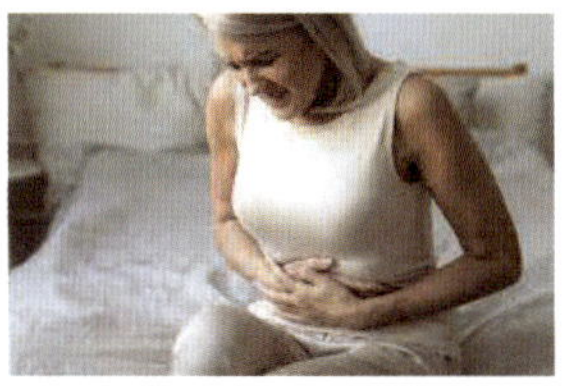

n 복통

= abdominal pain, bellyache, tummy ache
+ suffer from stomachache 복통을 앓다

Q: What usually causes a stomachache after eating certain foods?
특정 음식을 먹고 나면 보통 무엇이 복통을 유발하나요?

A: ....

1585 □□□

stove
[stoʊv]

n 난로, 스토브

= oven, cooker, range, heater
+ a gas[wood-burning] stove 가스스토브[장작] 난로

Q: Can you turn off the stove before leaving the kitchen?
주방을 떠나기 전에 가스레인지를 끌 수 있나요?

A: ....

1586 □□□

straighten
[ˈstreɪtn]

v 똑바르게 하다, 정리하다

= unbend, align, tidy, correct, rectify
+ straight **a** 곧은

Q: How do you straighten your hair without damaging it?
머리카락 손상 없이 어떻게 머리를 곧게 펴나요?

A: ....

1587 □□□

stranger
[ˈstreɪndʒər]

n 낯선 사람

= unknown person, foreigner, outsider, newcomer
+ strangeness **n** 이상함 **strange** **a** 이상한

Q: Would you offer help to a stranger who seemed lost in an unfamiliar part of the city? 낯선 도시에서 길을 잃은 듯 보이는 낯선 사람에게 도움을 주시겠어요?

A: ....

1588 □□□

strategy
[ˈstrætədʒi]

n 전략

= plan, tactic, approach, scheme, method
+ strategic **a** 전략적인 **strategically** **adv** 전략적으로

Q: What strategy will you use to increase sales this quarter?
이번 분기에 매출을 늘리기 위해 어떤 전략을 사용할 건가요?

A: ....

1589 □□□

stream
[striːm]

n 시내, 흐름 **v** 흐르다

= current, brook, creek, outpouring, continuous flow
+ live-stream **v** (인터넷에서) 실시간으로 방송하다, 실시간으로 시청하다
jet stream 제트 기류

Q: Is there a stream near your house where people go fishing?
당신 집 근처에 사람들이 낚시하러 가는 시냇물이 있나요?

A: ....

1590 □□□

strength
[streŋθ]

n 힘, 강점

= power, might, vigor, fortitude, advantage
+ strong **a** 강한 **strengthen** **v** 강화하다

Q: What do you consider your greatest strength when working in a team? 팀으로 일할 때 당신의 가장 큰 강점은 무엇이라고 생각하시나요?

A: ....

1591 □□□

stress
[stres]

n 스트레스, 강조 **v** 강조하다

= tension, pressure, emphasis, strain, emphasize, highlight

+ stressful **a** 스트레스가 많은 **stressed** **a** 스트레스 받은

Q: What techniques help you reduce stress after a long day?
긴 하루 후에 스트레스를 줄이는 데 어떤 기술들이 도움이 되나요?

A: ....

1592 □□□

stretch
[stretʃ]

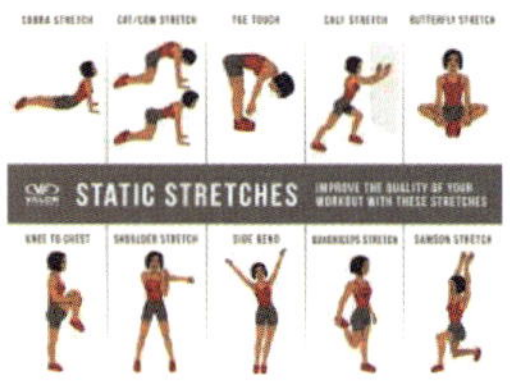

v 늘이다, 뻗다 **n** 늘림, 범위

= extend, lengthen, expand, reach, expanse, effort

+ at full stretch 전력을 기울여[(설비 등을) 최대한 가동하여]

Q: How often should you stretch before and after workouts?
운동 전후로 얼마나 자주 스트레칭 해야 하나요?

A: ....

1593 □□□

strict
[strɪkt]

a 엄격한, 엄밀한

= rigid, severe, stern, rigorous, precise

+ strictness **n** 엄격함 **strictly** **adv** 엄격하게

Q: Are the teachers at your school very strict with homework?
당신 학교 선생님들은 숙제에 대해 매우 엄격한가요?

A: ....

1594 □□□

strike
[straɪk]

v 치다, 파업하다, 떠오르다 **n** 파업, 타격

= hit, impact, assault, refuse to work, impress, discovery

+ air strike 공습 **strike out** 삼진[스트라이크 아웃]당하다[시키다]

Q: What will happen if the workers go on strike next week?
다음 주에 노동자들이 파업하면 어떻게 되나요?

A: ....

1595 □□□

string
[strɪŋ]

n 끈, 줄, 현악기 줄

= cord, thread, strand, series, sequence, tie

+ a piece[length] of string 끈[줄] 하나[한 가닥]

Q: Can you tie the package with a strong piece of string?
튼튼한 끈으로 소포를 묶을 수 있나요?

A: ....

1596 □□□

strip
[strɪp]

v 벗기다, 제거하다 **n** 가느다란 조각

= remove, peel, undress, narrow piece, sequence

+ landing strip 활주로(airstrip) **comic strip** (흔히 신문에서 연결된 사각형 박스들 속에 통일된 이야기를 담는) 만화

Q: Why did they strip the old paint off the wooden table?
왜 그들이 나무 테이블에서 오래된 페인트를 벗겨냈나요?

A: ....

1597 □□□

stripe
[straɪp]

n 줄무늬

= band, streak, line, chevron

+ striped a 줄무늬가 있는

Q: How many stripes are there on the national flag?
국기에는 줄무늬가 몇 개 있나요?

A: ....

1598 □□□

stroke
[stroʊk]

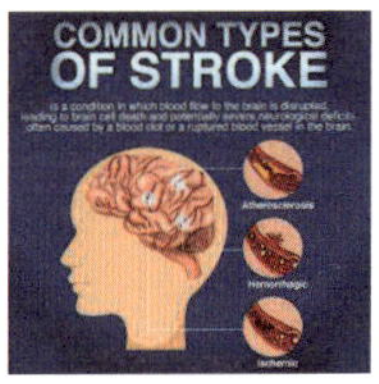

n 쓰다듬기, 뇌졸중, 타격 **v** 쓰다듬다

= caress, blow, paralysis, mark, sudden attack, pat

+ two-stroke a 2행정 사이클의 **four-stroke a** 4행정 사이클인

Q: What are the common symptoms of a stroke to watch for?
뇌졸중의 흔한 증상으로 무엇을 주의해야 하나요?

A: ....

1599 □□□

structure
[ˈstrʌktʃər]

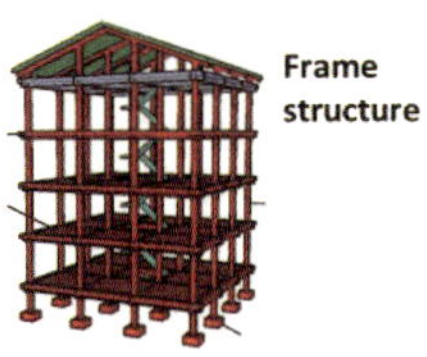

n 구조, 건물 **v** 구성하다

= organization, framework, building, form, arrange

+ structural a 구조적인

Q: How does the structure of this building withstand earthquakes?
이 건물의 구조는 어떻게 지진을 견뎌내나요?

A: ....

1600 □□□

struggle
[ˈstrʌgl]

n 고군분투, 싸움 **v** 고군분투하다

= strive, contend, fight, battle, effort, difficulty

+ class struggle 계급투쟁(특히 마르크스 이론에서 묘사된 사회 내 계급간의 대립)
a struggle for independence 독립 투쟁

Q: Why do some students struggle with learning a new language?
일부 학생들이 새로운 언어를 배우는 데 어려움을 겪는 이유는 무엇인가요?

A: ....

DAY 20 | DICTATION TEST

5회 반복 예문 QR

DICTATION TEST 예문 QR을 듣고 다음 빈칸에 올바른 단어를 쓰세요.

1581. Does a bee ______________ hurt more than a wasp ______________?

1582. How long should I ______________ the sauce to get the right consistency?

1583. Is the store well-______________ with fresh vegetables?

1584. What usually causes a ______________ after eating certain foods?

1585. Can you turn off the ______________ before leaving the kitchen?

1586. How do you ______________ your hair without damaging it?

1587. Would you offer help to a ______________ who seemed lost in an unfamiliar part of the city?

1588. What ______________ will you use to increase sales this quarter?

1589. Is there a ______________ near your house where people go fishing?

1590. What do you consider your greatest ______________ when working in a team?

1591. What techniques help you reduce ______________ after a long day?

1592. How often should you ______________ before and after workouts?

1593. Are the teachers at your school very ______________ with homework?

1594. What will happen if the workers go on ______________ next week?

1595. Can you tie the package with a strong piece of ______________?

1596. Why did they ______________ the old paint off the wooden table?

1597. How many ______________ are there on the national flag?

1598. What are the common symptoms of a ______________ to watch for?

1599. How does the ______________ of this building withstand earthquakes?

1600. Why do some students ______________ with learning a new language?

5회 반복 표제어 QR 5회 반복 예문 QR

DAY 21

30 days

AI 학습자료와 인강 youpass.co.kr

PREVIEW A 다음 단어의 뜻을 한국어로 써보세요.

- □ studio ____________
- □ stuff ____________
- □ subject ____________
- □ subjective ____________
- □ submit ____________
- □ substance ____________
- □ substitute ____________
- □ suburb ____________
- □ succeed ____________
- □ success ____________
- □ successful ____________
- □ successive ____________
- □ sudden ____________
- □ suffer ____________
- □ sufficient ____________
- □ suggest ____________
- □ suggestion ____________
- □ suit ____________
- □ suitable ____________
- □ sum ____________

PREVIEW B 사진을 보고 알맞은 영어 단어를 **PREVIEW A** 에서 찾아 써보세요.

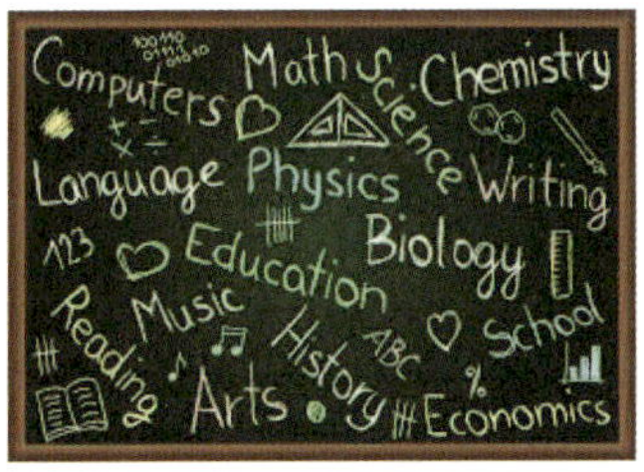

____

____

____

____

1601 □□□

studio
[ˈstuːdioʊ] [ˈstjuːdioʊ]

n 스튜디오, 작업실, 원룸 방

= workshop, atelier, office, set, soundstage
+ a design studio 디자인[설계]실

Q: Is the art studio open to visitors this weekend?
이번 주말에 미술 스튜디오가 방문객들에게 개방되나요?

A: ....

1602 □□□

stuff
[stʌf]

n 물건, 재료 v 채워 넣다

= material, things, belongings, fill, cram, pack
+ sticky stuff 끈적거리는 것

Q: Did you pack all your stuff for the trip?
여행 갈 짐 다 쌌나요?

A: ....

1603 □□□

subject
[ˈsʌbdʒekt] n [səbˈdʒekt] v

n 주제, 과목, 주어, 대상 v ~에 종속시키다

= topic, theme, matter, discipline, individual, impose, undergo
+ subjective a 주관적인

Q: What subject do you find most challenging at school?
학교에서 어떤 과목이 가장 어렵다고 생각하나요?

A: ....

1604 □□□

subjective
[səbˈdʒektɪv]

a 주관적인

= personal, biased, individual, arbitrary
+ subject n 주제, 과목, 신민, 피실험대상자 subjectivity n 주관성
subjectively adv 주관적으로

Q: Do you think opinions about art are mostly subjective?
미술에 대한 의견은 대부분 주관적이라고 생각하나요?

A: ....

1605 □□□

submit
[səbˈmɪt]

v 제출하다, 굴복하다

= present, hand in, surrender, yield, propose
+ submission n 제출, 항복 submissive a 순종적인

Q: When do we need to submit the final report for the project?
프로젝트 최종 보고서를 언제 제출해야 하나요?

A: ....

1606 □□□

substance
[ˈsʌbstəns]

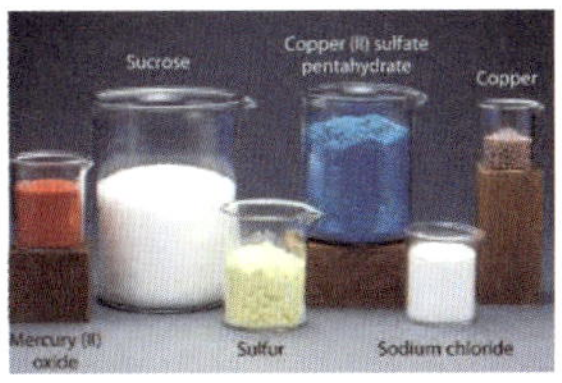

n 물질, 본질, 실체

= material, matter, essence, core, importance, reality

+ substantial a 상당한, 실질적인 substantially adv 상당히

Q: Can you identify the substance used in this chemical experiment?
이 화학 실험에 사용된 물질을 식별할 수 있나요?

A: ....

1607 □□□

substitute
[ˈsʌbstɪtuːt]

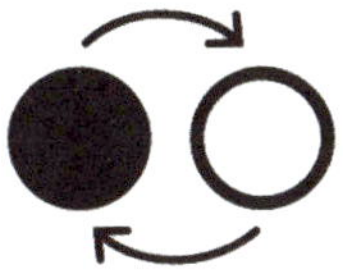

n 대용품, 대리인 v 대신하다

= replacement, stand-in, surrogate, exchange, replace

+ substitution n 대체 substitutable a 대체 가능한

Q: Who will substitute for the teacher during her absence?
선생님 부재중에 누가 대신할 건가요?

A: ....

1608 □□□

suburb
[ˈsʌbɜːrb]

n 교외

= outskirts, residential area, bedroom community

+ suburban a 교외의

Q: Do you prefer living in the city or in the suburbs?
도시와 교외 중 어디에 사는 것을 선호하나요?

A: ....

1609 □□□

succeed
[səkˈsiːd]

v 성공하다, 뒤를 잇다

= achieve, accomplish, thrive, follow, prosper

+ success n 성공 successor n 후임자 successful a 성공적인
successive a 연속적인

Q: What qualities do you think help someone succeed in business?
성공하는 데 어떤 자질이 도움이 된다고 생각하나요?

A: ....

1610 □□□

success
[səkˈses]

n 성공

= achievement, triumph, victory, accomplishment

+ succeed v 성공하다 successful a 성공적인

Q: How do you define success in your personal life?
개인적인 삶에서 성공을 어떻게 정의하나요?

A: ....

1611 □□□

successful
[sək'sesfl]

a 성공적인

= **prosperous, thriving, victorious, effective, favorable**

+ **success** **n** 성공 **successfully** **adv** 성공적으로

Q: What made the campaign so successful last year?
작년에 그 캠페인이 그렇게 성공적이었던 이유는 무엇인가요?

A: ....

1612 □□□

successive
[sək'sesɪv]

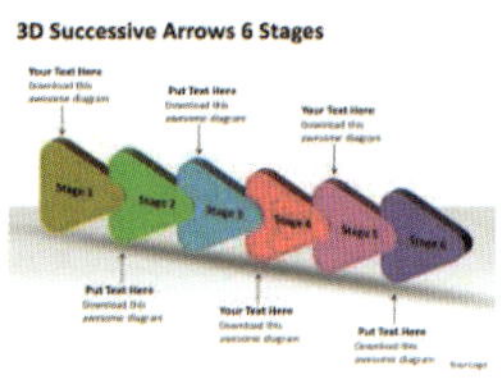

a 연속적인, 잇따른

= **consecutive, sequential, continuous, subsequent**

+ **successively** **adv** 연속적으로

Q: Have you ever won in two successive competitions?
연속으로 두 번의 대회에서 우승해 본 적이 있나요?

A: ....

1613 □□□

sudden
['sʌdn]

a 갑작스러운

= **abrupt, unexpected, rapid, swift, unforeseen**

+ **suddenly** **adv** 갑자기

Q: How did you react to the sudden change in your schedule?
갑작스러운 일정 변경에 어떻게 반응했나요?

A: ....

1614 □□□

suffer
['sʌfər]

v 고통 받다, 겪다

= **endure, undergo, experience, bear, tolerate**

+ **suffering** **n** 고통

Q: Why do some people suffer from allergies during spring?
일부 사람들이 봄에 알레르기로 고통 받는 이유는 무엇인가요?

A: ....

1615 □□□

sufficient
[sə'fɪʃnt]

a 충분한

= **enough, adequate, ample, satisfactory**

+ **sufficiency** **n** 충분함 **sufficiently** **adv** 충분히

Q: Is the budget sufficient to cover all the project expenses?
예산이 모든 프로젝트 비용을 충당하기에 충분한가요?

A: ....

1616 □□□

suggest
[səg'dʒest] [sə'dʒest]

v 제안하다, 암시하다

= propose, recommend, imply, hint, advise
+ suggestion **n** 제안

Q: Can you suggest a good restaurant near the airport?
공항 근처에 좋은 식당을 추천해 줄 수 있나요?

A: ....

1617 □□□

suggestion
[səg'dʒestʃən] [sə'dʒestʃən]

n 제안, 암시

= proposal, idea, recommendation, hint, advice
+ suggest **v** 제안하다

Q: Do you have any suggestion to improve the meeting process?
회의 과정을 개선하기 위한 제안이 있나요?

A: ....

1618 □□□

suit
[su:t]

n 정장, 소송 **v** 적합하다, 어울리다

= outfit, apparel, case, match, fit, be appropriate
+ suitable **a** 적합한

Q: Does this color suit you better than the other one?
이 색이 다른 색보다 당신에게 더 잘 어울리나요?

A: ....

1619 □□□

suitable
['su:təbl]

a 적합한, 적절한

= appropriate, proper, fitting, apt, convenient
+ suitability **n** 적합성 **suitably** **adv** 적합하게

Q: Is this dress suitable for the formal event tonight?
이 드레스가 오늘 밤 공식 행사에 적합한가요?

A: ....

1620 □□□

sum
[sʌm]

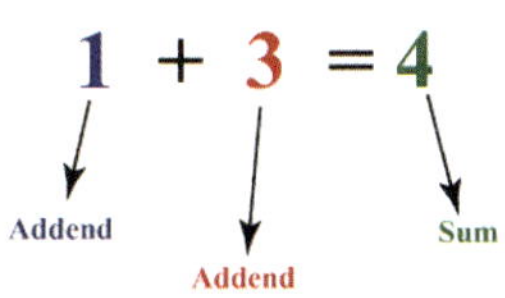

n 합계, 총액 **v** 합산하다

= total, amount, aggregate, calculate, summarize
+ the sum of 6 and 8 6과 8의 합계

Q: Can you calculate the sum of these two numbers quickly?
이 두 숫자의 합계를 빠르게 계산할 수 있나요?

A: ....

DAY 21 | DICTATION TEST

5회 반복 예문 QR

DICTATION TEST 예문 QR을 듣고 다음 빈칸에 올바른 단어를 쓰세요.

1601. Is the art ______________ open to visitors this weekend?

1602. Did you pack all your ______________ for the trip?

1603. What ______________ do you find most challenging at school?

1604. Do you think opinions about art are mostly ______________?

1605. When do we need to ______________ the final report for the project?

1606. Can you identify the ______________ used in this chemical experiment?

1607. Who will ______________ for the teacher during her absence?

1608. Do you prefer living in the city or in the ______________?

1609. What qualities do you think help someone ______________ in business?

1610. How do you define ______________ in your personal life?

1611. What made the campaign so ______________ last year?

1612. Have you ever won in two ______________ competitions?

1613. How did you react to the ______________ change in your schedule?

1614. Why do some people ______________ from allergies during spring?

1615. Is the budget ______________ to cover all the project expenses?

1616. Can you ______________ a good restaurant near the airport?

1617. Do you have any ______________ to improve the meeting process?

1618. Does this color ______________ you better than the other one?

1619. Is this dress ______________ for the formal event tonight?

1620. Can you calculate the ______________ of these two numbers quickly?

5회 반복 표제어 QR   5회 반복 예문 QR

DAY 22

30 days

PREVIEW A 다음 단어의 뜻을 한국어로 써보세요.

- ☐ summarize ______
- ☐ summary ______
- ☐ superior ______
- ☐ supervise ______
- ☐ supper ______
- ☐ supply ______
- ☐ support ______
- ☐ suppose ______
- ☐ surface ______
- ☐ surgery ______
- ☐ surprisingly ______
- ☐ surround ______
- ☐ survey ______
- ☐ survive ______
- ☐ suspect ______
- ☐ suspend ______
- ☐ suspension ______
- ☐ sustainable ______
- ☐ swallow ______
- ☐ swear ______

PREVIEW B 사진을 보고 알맞은 영어 단어를 PREVIEW A 에서 찾아 써보세요.

______

______

______

______

1621 □□□

summarize
[ˈsʌməraɪz]

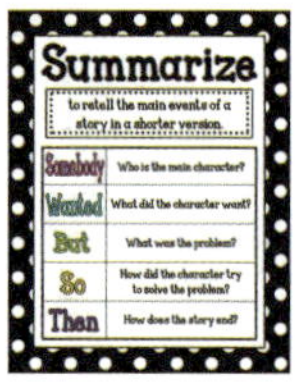

v 요약하다

= abridge, condense, outline, precis, encapsulate

+ summary **n** 요약

Q: Can you summarize the main points of the meeting?
회의 주요 내용을 요약해 줄 수 있나요?

A: ....

1622 □□□

summary
[ˈsʌməri]

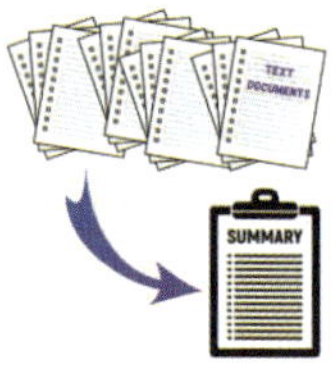

n 요약

= synopsis, abstract, brief, precis, overview

+ summarize **v** 요약하다

Q: Did you read the summary of the latest report?
최신 보고서 요약을 읽었나요?

A: ....

1623 □□□

superior
[suːˈpɪriər]

a 우월한, 상위의 **n** 상사

= higher, better, greater, excellent, top-notch

+ superiority **n** 우월성

Q: Do you think this model is superior to the previous one?
이 모델이 이전 모델보다 우수하다고 생각하나요?

A: ....

1624 □□□

supervise
[ˈsuːpərvaɪz]

v 감독하다, 관리하다

= oversee, manage, direct, monitor, guide

+ supervision **n** 감독 **supervisor** **n** 감독관

Q: Who will supervise the interns during their training?
인턴 교육 중 누가 인턴을 감독할 건가요?

A: ....

1625 □□□

supper
[ˈsʌpər]

n 저녁 식사

= dinner, evening meal

+ the Last Supper (그리스도가 십자가에 못 박히기 전날 밤에 제자들과 같이 한) 최후의 만찬

Q: What time do you usually have supper on weekdays?
평일에 보통 몇 시에 저녁 식사를 하나요?

A: ....

1626 □□□

supply
[sə'plaɪ]

n 공급, 비축 **v** 공급하다

= provide, furnish, deliver, provision, stock, reserve

+ water supply 상수도 supply line 보급로

Q: Is the supply of raw materials enough for this month's production?
이번 달 생산량을 위한 원자재 공급이 충분한가요?

A: ....

1627 □□□

support
[sə'pɔːrt]

n 지지, 지원 **v** 지지하다, 부양하다

= uphold, sustain, assist, encourage, backing, aid

+ supporter **n** 지지자 supportive **a** 지지하는

Q: How can we support our colleagues better during busy periods?
바쁜 시기에 동료들을 어떻게 더 잘 지원할 수 있을까요?

A: ....

1628 □□□

suppose
[sə'poʊz]

v 가정하다, 생각하다

= assume, presume, imagine, believe, guess

+ supposition **n** 가정 supposed **a** 추정된 supposedly **adv** 추정컨대

+ is[am/are] supposed to + v ~하기로 되어 있다(예정, 규칙, 관례), ~해야 한다(의무, 책임), ~라고 여겨진다(일반적인 생각), ~인 줄 알았다(오해)

+ was[were] supposed to + v ~할 예정이었는데 하지 못했다(의무 불이행), ~해야 했었는데 하지 않았다(의무 불이행)

Q: What do you suppose will happen if we delay the project?
프로젝트를 지연하면 어떤 일이 일어날 것이라고 생각하나요?

A: ....

1629 □□□

surface
['sɜːrfɪs]

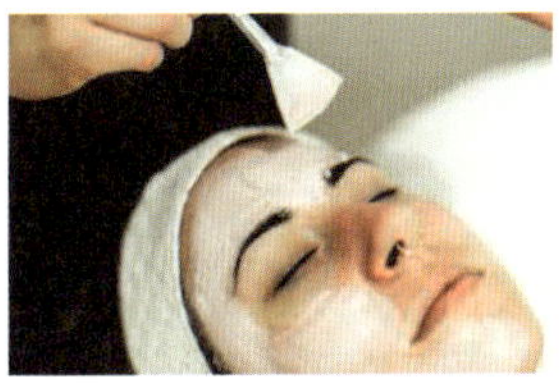

n 표면 **v** 떠오르다

= exterior, facade, outside, emerge, appear, rise

+ surface-to-surface **a** 지대지의 air-to-surface **a** 공대지의

Q: When will the new road surface be completed by the contractors?
계약업체들이 새로운 도로 표면을 언제까지 완성할 건가요?

A: ....

1630 □□□

surgery
['sɜːrdʒəri]

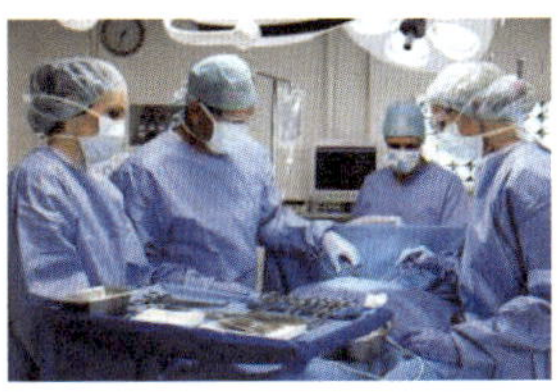

n 수술

= operation, intervention, medical procedure

+ surgeon **n** 외과 의사 surgical **a** 외과의

Q: How long does it usually take to perform the surgery?
수술은 보통 얼마나 걸리나요?

A: ....

1631 □□□

surprisingly
[sər'praɪzɪŋli]

adv 놀랍게도

= unexpectedly, astonishingly, remarkably, amazingly

+ surprise **v** 놀라게 하다 **surprising** **a** 놀라운 **surprised** **a** 놀란

Q: Did the team surprisingly win the championship?
그 팀이 놀랍게도 챔피언십에서 우승했나요?

A: ....

1632 □□□

surround
[sə'raʊnd]

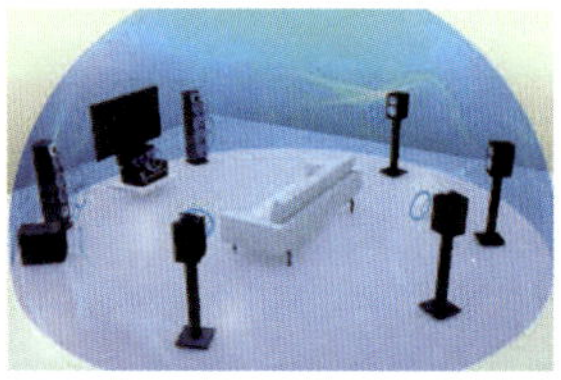

v 둘러싸다

= encircle, enclose, encompass, environ, beset

+ surroundings **n** 환경, 주위

Q: Are we surrounded by enough resources to finish on time?
제시간에 마치기 위한 충분한 자원에 둘러싸여 있나요?

A: ....

1633 □□□

survey
['sɜːrveɪ] **n** [sər'veɪ] **v**

n 조사, 설문조사 **v** 조사하다

= poll, questionnaire, inspection, scrutinize, examine

+ an aerial survey 항공 측량

Q: Have you completed the customer satisfaction survey?
고객 만족도 조사를 완료했나요?

A: ....

1634 □□□

survive
[sər'vaɪv]

v 살아남다, 생존하다

= live, subsist, outlive, endure, last

+ survival **n** 생존 **survivor** **n** 생존자 **surviving** **a** 살아남은

Q: Do you think it's possible for some species to survive the effects of climate change? 일부 종들이 기후 변화의 영향에서 살아남는 것이 가능하다고 생각하시나요?

A: ....

1635 □□□

suspect
['sʌspekt] **n** [sə'spekt] **v**

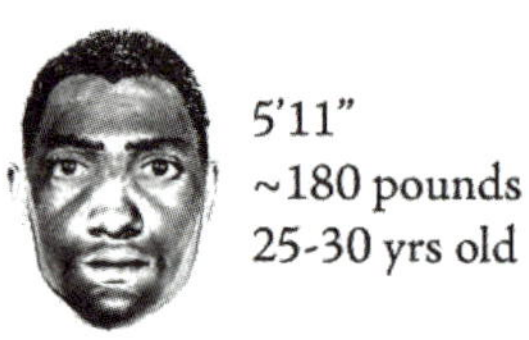

v 의심하다, 짐작하다 **n** 용의자

= doubt, mistrust, believe, guess, criminal, likely

+ suspicion **n** 의심 **suspicious** **a** 의심스러운 **suspect A of B** A가 B했다고 의심하다

Q: Do you suspect anyone of leaking the confidential information?
기밀 정보 유출을 누구라도 의심하나요?

A: ....

1636 □□□

suspend
[sə'spend]

v 매달다, 중단하다, 정학시키다

= hang, postpone, stop, defer, interrupt, debar
+ suspension **n** 정지, 유예

Q: Why did the company temporarily suspend production?
회사가 왜 일시적으로 생산을 중단했나요?

A: ....

1637 □□□

suspension
[sə'spenʃn]

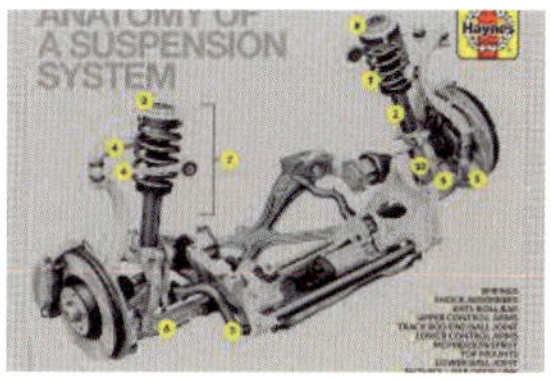

n 중단, 정학, 서스펜션

= hanging, postponement, halt, interruption, deferral
+ suspend **v** 중단하다, 매달다

Q: How long is the suspension period for employees who break rules?
규칙을 위반하는 직원들의 정직 기간은 얼마나 되나요?

A: ....

1638 □□□

sustainable
[sə'steɪnəbl]

a 지속 가능한

= ecological, viable, renewable, maintainable, durable
+ sustainability **n** 지속가능성 **sustain** **v** 지속하다

Q: What is the sustainable environmental protection policy your company follows? 당신 회사가 따르고 있는 지속 환경 보호 정책은 무엇인가요?

A: ....

1639 □□□

swallow
['swɑːloʊ]

v 삼키다 **n** (조류) 제비

= ingest, gulp, consume, accept, believe, bird
+ before swallowing it 삼키기 전에

Q: Can you swallow pills without water?
물 없이도 알약을 삼킬 수 있나요?

A: ....

1640 □□□

swear
[swer]

v 맹세하다, 욕하다

= vow, promise, pledge, curse, utter profanity
+ swear word 욕, 욕설

Q: Did he swear to keep the secret confidential during the meeting?
회의 중에 그는 비밀을 기밀로 유지하겠다고 맹세했나요?

A: ....

DAY 22 | DICTATION TEST

5회 반복 예문 QR

DICTATION TEST 예문 QR을 듣고 다음 빈칸에 올바른 단어를 쓰세요.

1621. Can you ______________ the main points of the meeting?

1622. Did you read the ______________ of the latest report?

1623. Do you think this model is ______________ to the previous one?

1624. Who will ______________ the interns during their training?

1625. What time do you usually have ______________ on weekdays?

1626. Is the ______________ of raw materials enough for this month's production?

1627. How can we ______________ our colleagues better during busy periods?

1628. What do you ______________ will happen if we delay the project?

1629. When will the new road ______________ be completed by the contractors?

1630. How long does it usually take to perform the ______________?

1631. Did the team ______________ win the championship?

1632. Are we ______________ by enough resources to finish on time?

1633. Have you completed the customer satisfaction ______________?

1634. Do you think it's possible for some species to ______________ the effects of climate change?

1635. Do you ______________ anyone of leaking the confidential information?

1636. Why did the company temporarily ______________ production?

1637. How long is the ______________ period for employees who break rules?

1638. What is the ______________ environmental protection policy your company follows?

1639. Can you ______________ pills without water?

1640. Did he ______________ to keep the secret confidential during the meeting?

5회 반복 표제어 QR   5회 반복 예문 QR

DAY 23

30 days

AI 학습자료와 인강 youpass.co.kr

PREVIEW A 다음 단어의 뜻을 한국어로 써보세요.

□ sweat ______	□ tap ______
□ sweep ______	□ target ______
□ switch ______	□ task ______
□ symbol ______	□ tax ______
□ sympathy ______	□ tease ______
□ symptom ______	□ technical ______
□ system ______	□ technician ______
□ tag ______	□ technology ______
□ tale ______	□ temper ______
□ talented ______	□ temperature ______

PREVIEW B 사진을 보고 알맞은 영어 단어를 **PREVIEW A** 에서 찾아 써보세요.

______

______

______

______

1641 □□□

sweat
[swet]

n 땀 **v** 땀 흘리다

= perspire, exude, labor, perspiration, moisture

+ no sweat (상대방의 감사 · 부탁에 대한 대꾸로**)** 이 정도는 별 거 아냐 **cold sweat** 식은땀

Q: Do you sweat a lot when you exercise?
운동할 때 땀을 많이 흘리나요?

A: ....

1642 □□□

sweep
[swi:p]

v 쓸다, 청소하다

= clean, brush, clear, move quickly, pervade

+ chimney sweep 굴뚝 청소부

Q: Who usually sweeps the floor in your office?
사무실 바닥은 보통 누가 쓸어요?

A: ....

1643 □□□

switch
[swɪtʃ]

n 스위치, 전환 **v** 바꾸다, 전환하다

= change, alter, shift, substitute, exchange, lever

+ switch off 신경을 끄다

Q: Did you switch your phone to silent mode?
휴대폰을 무음 모드로 바꿨나요?

A: ....

1644 □□□

symbol
[ˈsɪmbl]

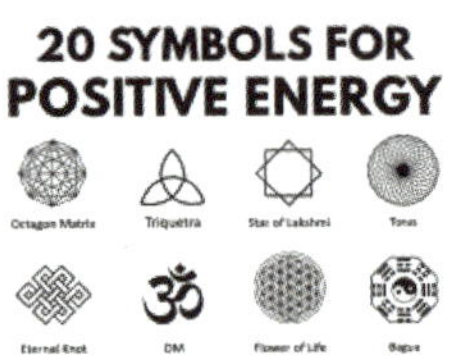

n 상징

= emblem, sign, representation, icon, token

+ symbolic a 상징적인 **symbolize v** 상징하다

Q: What does this symbol represent on the map?
이 기호는 지도에서 무엇을 나타내나요?

A: ....

1645 □□□

sympathy
[ˈsɪmpəθi]

n 동정, 공감

= compassion, pity, empathy, understanding, commiseration

+ sympathetic a 동정적인 **sympathetically adv** 동정적으로

Q: Did you send your sympathy to the family after the loss?
상실 후에 가족에게 위로를 전했나요?

A: ....

1646 □□□

symptom
[ˈsɪmptəm]

n 증상

= **sign, indication, manifestation, signal, clue**
\+ **symptomatic** **a** 증상적인
Q: Are fever and cough common symptoms of the flu?
열과 기침은 독감의 흔한 증상인가요?
A: ....

1647 □□□

system
[ˈsɪstəm]

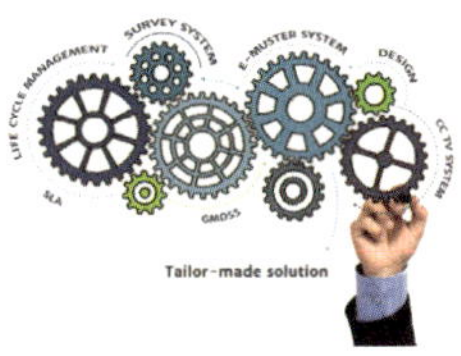

n 시스템, 체계

= **method, arrangement, scheme, structure, network**
\+ **systematic** **a** 체계적인 **systematically** **adv** 체계적으로
Q: Is the new computer system working properly now?
새 컴퓨터 시스템이 지금 제대로 작동하나요?
A: ....

1648 □□□

tag
[tæg]

n 꼬리표, 태그 **v** 꼬리표를 붙이다

= **label, mark, identify, attach, follow, trail**
\+ **price tag** 가격표
Q: Did you put a price tag on all the clothes for the garage sale?
차고 세일할 옷들에 가격표를 다 붙였나요?
A: ....

1649 □□□

tale
[teɪl]

n 이야기

= **story, narrative, legend, fable, account**
\+ **tail** **n** (동물의) 꼬리 **fairy tale** 동화
Q: Have you heard the old tale about the haunted house?
유령의 집에 대한 옛날이야기를 들어본 적 있나요?
A: ....

1650 □□□

talented
[ˈtæləntɪd]

a 재능 있는

= **gifted, skilled, artistic, accomplished, adept**
\+ **talent** **n** 재능
Q: Do you think she is talented enough to join the team?
그녀가 팀에 합류할 만큼 재능 있다고 생각하나요?
A: ....

1651 □□□

tap
[tæp]

n 수도꼭지, 가볍게 두드림 **v** 가볍게 두드리다

= **faucet, spigot, hit, strike, draw on, extract**
+ **tap time** 똑똑 박자를 맞추다

Q: Can I tap the screen to open the app?
앱을 열려면 화면을 탭하면 되나요?

A:

1652 □□□

target
[ˈtɑːrgɪt]

n 목표, 표적 **v** 목표로 하다

= **goal, aim, objective, mark, direct, focus on**
+ **soft target** (공격의) 쉬운 목표물 **moving target** 움직이는 목표물

Q: What is the sales target for this quarter?
이번 분기 판매 목표는 무엇인가요?

A:

1653 □□□

task
[tæsk]

n 과업, 임무

= **assignment, duty, chore, job, mission**
+ **task force** (군대의) 기동 부대

Q: How long will it take to complete this task?
이 작업을 완료하는 데 얼마나 걸릴까요?

A:

1654 □□□

tax
[tæks]

n 세금 **v** 세금을 부과하다

= **levy, duty, impost, burden, impose, demand**
+ **taxation** **n** 과세 **taxable** **a** 과세 대상의

Q: Do you know how much tax you have to pay this year?
올해 얼마의 세금을 내야 하는지 아나요?

A:

1655 □□□

tease
[tiːz]

v 놀리다, 괴롭히다

= **bother, provoke, taunt, torment, playful vexation**
+ **tease for candy** 캔디를 달라고 졸라대다[집적거리다]

Q: Why do you always tease your little brother?
왜 항상 네 남동생을 놀리나요?

A:

1656 □□□

technical
[ˈteknɪkl]

a 기술적인, 전문적인

= practical, mechanical, specialized, specific, expert

+ technique **n** 기술 technology **n** 기술 technician **n** 기술자
technically **adv** 기술적으로

Q: Is this issue related to a technical problem?
이 문제는 기술적인 문제와 관련이 있나요?

A: ....

1657 □□□

technician
[tekˈnɪʃn]

n 기술자

= engineer, specialist, expert, operative

+ technology **n** 기술 technique **n** 기술

Q: When will the technician arrive to fix the machine?
기계 고치러 기술자가 언제 도착할까요?

A: ....

1658 □□□

technology
[tekˈnɑːlədʒi]

n 기술

= innovation, machinery, applied science, methods

+ technological **a** 기술적인 technologically **adv** 기술적으로

Q: How has technology changed the way we work?
기술이 우리가 일하는 방식을 어떻게 변화시켰나요?

A: ....

1659 □□□

temper
[ˈtempər]

n 성질, 기질

= disposition, mood, anger, soothe, harden

+ temperamental **a** 변덕스러운

Q: Do you lose your temper easily under stress?
스트레스 받으면 쉽게 화를 내나요?

A: ....

1660 □□□

temperature
[ˈtemprətʃər]

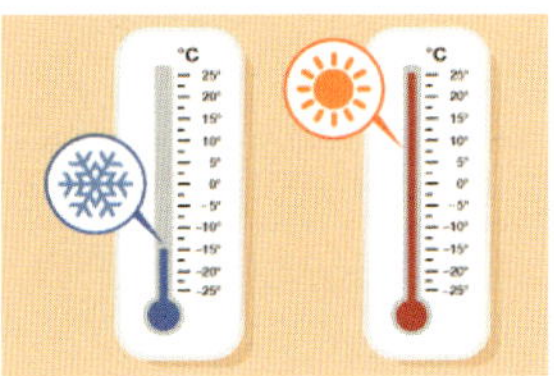

n 온도, 기온

= heat, coldness, fever, degree, warmth

+ room temperature (건물 내의) 상온[평상시 온도] absolute temperature 절대 온도

Q: What's the temperature like outside today?
오늘 밖에 기온이 어떤가요?

A: ....

DAY 23 | DICTATION TEST

5회 반복 예문 QR

DICTATION TEST 예문 QR을 듣고 다음 빈칸에 올바른 단어를 쓰세요.

1641. Do you ______________ a lot when you exercise?

1642. Who usually ______________ the floor in your office?

1643. Did you ______________ your phone to silent mode?

1644. What does this ______________ represent on the map?

1645. Did you send your ______________ to the family after the loss?

1646. Are fever and cough common ______________ of the flu?

1647. Is the new computer ______________ working properly now?

1648. Did you put a price ______________ on all the clothes for the garage sale?

1649. Have you heard the old ______________ about the haunted house?

1650. Do you think she is ______________ enough to join the team?

1651. Can I ______________ the screen to open the app?

1652. What is the sales ______________ for this quarter?

1653. How long will it take to complete this ______________?

1654. Do you know how much ______________ you have to pay this year?

1655. Why do you always ______________ your little brother?

1656. Is this issue related to a ______________ problem?

1657. When will the ______________ arrive to fix the machine?

1658. How has ______________ changed the way we work?

1659. Do you lose your ______________ easily under stress?

1660. What's the ______________ like outside today?

5회 반복 표제어 QR 5회 반복 예문 QR

DAY 24

30 days

AI 학습자료와 인강 youpass.co.kr

PREVIEW A 다음 단어의 뜻을 한국어로 써보세요.

- □ temporary ____________
- □ tend ____________
- □ tendency ____________
- □ tender ____________
- □ tense ____________
- □ tension ____________
- □ term ____________
- □ terrible ____________
- □ terribly ____________
- □ terrific ____________
- □ territory ____________
- □ theme ____________
- □ theory ____________
- □ therapy ____________
- □ therefore ____________
- □ thirst ____________
- □ thoughtful ____________
- □ thread ____________
- □ threat ____________
- □ threaten ____________

PREVIEW B 사진을 보고 알맞은 영어 단어를 PREVIEW A 에서 찾아 써보세요.

____

____

____

____

1661 □□□

temporary
[ˈtempəreri]

a 일시적인

= **provisional, transient, fleeting, short-term**
+ **temporarily** adv 일시적으로

Q: Is this job only temporary or permanent?
이 직업은 임시직인가요, 아니면 영구직인가요?

A: ....

1662 □□□

tend
[tend]

v ~하는 경향이 있다, 돌보다

= **incline, lean, be prone, care for, look after**
+ **tendency** n 경향 **tend to do** ~하는 경향이 있다, ~하는 편이다

Q: Do you tend to wake up early or late?
일찍 일어나는 편인가요, 아니면 늦게 일어나는 편인가요?

A: ....

1663 □□□

tendency
[ˈtendənsi]

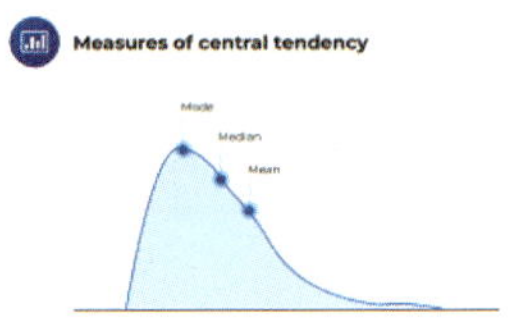

n 경향, 추세

= **inclination, predisposition, propensity, trend**
+ **tend** v ~하는 경향이 있다

Q: Do you have a tendency to procrastinate before deadlines?
마감 기한 전에 미루는 경향이 있나요?

A: ....

1664 □□□

tender
[ˈtendər]

a 부드러운, 다정한 **n** 보살핌, 입찰

= **soft, gentle, delicate, affectionate, offer, bid**
+ **tenderness** n 부드러움 **tenderly** adv 부드럽게

Q: Is the meat tender enough to eat?
고기가 먹기에 충분히 부드러운가요?

A: ....

1665 □□□

tense
[tens]

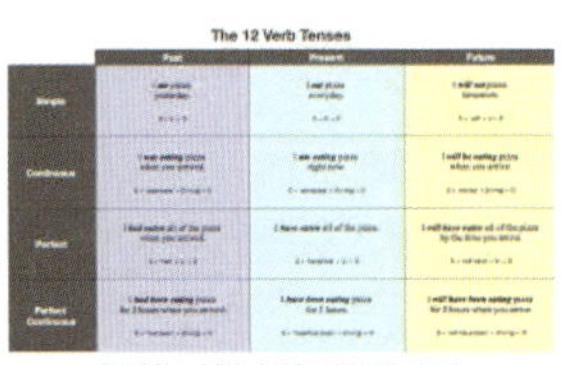

a 긴장한, 팽팽한 **n** 시제

= **tight, strained, nervous, anxious, rigid, period**
+ **tension** n 긴장 **tensely** adv 긴장하여

Q: Why do you feel so tense before presentations?
발표 전에 왜 그렇게 긴장하나요?

A: ....

1666 □□□

tension
[ˈtenʃn]

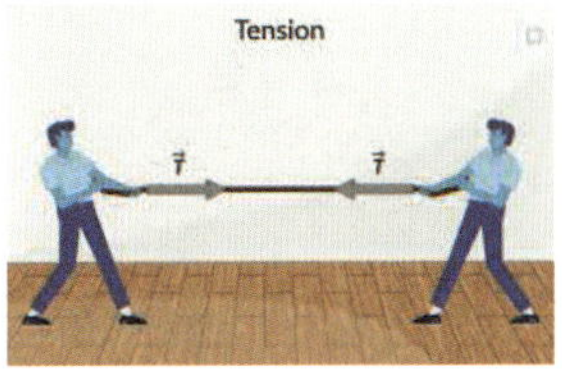

n 긴장, 갈등

= strain, stress, pressure, anxiety, friction

\+ tense a 긴장한

Q: Can you sense any tension in the meeting room?
회의실에 어떤 긴장감이라도 감지할 수 있나요?

A: ....

1667 □□□

term
[tɜːrm]

n 용어, 기간, 조건 v 칭하다

= word, expression, period, condition, quarter, duration

\+ terms n 조건, 용어

Q: How long is the term for this lease agreement?
이 임대 계약의 기간은 얼마나 되나요?

A: ....

1668 □□□

terrible
[ˈterəbl]

a 끔찍한, 지독한

= dreadful, awful, horrible, unpleasant, severe

\+ terribleness n 끔찍함 terribly adv 몹시, 끔찍하게

Q: Did you have a terrible day at work today?
오늘 직장에서 끔찍한 하루를 보냈나요?

A: ....

1669 □□□

terribly
[ˈterəbli]

adv 몹시, 지독하게

= awfully, dreadfully, extremely, severely, very

\+ terrible a 끔찍한

Q: Are you feeling terribly tired after the long trip?
긴 여행 후에 몹시 피곤한가요?

A: ....

1670 □□□

terrific
[təˈrɪfɪk]

a 멋진, 훌륭한

= wonderful, excellent, great, splendid, huge

\+ terrifically adv 굉장히

Q: Did you have a terrific time at the concert last night?
어젯밤 콘서트에서 정말 멋진 시간을 보냈나요?

A: ....

1671 □□□

territory
[ˈterətɔːri]

n 영토, 영역

= area, region, land, domain, realm

+ territorial **a** 영토의

Q: Is this territory safe for tourists to visit?
이 지역이 관광객들이 방문하기에 안전한가요?

A: ....

1672 □□□

theme
[θiːm]

n 주제, 테마

= subject, topic, motif, dominant idea, concept

+ thematic **a** 주제와 관련된

Q: What is the main theme of the movie you watched?
당신이 본 영화의 주요 주제는 무엇인가요?

A: ....

1673 □□□

theory
[ˈθiːəri]

n 이론

= hypothesis, principle, concept, speculation, assumption

+ theorist **n** 이론가 **theorize** **v** 이론화하다 **theoretical** **a** 이론적인

Q: Do you agree with this scientific theory?
이 과학 이론에 동의하나요?

A: ....

1674 □□□

therapy
[ˈθerəpi]

n 치료, 요법

= treatment, cure, rehabilitation, healing, counseling

+ therapist **n** 치료사 **therapeutic** **a** 치료적인

Q: Have you tried any therapy to relieve stress?
스트레스 해소를 위해 어떤 치료법을 시도해 본 적 있나요?

A: ....

1675 □□□

therefore
[ˈðerfɔːr]

adv 그러므로, 따라서

= thus, hence, consequently, accordingly, so

+ therefor **adv** 그것에 대해, 그것을 위해, 그에 대한 대가로
and therefore 그 때문에, 그래서

Q: We've missed the deadline; therefore, will we face any penalties?
마감 기한을 놓쳤습니다. 따라서 어떤 불이익을 받게 될까요?

A: ....

1676 □□□

thirst
[θɜːrst]

n 갈증, 갈망

= craving, desire, dryness, parchedness, longing
+ thirsty a 목마른

Q: Do you feel thirstier after exercising outdoors?
야외에서 운동한 후에 더 목마른가요?

A: ....

1677 □□□

thoughtful
[ˈθɔːtfl]

a 사려 깊은, 생각에 잠긴

= considerate, reflective, pensive, deep, caring
+ thought n 생각 thoughtfulness n 사려 깊음 thoughtfully adv 사려 깊게

Q: Was your gift thoughtful enough to please her?
당신의 선물이 그녀를 기쁘게 할 만큼 사려 깊었나요?

A: ....

1678 □□□

thread
[θred]

n 실, 줄거리 v 실을 꿰다

= fiber, yarn, strand, connection, theme, string
+ thread vein 실핏줄

Q: Do you know what kind of thread I should use to sew this delicate silk fabric? 이 섬세한 실크 천을 바느질하려면 어떤 종류의 실을 사용해야 하는지 아세요?

A: ....

1679 □□□

threat
[θret]

n 위협

= menace, danger, peril, warning, intimidation
+ threaten v 위협하다 threatening a 위협적인

Q: Is there any threat to the local wildlife in this area?
이 지역 야생동물에게 어떤 위협이 있나요?

A: ....

1680 □□□

threaten
[ˈθretn]

v 위협하다

= menace, intimidate, imperil, endanger, warn
+ threat n 위협

Q: Do these dark clouds threaten to bring a severe thunderstorm later today? 이 먹구름이 오늘 오후에 심한 뇌우를 몰고 올 것 같나요?

A: ....

DAY 24 | DICTATION TEST

5회 반복 예문 QR

DICTATION TEST 예문 QR을 듣고 다음 빈칸에 올바른 단어를 쓰세요.

1661. Is this job only ______________ or permanent?

1662. Do you ______________ to wake up early or late?

1663. Do you have a ______________ to procrastinate before deadlines?

1664. Is the meat ______________ enough to eat?

1665. Why do you feel so ______________ before presentations?

1666. Can you sense any ______________ in the meeting room?

1667. How long is the ______________ for this lease agreement?

1668. Did you have a ______________ day at work today?

1669. Are you feeling ______________ tired after the long trip?

1670. Did you have a ______________ time at the concert last night?

1671. Is this ______________ safe for tourists to visit?

1672. What is the main ______________ of the movie you watched?

1673. Do you agree with this scientific ______________?

1674. Have you tried any ______________ to relieve stress?

1675. We've missed the deadline; ______________, will we face any penalties?

1676. Do you feel ______________ after exercising outdoors?

1677. Was your gift ______________ enough to please her?

1678. Do you know what kind of ______________ I should use to sew this delicate silk fabric?

1679. Is there any ______________ to the local wildlife in this area?

1680. Do these dark clouds ______________ to bring a severe thunderstorm later today?

5회 반복 표제어 QR　　5회 반복 예문 QR

DAY 25

30 days

AI 학습자료와 인강 youpass.co.kr

PREVIEW A 다음 단어의 뜻을 한국어로 써보세요.

□ thrilling ____________	□ tough ____________
□ throat ____________	□ trace ____________
□ tide ____________	□ tragedy ____________
□ tidy ____________	□ tragic ____________
□ tight ____________	□ trail ____________
□ tissue ____________	□ trait ____________
□ tolerate ____________	□ transfer ____________
□ tomb ____________	□ transform ____________
□ tone ____________	□ translate ____________
□ totally ____________	□ transmit ____________

PREVIEW B 사진을 보고 알맞은 영어 단어를 **PREVIEW A**에서 찾아 써보세요.

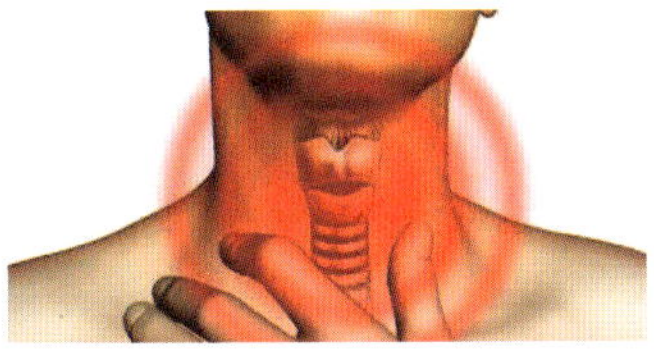

____

____

____

____

1681 □□□

thrilling
['θrɪlɪŋ]

a 스릴 넘치는, 신나는

= exciting, exhilarating, gripping, suspenseful
+ thrill **n** 스릴

Q: Was the roller coaster ride thrilling enough for you?
롤러코스터 타는 것이 당신에게 충분히 스릴 있었나요?

A:

1682 □□□

throat
[θroʊt]

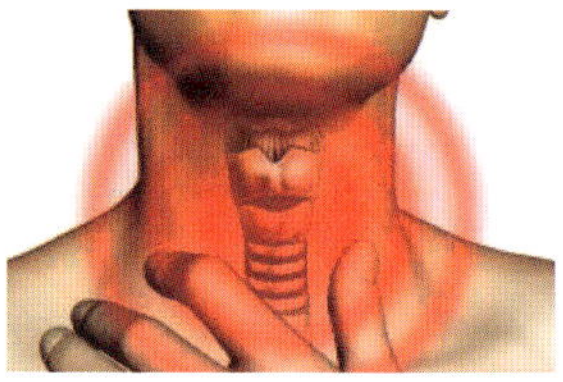

n 목구멍

= gullet, pharynx, gorge, voice box
+ a throat spray 목 아픈 데 뿌리는 스프레이

Q: Do you have a sore throat or just feel a bit dry?
목이 아픈가요, 아니면 그냥 좀 건조한가요?

A:

1683 □□□

tide
[taɪd]

n 조수, 흐름

= current, flow, trend, surge, ebb and flow
+ high tide 만조 **low tide** 간조

Q: Can you predict the tide levels for tomorrow's beach trip?
내일 해변 여행을 위한 조수 간만의 차를 예측할 수 있나요?

A:

1684 □□□

tidy
['taɪdi]

a 깔끔한, 단정한 **v** 정리하다

= neat, orderly, clean, organize, arrange, straighten
+ tidiness **n** 깔끔함 **tidily** **adv** 깔끔하게

Q: Did you tidy your desk before leaving the office?
사무실을 떠나기 전에 책상을 정리했나요?

A:

1685 □□□

tight
[taɪt]

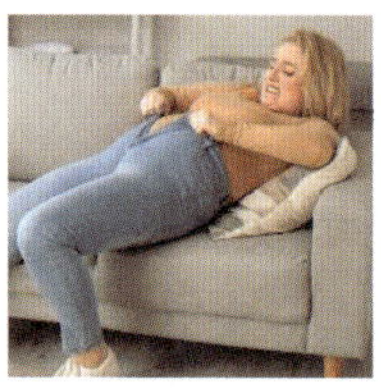

a 꽉 죄는, 단단한 **adv** 단단히

= snug, firm, close, rigid, difficult, strict
+ tightness **n** 꽉 조임 **tighten** **v** 꽉 조이다 **tightly** **adv** 꽉

Q: Is the lid on the jar tight enough to prevent leaks?
병뚜껑이 새지 않도록 충분히 단단히 닫혔나요?

A:

1686 □□□

tissue
[ˈtɪʃuː]

n 조직, 화장지, 티슈

= fabric, paper, cell (biology), bodily substance
+ soft tissue (몸에서 뼈나 연골이 아닌) 연조직

Q: Could you pass me a tissue for my runny nose?
콧물 때문에 휴지 좀 건네줄 수 있나요?

A: ....

1687 □□□

tolerate
[ˈtɑːləreɪt]

v 참다, 용인하다

= endure, bear, accept, permit, put up with
+ tolerance **n** 관용, 내성 tolerant **a** 관대한

Q: Can you really tolerate his constant complaining?
그의 끊임없는 불평을 정말로 참을 수 있나요?

A: ....

1688 □□□

tomb
[tuːm]

n 무덤

= grave, crypt, burial place, mausoleum
+ entomb **v** (완전히) 파묻다[뒤덮다] womb to tomb 태어나서 죽을 때까지 일생의

Q: Have you ever visited an ancient tomb on a historical tour?
역사 여행 중에 고대 무덤을 방문한 적 있나요?

A: ....

1689 □□□

tone
[toʊn]

n 어조, 음색, 색조

= pitch, timbre, mood, attitude, accent, nuance
+ tonal **a** 음조의

Q: Did you notice the change in his tone during the meeting?
회의 중에 그의 어조 변화를 알아차렸나요?

A: ....

1690 □□□

totally
[ˈtoʊtəli]

adv 완전히, 전적으로

= completely, entirely, wholly, utterly, absolutely
+ total **a** 전체의

Q: Do you totally agree with the new company policy?
새로운 회사 정책에 전적으로 동의하나요?

A: ....

1691 □□□

tough
[tʌf]

a 질긴, 힘든, 강인한

= strong, durable, difficult, resilient, robust, harsh

+ toughness n 강인함 toughly adv 강인하게

Q: Was the exam tougher than you expected?
시험이 예상보다 더 어려웠나요?

A: ....

1692 □□□

trace
[treɪs]

n 흔적, 소량 v 추적하다, 따라가다

= outline, remnant, vestige, track, follow, detect

+ traceable a 추적 가능한

Q: Can you trace the origin of this old family recipe?
이 오래된 가족 레시피의 기원을 추적할 수 있나요?

A: ....

1693 □□□

tragedy
[ˈtrædʒədi]

n 비극

= disaster, catastrophe, calamity, misfortune, drama

+ tragic a 비극적인 tragically adv 비극적으로

Q: How did the community respond to the recent tragedy?
지역 사회는 최근 비극에 어떻게 대응했나요?

A: ....

1694 □□□

tragic
[ˈtrædʒɪk]

a 비극적인

= disastrous, catastrophic, sad, unfortunate, mournful

+ tragedy n 비극 tragically adv 비극적으로

Q: Was the accident as tragic as the news reported?
그 사고가 뉴스에서 보도된 만큼 비극적이었나요?

A: ....

1695 □□□

trail
[treɪl]

n 오솔길, 흔적 v 뒤쫓다, 끌고 가다

= path, track, scent, follow, pursue, drag

+ trail bike 트레일 바이크(험한 길 위로 달릴 수 있는 경량 오토바이)

Q: Have you ever hiked the trail that leads to the waterfall?
폭포로 이어지는 길을 하이킹해 본 적 있나요?

A: ....

1696 □□□

trait
[treɪt]

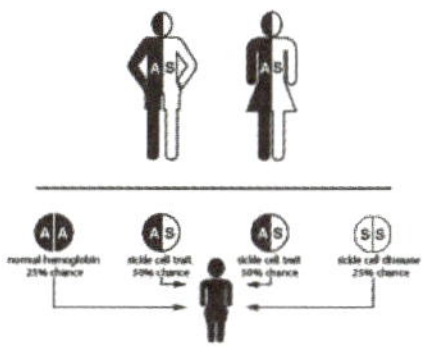

n 특성, 특징

= characteristic, feature, attribute, quality, peculiarity

+ a predominant trait 눈에 띄는 특징 **an inheritable trait** 유전하는 특성

Q: What trait do you value most in a good friend?
좋은 친구에게서 가장 중요하게 여기는 특성은 무엇인가요?

A: ....

1697 □□□

transfer
[ˈtrænsfɜːr] **n** [trænsˈfɜːr] **v**

v 이동하다, 전송하다 **n** 이동, 전송

= move, relocate, transmit, assign, convey, shift

+ electronic data transfer 전자 데이터 이동[전송]

Q: Are you planning to transfer to another department?
다른 부서로 전근 갈 계획인가요?

A: ....

1698 □□□

transform
[trænsˈfɔːrm]

v 변형시키다, 변화시키다

= convert, change, alter, modify, reshape

+ transformation n 변형, 변화

Q: How can we transform our ideas into real projects?
우리의 아이디어를 실제 프로젝트로 어떻게 바꿀 수 있을까요?

A: ....

1699 □□□

translate
[trænsˈleɪt]

v 번역하다

= interpret, render, convert, decipher, express

+ translation n 번역 **translator n** 번역가 **translatable a** 번역 가능한

Q: Can you translate this document into English by tomorrow?
내일까지 이 문서를 영어로 번역해 줄 수 있나요?

A: ....

1700 □□□

transmit
[trænzˈmɪt]

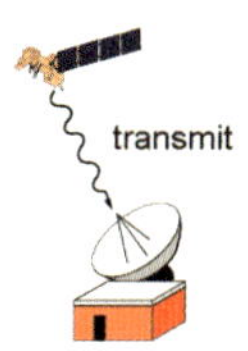

v 전송하다, 전달하다, 전염되다

= send, convey, communicate, broadcast, transfer

+ transmission n 전송, 전달

Q: Can some diseases transmit through casual contact, like shaking hands? 일부 질병은 악수와 같은 가벼운 접촉을 통해 전염될 수 있나요?

A: ....

DAY 25 | DICTATION TEST

5회 반복 예문 QR

DICTATION TEST 예문 QR을 듣고 다음 빈칸에 올바른 단어를 쓰세요.

1681. Was the roller coaster ride ______________ enough for you?

1682. Do you have a sore ______________ or just feel a bit dry?

1683. Can you predict the ______________ levels for tomorrow's beach trip?

1684. Did you ______________ your desk before leaving the office?

1685. Is the lid on the jar ______________ enough to prevent leaks?

1686. Could you pass me a ______________ for my runny nose?

1687. Can you really ______________ his constant complaining?

1688. Have you ever visited an ancient ______________ on a historical tour?

1689. Did you notice the change in his ______________ during the meeting?

1690. Do you ______________ agree with the new company policy?

1691. Was the exam ______________ than you expected?

1692. Can you ______________ the origin of this old family recipe?

1693. How did the community respond to the recent ______________?

1694. Was the accident as ______________ as the news reported?

1695. Have you ever hiked the ______________ that leads to the waterfall?

1696. What ______________ do you value most in a good friend?

1697. Are you planning to ______________ to another department?

1698. How can we ______________ our ideas into real projects?

1699. Can you ______________ this document into English by tomorrow?

1700. Can some diseases ______________ through casual contact, like shaking hands?

5회 반복 표제어 QR　5회 반복 예문 QR

DAY 26

30 days

AI 학습자료와 인강 youpass.co.kr

PREVIEW A 다음 단어의 뜻을 한국어로 써보세요.

□ **transport**	________	□ **trigger**	________
□ **transportation**	________	□ **troop**	________
□ **trap**	________	□ **tropical**	________
□ **treasure**	________	□ **truly**	________
□ **treat**	________	□ **trust**	________
□ **treatment**	________	□ **tune**	________
□ **trend**	________	□ **twist**	________
□ **trial**	________	□ **typhoon**	________
□ **tribe**	________	□ **typical**	________
□ **trick**	________	□ **ultimate**	________

PREVIEW B 사진을 보고 알맞은 영어 단어를 **PREVIEW A**에서 찾아 써보세요.

____

____

____

____

1701 □□□

transport
['trænspɔːrt] n
[træns'pɔːrt] v

v 운송하다, 수송하다 n 운송, 수송

= convey, carry, move, transfer, transportation, vehicle
+ transportation n 운송
Q: What's the best way to transport fragile items safely?
깨지기 쉬운 물건을 안전하게 운송하는 가장 좋은 방법은 무엇인가요?
A:

1702 □□□

transportation
[ˌtrænspər'teɪʃn]

n 운송, 교통수단

= transit, conveyance, transport, movement
+ transport v 운송하다
Q: Does the company provide transportation for its employees?
회사가 직원들에게 교통편을 제공하나요?
A:

1703 □□□

trap
[træp]

n 덫, 함정 v 덫으로 잡다, 가두다

= snare, net, ambush, trick, catch, ensnare
+ booby trap 부비트랩(건드리면 터지는 위장 폭탄)
Q: How do you set a trap to catch these animals?
그 동물들을 잡기 위해 덫을 어떻게 놓나요?
A:

1704 □□□

treasure
['treʒər]

n 보물 v 소중히 여기다

= valuable, gem, hoard, cherish, prize
+ treasure hunt 보물찾기
Q: Have you ever found a hidden treasure?
숨겨진 보물을 발견해 본 적이 있나요?
A:

1705 □□□

treat
[triːt]

v 다루다, 치료하다, 대접하다 n 특별한 즐거움

= handle, deal with, cure, process, entertain, delicacy
+ treatment n 치료, 대우
Q: How should I treat a minor burn at home?
집에서 경미한 화상을 어떻게 치료해야 하나요?
A:

1706 □□□

treatment
[ˈtriːtmənt]

n 치료, 대우

= therapy, care, handling, approach, procedure
+ treat **v** 다루다, 치료하다

Q: Is this treatment effective for common cold symptoms?
이 치료법이 일반적인 감기 증상에 효과적인가요?

A: ....

1707 □□□

trend
[trend]

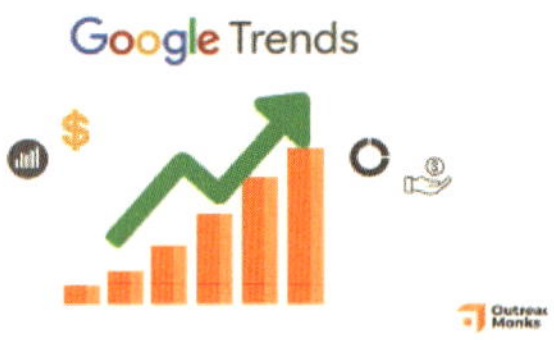

n 경향, 유행

= tendency, direction, fashion, inclination, movement
+ trendy **a** 유행하는

Q: What's the latest trend in mobile app development?
모바일 앱 개발의 최신 트렌드는 무엇인가요?

A: ....

1708 □□□

trial
[ˈtraɪəl]

n 재판, 시도, 시련

= test, experiment, hearing, ordeal, attempt
+ trial and error 시행착오

Q: When will the trial period for the new software end?
새 소프트웨어의 시험 사용 기간은 언제 끝나나요?

A: ....

1709 □□□

tribe
[traɪb]

n 부족, 종족

= clan, ethnic group, family, kin
+ tribal **a** 부족의

Q: Have you learned about the customs of any indigenous tribes?
어떤 원주민 부족의 관습에 대해 배워본 적 있나요?

A: ....

1710 □□□

trick
[trɪk]

n 속임수, 묘기 **v** 속이다

= deception, hoax, prank, ploy, deceive, fool
+ hat-trick **n** 해트 트릭(특정한 한 경기에서 한 명의 선수가 3점[골 등]을 올리는 것)
trick or treat 과자를 안 주면 장난칠 거예요(핼러윈(Halloween) 때 아이들이 집집마다 다니며 하는 말)

Q: What's a useful trick to remember long vocabulary lists?
긴 어휘 목록을 기억하는 데 유용한 요령은 무엇인가요?

A: ....

1711 □□□

trigger
[ˈtrɪgər]

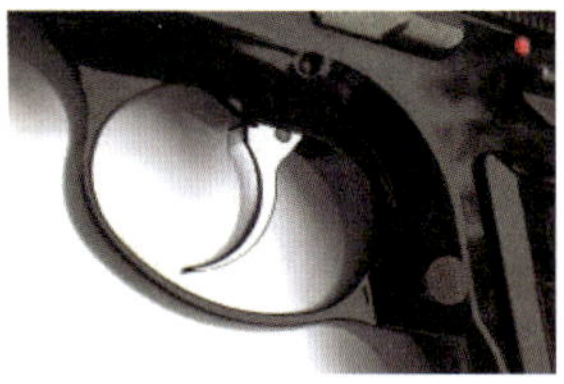

n 방아쇠, 계기 **v** 유발하다, 작동시키다

= **initiate, activate, cause, prompt, mechanism, stimulus**

+ **trigger an alarm** 경보기를 작동시키다

Q: What might trigger allergic reactions in some people?
어떤 것이 일부 사람들에게 알레르기 반응을 유발할 수 있나요?

A: ....

1712 □□□

troop
[tru:p]

n 무리, 부대

= **squad, unit, group, company, gather, march**

+ **troop carrier** 수송기[선/차], 보병용 장갑차 **troop train** 군용 열차

Q: How many troops were deployed during the Gulf War?
걸프전 중 얼마나 많은 병력이 배치되었나요?

A: ....

1713 □□□

tropical
[ˈtrɑ:pɪkl]

a 열대의

= **hot, humid, equatorial, lush, exotic**

+ **tropics** **n** 열대 지방

Q: Have you ever visited a tropical island for vacation?
휴가로 열대 섬을 방문한 적 있나요?

A: ....

1714 □□□

truly
[ˈtru:li]

adv 진정으로, 정말로

= **genuinely, really, indeed, sincerely, authentically**

+ **true** **a** 진실된 **truth** **n** 진실

Q: Do you truly believe that hard work guarantees success?
열심히 일하는 것이 성공을 보장한다고 진정으로 믿나요?

A: ....

1715 □□□

trust
[trʌst]

n 신뢰 **v** 신뢰하다

= **faith, confidence, reliance, believe, depend on**

+ **trustworthy** **a** 신뢰할 수 있는

Q: Can you trust this source of information completely?
이 정보 출처를 완전히 신뢰할 수 있나요?

A: ....

1716 □□□

tune
[tu:n] [tʃu:n]

n 곡조, 음조 **v** 조율하다

= melody, harmony, adjust, align, conform
+ fine-tune **v** 미세 조정을 하다

Q: Can you tune the guitar before the concert starts?
콘서트 시작 전에 기타를 조율해 줄 수 있나요?

A:

1717 □□□

twist
[twɪst]

v 비틀다, 왜곡하다 **n** 비틀기, 반전

= turn, intertwine, distort, curve, bend, spin
+ twist somebody's arm (어떤 일을 하도록) ~를 설득[강요]하다

Q: How did the story take such a surprising twist?
이야기가 어떻게 그렇게 놀라운 반전을 맞이했나요?

A:

1718 □□□

typhoon
[taɪˈfu:n]

n 태풍

= hurricane, cyclone, storm, tempest
+ a destructive typhoon 파괴적인 태풍

Q: When is the typhoon expected to hit the coastal area?
태풍이 해안 지역에 언제 상륙할 것으로 예상되나요?

A:

1719 □□□

typical
[ˈtɪpɪkl]

a 전형적인, 대표적인

= characteristic, representative, standard, average, classic
+ type **v** 유형 typically **adv** 전형적으로

Q: Is this typical weather for this region in spring?
이것이 이 지역의 봄철 전형적인 날씨인가요?

A:

1720 □□□

ultimate
[ˈʌltɪmət]

a 궁극적인, 최종적인

= final, supreme, utmost, fundamental
+ ultimately **adv** 궁극적으로

Q: What is the ultimate goal of your new project?
새 프로젝트의 궁극적인 목표는 무엇인가요?

A:

DAY 26 | DICTATION TEST

5회 반복 예문 QR

DICTATION TEST 예문 QR을 듣고 다음 빈칸에 올바른 단어를 쓰세요.

1701. What's the best way to ______________ fragile items safely?

1702. Does the company provide ______________ for its employees?

1703. How do you set a ______________ to catch these animals?

1704. Have you ever found a hidden ______________?

1705. How should I ______________ a minor burn at home?

1706. Is this ______________ effective for common cold symptoms?

1707. What's the latest ______________ in mobile app development?

1708. When will the ______________ period for the new software end?

1709. Have you learned about the customs of any indigenous ______________?

1710. What's a useful ______________ to remember long vocabulary lists?

1711. What might ______________ allergic reactions in some people?

1712. How many ______________ were deployed during the Gulf War?

1713. Have you ever visited a ______________ island for vacation?

1714. Do you ______________ believe that hard work guarantees success?

1715. Can you ______________ this source of information completely?

1716. Can you ______________ the guitar before the concert starts?

1717. How did the story take such a surprising ______________?

1718. When is the ______________ expected to hit the coastal area?

1719. Is this ______________ weather for this region in spring?

1720. What is the ______________ goal of your new project?

5회 반복 표제어 QR　5회 반복 예문 QR

DAY 27

30 days

AI 학습자료와 인강 youpass.co.kr

PREVIEW A 다음 단어의 뜻을 한국어로 써보세요.

- ☐ unbelievable ____________
- ☐ undergo ____________
- ☐ underground ____________
- ☐ underwater ____________
- ☐ uneasy ____________
- ☐ unexpected ____________
- ☐ unfortunately ____________
- ☐ unhealthy ____________
- ☐ unify ____________
- ☐ union ____________
- ☐ unique ____________
- ☐ unit ____________
- ☐ unite ____________
- ☐ universal ____________
- ☐ universe ____________
- ☐ university ____________
- ☐ unreasonable ____________
- ☐ unusual ____________
- ☐ upset ____________
- ☐ upward ____________

PREVIEW B 사진을 보고 알맞은 영어 단어를 **PREVIEW A** 에서 찾아 써보세요.

____

____

____

____

1721 □□□

unbelievable
[ˌʌnbɪˈliːvəbl]

a 믿을 수 없는

= **incredible, astonishing, astounding, implausible**
+ **unbelievability** **n** 믿을 수 없음 **unbelievably** **adv** 믿을 수 없을 정도로

Q: Did you hear that unbelievable news about the company?
회사에 대한 그 믿을 수 없는 소식을 들었나요?

A: ....

1722 □□□

undergo
[ˌʌndərˈgoʊ]

v 겪다, 경험하다

= **experience, suffer, go through, endure, submit to**
+ **undergoing** **n** 겪는 중

Q: How long will the patient undergo treatment in the hospital?
환자는 병원에서 얼마나 오래 치료를 받을 건가요?

A: ....

1723 □□□

underground
[ˌʌndərˈgraʊnd] **a**
[ˈʌndərgraʊnd] **n**

a 지하의 **n** 지하철

= **subterranean, hidden, secret, subversive, subway**
+ **an underground garage** 지하 차고[주차장] **the London Underground** 런던 지하철

Q: Are there any underground tunnels in this old city?
이 오래된 도시에 지하 터널이 있나요?

A: ....

1724 □□□

underwater
[ˌʌndərˈwɔːtər]

a 수중의 **adv** 수중에서

= **submerged, aquatic, below surface**
+ **underwater creatures** 수중 생물

Q: Have you ever seen underwater creatures while diving?
다이빙하면서 수중 생물을 본 적 있나요?

A: ....

1725 □□□

uneasy
[ʌnˈiːzi]

a 불안한, 불편한

= **anxious, uncomfortable, restless, apprehensive, troubled**
+ **uneasiness** **n** 불안함 **uneasily** **adv** 불안하게

Q: Why do you feel uneasy about the upcoming presentation?
다가오는 발표에 대해 왜 불안감을 느끼나요?

A: ....

1726 □□□

unexpected
[ˌʌnɪkˈspektɪd]

a 예상치 못한

= **unforeseen, sudden, surprising, abrupt, unanticipated**
\+ **unexpectedly** **adv** 뜻밖에

Q: Did the team face any unexpected challenges during the event?
팀이 행사 중에 예상치 못한 어려움에 직면했었나요?

A: ....

1727 □□□

unfortunately
[ʌnˈfɔːrtʃənətli]

adv 불행히도

= **regrettably, sadly, unluckily, alas**
\+ **unfortunate** **a** 불운한

Q: Unfortunately, will we have to cancel the outdoor picnic if it rains tomorrow? 안타깝게도, 내일 비가 오면 야외 소풍을 취소해야 할까요?

A: ....

1728 □□□

unhealthy
[ʌnˈhelθi]

a 건강에 해로운, 건강하지 못한

= **sick, ill, detrimental, noxious, unsound**
\+ **health** **n** 건강

Q: Do you think eating fast food regularly is unhealthy?
패스트푸드를 정기적으로 먹는 것이 건강에 해롭다고 생각하나요?

A: ....

1729 □□□

unify
[ˈjuːnɪfaɪ]

v 통합하다, 통일하다

= **unite, consolidate, integrate, merge, combine**
\+ **unification** **n** 통합 **unified** **a** 통합된

Q: How can we unify the different departments for better cooperation?
더 나은 협력을 위해 다른 부서들을 어떻게 통합할 수 있을까요?

A: ....

1730 □□□

union
[ˈjuːnjən]

n 연합, 조합, 노조

= **alliance, association, merger, coalition, marriage**
\+ **trade union** 노동조합(**labor union**) **Union Jack** 유니언잭(영국 국기)

Q: Is the labor union planning to negotiate new contracts?
노동조합은 새 계약을 협상할 계획인가요?

A: ....

1731 □□□

unique
[juˈniːk]

a 독특한, 유일한

= **distinct, unparalleled, singular, sole, one-of-a-kind**

+ **uniqueness** **n** 독특함 **uniquely** **adv** 독특하게

Q: What makes this artwork unique compared to others in the gallery?
이 작품을 갤러리의 다른 작품들과 비교했을 때 무엇이 독특하게 만드나요?

A: ....

1732 □□□

unit
[ˈjuːnɪt]

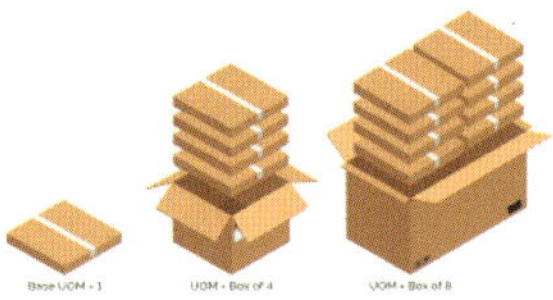

n 단위, 부대

= **component, module, section, individual, standard**

+ **army[military/police] units** 육군[군사/경찰] 부대

Q: How many units of the product did the company sell last month?
회사가 지난달에 제품 몇 단위를 팔았나요?

A: ....

1733 □□□

unite
[juˈnaɪt]

v 연합하다, 통합하다

= **join, combine, merge, link, unify**

+ **unity** **n** 통일, 단결 **united** **a** 연합된

Q: Can sports events unite people from diverse backgrounds effectively? 스포츠 행사가 다양한 배경을 가진 사람들을 효과적으로 단결시킬 수 있나요?

A: ....

1734 □□□

universal
[ˌjuːnɪˈvɜːrsl]

a 보편적인, 전 세계적인

= **global, comprehensive, widespread, general, pervasive**

+ **universe** **n** 우주 **universality** **n** 보편성 **universally** **adv** 보편적으로

Q: Is there a universal language that most people understand?
대부분의 사람들이 이해하는 보편적인 언어가 있나요?

A: ....

1735 □□□

universe
[ˈjuːnɪvɜːrs]

n 우주

= **cosmos, galaxy, creation, existence, world**

+ **universal** **a** 보편적인

Q: Do you ever wonder how big the universe really is?
우주가 정말 얼마나 큰지 궁금해 본 적 있나요?

A: ....

1736 □□□

university
[ˌjuːnɪˈvɜːrsəti]

n 대학교

= college, academy, institution of higher learning

+ state university (미국) 주립 대학

Q: Which university are you planning to apply to next year?
내년에 어느 대학교에 지원할 계획인가요?

A:

1737 □□□

unreasonable
[ʌnˈriːznəbl]

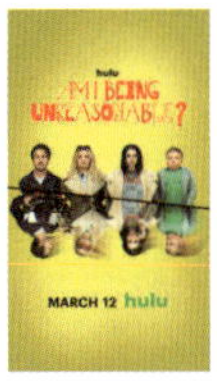

a 비합리적인, 터무니없는

= illogical, unfair, excessive, irrational, absurd

+ reason **n** 이유 **unreasonably** **adv** 부당하게

Q: Don't you think his request was a bit unreasonable?
그의 요청이 좀 불합리했다고 생각하지 않나요?

A:

1738 □□□

unusual
[ʌnˈjuːʒuəl]

a 특이한, 평범하지 않은

= uncommon, rare, strange, extraordinary, atypical

+ unusualness **n** 특이함 **unusually** **adv** 이례적으로

Q: Is it unusual for the weather to be this warm in January?
1월에 날씨가 이렇게 따뜻한 것은 이례적인 일인가요?

A:

1739 □□□

upset
[ʌpˈset]

a 속상한, 화난 **v** 속상하게 하다, 뒤엎다

= disturbed, distressed, angry, overthrow, overturn, bother

+ an upset stomach 배탈

Q: Why did she get so upset over a small mistake?
왜 그녀는 작은 실수 하나에 그렇게 화를 냈나요?

A:

1740 □□□

upward
[ˈʌpwərd]

adv 위쪽으로 **a** 위쪽을 향한

= rising, ascending, increasing, elevated, upwards

+ upwards **adv** 위쪽으로

Q: Has the company shown any upward trend in sales this quarter?
이번 분기에 회사의 매출이 상승세를 보였나요?

A:

DAY 27 | DICTATION TEST

5회 반복 예문 QR

DICTATION TEST 예문 QR을 듣고 다음 빈칸에 올바른 단어를 쓰세요.

1721. Did you hear that ______________ news about the company?

1722. How long will the patient ______________ treatment in the hospital?

1723. Are there any ______________ tunnels in this old city?

1724. Have you ever seen ______________ creatures while diving?

1725. Why do you feel ______________ about the upcoming presentation?

1726. Did the team face any ______________ challenges during the event?

1727. ______________, will we have to cancel the outdoor picnic if it rains tomorrow?

1728. Do you think eating fast food regularly is ______________?

1729. How can we ______________ the different departments for better cooperation?

1730. Is the labor ______________ planning to negotiate new contracts?

1731. What makes this artwork ______________ compared to others in the gallery?

1732. How many ______________ of the product did the company sell last month?

1733. Can sports events ______________ people from diverse backgrounds effectively?

1734. Is there a ______________ language that most people understand?

1735. Do you ever wonder how big the ______________ really is?

1736. Which ______________ are you planning to apply to next year?

1737. Don't you think his request was a bit ______________?

1738. Is it ______________ for the weather to be this warm in January?

1739. Why did she get so ______________ over a small mistake?

1740. Has the company shown any ______________ trend in sales this quarter?

5회 반복 표제어 QR　5회 반복 예문 QR

DAY 28

30 days

AI 학습자료와 인강 youpass.co.kr

PREVIEW A 다음 단어의 뜻을 한국어로 써보세요.

□ urban	______	□ variety	______
□ urge	______	□ various	______
□ urgent	______	□ vary	______
□ utilize	______	□ vast	______
□ vacation	______	□ vehicle	______
□ valid	______	□ version	______
□ valley	______	□ vertical	______
□ valuable	______	□ vet	______
□ value	______	□ via	______
□ variable	______	□ victim	______

PREVIEW B 사진을 보고 알맞은 영어 단어를 **PREVIEW A** 에서 찾아 써보세요.

______　______　______　______

1741 □□□

urban
['ɜːrbən]

a 도시의

= city, metropolitan, municipal, town
+ urbanization n 도시화 urbanize v 도시화하다

Q: Are you planning to move to an urban area after graduation?
졸업 후에 도시 지역으로 이사할 계획인가요?

A: ……………………

1742 □□□

urge
[ɜːrdʒ]

n 충동, 강한 욕구 v 촉구하다, 재촉하다

= impulse, desire, compulsion, push, encourage, exhort
+ urgent a 긴급한

Q: What made you feel the urge to speak up at the meeting?
회의에서 발언해야겠다는 충동을 느끼게 한 것은 무엇인가요?

A: ……………………

1743 □□□

urgent
['ɜːrdʒənt]

a 긴급한, 다급한

= pressing, critical, immediate, vital, compelling
+ urgency n 긴급성 urgently adv 긴급하게

Q: Is there an urgent matter we need to deal with right now?
지금 당장 처리해야 할 긴급한 사안이 있나요?

A: ……………………

1744 □□□

utilize
['juːtəlaɪz]

v 활용하다, 이용하다

= use, employ, apply, harness, make use of
+ utilization n 활용 usable a 사용 가능한

Q: How can we better utilize our time and resources?
시간과 자원을 어떻게 더 잘 활용할 수 있을까요?

A: ……………………

1745 □□□

vacation
[veɪ'keɪʃn] [və'keɪʃn]

n 방학, 휴가

= holiday, break, recess, trip, leave
+ a two-week vacation 2주일 동안의 휴가[방학]

Q: Where would you like to go for your next vacation?
다음 휴가 때 어디로 가고 싶나요?

A: ……………………

1746 □□□

valid
[ˈvælɪd]

a 유효한, 타당한

= legitimate, sound, legal, authentic, justifiable
+ validity **n** 유효성 validate **v** 유효성을 확인하다 validly **adv** 유효하게

Q: Is your driver's license still valid for international travel?
당신의 운전면허증이 국제 여행에도 여전히 유효한가요?

A: ....

1747 □□□

valley
[ˈvæli]

n 계곡, 골짜기

= dale, glen, hollow, basin, depression
+ Silicon Valley 실리콘 밸리(컴퓨터 및 전자 산업체가 많이 모여 있는, 미국 캘리포니아 주 샌프란시스코 남동부 지역)

Q: Have you ever hiked through a deep mountain valley?
깊은 산골짜기를 하이킹해 본 적 있나요?

A: ....

1748 □□□

valuable
[ˈvæljuəbl]

a 가치 있는, 귀중한

= precious, costly, estimable, cherished, important
+ value **n** 가치 valuation **n** 가치 평가 valuably **adv** 가치 있게

Q: Which experience taught you the most valuable skill?
어떤 경험이 당신에게 가장 귀중한 기술을 가르쳐 주었나요?

A: ....

1749 □□□

value
[ˈvælju:]

n 가치, 중요성 **v** 소중히 여기다, 평가하다

= worth, merit, price, importance, appreciate, cherish
+ valuable **a** 가치 있는 valueless **a** 가치 없는

Q: How do you value teamwork in achieving success?
성공을 달성하는 데 팀워크를 어떻게 평가하나요?

A: ....

1750 □□□

variable
[ˈveriəbl]

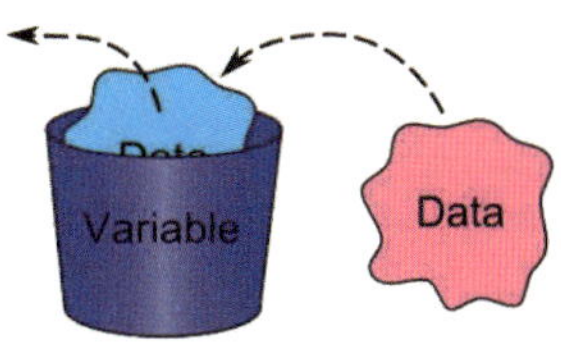

n 변수 **a** 변하기 쉬운

= changeable, fluctuating, inconsistent, factor, element
+ variation **n** 변화 vary **v** 다르다

Q: What variable affects your decision the most?
어떤 변수가 당신의 결정에 가장 큰 영향을 미치나요?

A: ....

1751 □□□

variety
[vəˈraɪəti]

n 다양성, 여러 종류

= diversity, assortment, range, mixture, selection
+ various a 다양한

Q: Do you enjoy trying a variety of cuisines when dining out?
외식할 때 다양한 요리를 시도하는 것을 즐기나요?

A: ....

1752 □□□

various
[ˈveriəs]

a 다양한

= diverse, different, assorted, numerous, sundry
+ variety n 다양성 **variously adv** 다양하게

Q: Have you considered the various factors before choosing a new home? 새 집을 선택하기 전에 다양한 요소들을 고려해 봤나요?

A: ....

1753 □□□

vary
[ˈveri]

v 다양하다, 달라지다

= differ, change, fluctuate, diverge, diversify
+ variation n 변화 **variety n** 다양성 **various a** 다양한

Q: How do the prices vary depending on the size or quality?
가격이 크기나 품질에 따라 어떻게 달라지나요?

A: ....

1754 □□□

vast
[væst]

a 광대한, 거대한

= enormous, huge, immense, extensive, wide
+ vastness n 광대함 **vastly adv** 막대하게

Q: Isn't the desert a vast and empty place to travel through?
사막은 여행하기에 광대하고 텅 빈 곳 아닌가요?

A: ....

1755 □□□

vehicle
[ˈviːɪkl]

n 차량, 운송 수단

= conveyance, transport, car, medium, means
+ sport utility vehicle 스포츠 유틸리티 카**(SUV)**

Q: What kind of vehicle do you usually use for commuting?
통근할 때 보통 어떤 종류의 차량을 이용하나요?

A: ....

1756 □□□

version
[ˈvɜːrʒn]

n 버전, 판, 형태

= edition, rendition, interpretation, variant, form

\+ **beta version** (특히 컴퓨터 소프트웨어의) 베타 판[버전]

Q: Have you updated to the latest version of the software?
소프트웨어 최신 버전으로 업데이트했나요?

A: ....

1757 □□□

vertical
[ˈvɜːrtɪkl]

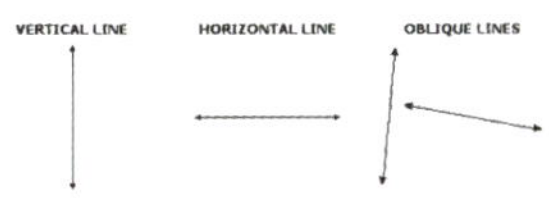

a 수직의

= upright, perpendicular, erect, plum

\+ **vertically** **adv** 수직으로

Q: Can this image be adjusted to a vertical layout?
이 이미지를 세로 레이아웃으로 조절할 수 있나요?

A: ....

1758 □□□

vet
[vet]

n 수의사 **v** 심사하다

= examine, check, screen, approve, animal doctor, veterinarian

\+ **veterinarian** **n** 수의사 **veterinary surgeon** **n** 수의사

Q: Do you take your dog to the vet for its annual check-up?
강아지를 연례 검진을 위해 수의사에게 데려가나요?

A: ....

1759 □□□

via
[ˈvaɪə] [ˈviːə]

prep ~을 통하여, ~경유로

= through, by way of, by means of, using

\+ **via Dubai** 두바이를 경유하여, 두바이를 통해

Q: Are we sending the documents via email or regular mail?
문서를 이메일로 보내나요, 아니면 일반 우편으로 보내나요?

A: ....

1760 □□□

victim
[ˈvɪktɪm]

n 희생자, 피해자

= casualty, sufferer, prey, target, injured party

\+ **victimization** **n** 희생, 희생자 만들기 **victimize** **v** 희생시키다

Q: Who was the victim in the recent case mentioned on the news?
뉴스에 언급된 최근 사건의 피해자는 누구였나요?

A: ....

DAY 28 | DICTATION TEST

5회 반복 예문 QR

DICTATION TEST 예문 QR을 듣고 다음 빈칸에 올바른 단어를 쓰세요.

1741. Are you planning to move to an ______________ area after graduation?

1742. What made you feel the ______________ to speak up at the meeting?

1743. Is there an ______________ matter we need to deal with right now?

1744. How can we better ______________ our time and resources?

1745. Where would you like to go for your next ______________?

1746. Is your driver's license still ______________ for international travel?

1747. Have you ever hiked through a deep mountain ______________?

1748. Which experience taught you the most ______________ skill?

1749. How do you ______________ teamwork in achieving success?

1750. What ______________ affects your decision the most?

1751. Do you enjoy trying a ______________ of cuisines when dining out?

1752. Have you considered the ______________ factors before choosing a new home?

1753. How do the prices ______________ depending on the size or quality?

1754. Isn't the desert a ______________ and empty place to travel through?

1755. What kind of ______________ do you usually use for commuting?

1756. Have you updated to the latest ______________ of the software?

1757. Can this image be adjusted to a ______________ layout?

1758. Do you take your dog to the ______________ for its annual check-up?

1759. Are we sending the documents ______________ email or regular mail?

1760. Who was the ______________ in the recent case mentioned on the news?

5회 반복 표제어 QR　5회 반복 예문 QR

DAY 29

30 days

PREVIEW A 다음 단어의 뜻을 한국어로 써보세요.

- ☐ victory ______
- ☐ violate ______
- ☐ violence ______
- ☐ violent ______
- ☐ virtual ______
- ☐ virtue ______
- ☐ visible ______
- ☐ vision ______
- ☐ visitor ______
- ☐ visual ______
- ☐ vital ______
- ☐ vivid ______
- ☐ vocation ______
- ☐ voluntary ______
- ☐ volunteer ______
- ☐ wage ______
- ☐ wander ______
- ☐ warn ______
- ☐ waterproof ______
- ☐ wavy ______

PREVIEW B 사진을 보고 알맞은 영어 단어를 **PREVIEW A**에서 찾아 써보세요.

______

______

______

______

1761 □□□

victory
[ˈvɪktəri]

n 승리

= **triumph, win, conquest, success, achievement**
+ **victorious** **a** 승리한 **victoriously** **adv** 승리하여

Q: How did the team celebrate their surprising victory?
팀은 놀라운 승리를 어떻게 축하했나요?

A: ……………………

1762 □□□

violate
[ˈvaɪəleɪt]

v 위반하다, 침해하다

= **break, infringe, transgress, breach, desecrate**
+ **violation** **n** 위반 **violence** **n** 폭력 **violent** **a** 폭력적인

Q: What happens if someone violates the company's policies?
누군가 회사 정책을 위반하면 어떻게 되나요?

A: ……………………

1763 □□□

violence
[ˈvaɪələns]

n 폭력

= **aggression, brutality, force, savagery, harm**
+ **violent** **a** 폭력적인

Q: Why has there been a rise in violence in that region lately?
최근 그 지역에서 폭력이 왜 증가했나요?

A: ……………………

1764 □□□

violent
[ˈvaɪələnt]

a 폭력적인, 맹렬한

= **aggressive, brutal, fierce, intense, strong**
+ **violence** **n** 폭력 **violently** **adv** 폭력적으로

Q: Was the movie too violent for young children to watch?
영화가 어린아이들이 보기에는 너무 폭력적이었나요?

A: ……………………

1765 □□□

virtual
[ˈvɜːrtʃuəl]

a 가상의, 사실상의

= **almost, simulated, actual, inherent, digital**
+ **virtuality** **n** 가상성 **virtually** **adv** 사실상, 거의

Q: Are most of your classes still held in a virtual format?
대부분의 수업이 여전히 가상 형식으로 진행되나요?

A: ……………………

1766 □□□

virtue
[ˈvɜːrtʃuː]

n 미덕, 장점

= goodness, morality, integrity, advantage, asset
+ virtuous **a** 덕이 있는 virtuously **adv** 덕성스럽게

Q: Which virtue do you believe is most important in a leader?
리더에게 가장 중요하다고 생각하는 덕목은 무엇인가요?

A: ....

1767 □□□

visible
[ˈvɪzəbl]

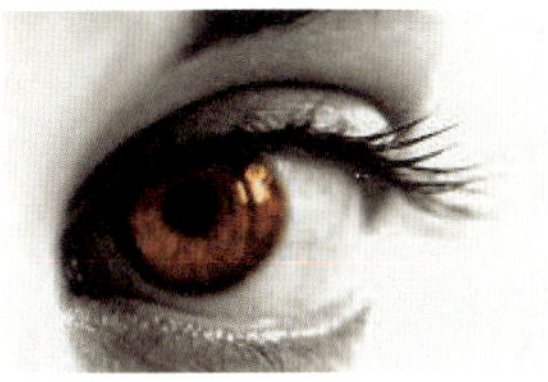

a 보이는, 눈에 띄는

= observable, apparent, detectable, perceptible, clear
+ visibility **n** 가시성 visibly **adv** 눈에 띄게

Q: Is the mountain clearly visible from this viewpoint?
이 지점에 산이 명확하게 보이나요?

A: ....

1768 □□□

vision
[ˈvɪʒn]

n 시력, 시야, 비전

= sight, eyesight, imagination, foresight, dream, concept
+ visual **a** 시각적인 visionary **a** 선견지명이 있는

Q: What's your long-term vision for your career path?
당신의 경력 경로에 대한 장기적인 비전은 무엇인가요?

A: ....

1769 □□□

visitor
[ˈvɪzɪtər]

n 방문객

= guest, caller, tourist, company, frequenter
+ visit **v** 방문하다

Q: How many visitors does the museum receive each year?
박물관은 매년 몇 명의 방문객을 받나요?

A: ....

1770 □□□

visual
[ˈvɪʒuəl]

a 시각적인

= optic, visible, graphic, pictorial, imagery
+ vision **n** 시력, 시각 visualize **v** 시각화하다 visually **adv** 시각적으로

Q: Do you prefer visual aids when learning something new?
새로운 것을 배울 때 시각 자료를 선호하나요?

A: ....

1771 □□□

vital
[ˈvaɪtl]

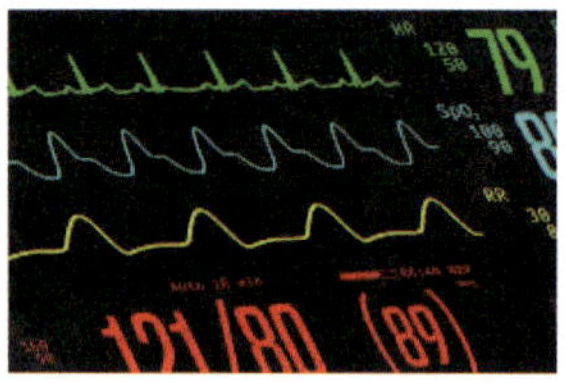

a 필수적인, 활기찬

= essential, crucial, indispensable, energetic, living
+ vitality **n** 활력 **vitally** **adv** 필수적으로

Q: Why is sleep so vital for maintaining good health?
건강을 유지하는 데 왜 수면이 그렇게 중요한가요?

A: ______________________________

1772 □□□

vivid
[ˈvɪvɪd]

a 생생한, 선명한

= clear, graphic, bright, lively, striking, expressive
+ vividness **n** 생생함 **vividly** **adv** 생생하게

Q: Do you still have a vivid memory of your childhood?
여전히 어린 시절에 대한 생생한 기억이 있나요?

A: ______________________________

1773 □□□

vocation
[voʊˈkeɪʃn]

n 천직, 소명

= calling, profession, career, trade, occupation
+ vocational **a** 직업의

Q: How did you discover your true vocation in life?
인생에서 진정한 천직을 어떻게 발견했나요?

A: ______________________________

1774 □□□

voluntary
[ˈvɑːlənteri]

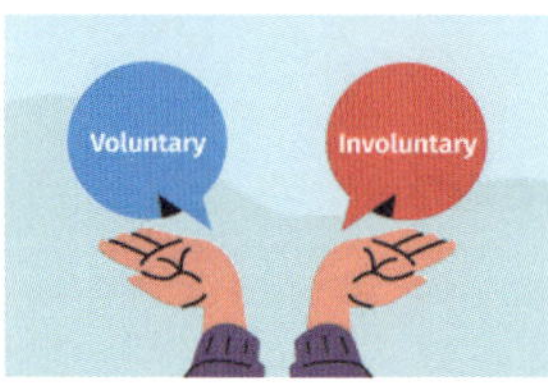

a 자발적인

= optional, spontaneous, chosen, unforced, willing
+ volunteer **n** 자원봉사자 **voluntarily** **adv** 자발적으로

Q: Is participation in this event completely voluntary?
이 행사의 참여는 전적으로 자발적인가요?

A: ______________________________

1775 □□□

volunteer
[ˌvɑːlənˈtɪr]

n 자원봉사자 **v** 자원하다

= undertake, provide, unpaid helper, freely offer
+ voluntary **a** 자발적인

Q: Have you ever worked as a volunteer abroad?
해외에서 자원봉사자로 일해본 적 있나요?

A: ______________________________

1776 □□□

wage
[weɪdʒ]

n 임금, 급료 **v** (전쟁 등을) 벌이다

= **salary, pay, earnings, conduct, carry on**

+ **a wage raise** 임금 인상

Q: Are the workers satisfied with the current minimum wage?
노동자들은 현재 최저 임금에 만족하고 있나요?

A:

1777 □□□

wander
[ˈwɑːndər]

v 방랑하다, 헤매다

= **roam, stroll, stray, meander, drift**

+ **wanderer** **n** 방랑자

Q: Why did the child wander off alone in the park?
아이는 왜 공원에서 혼자 돌아다녔나요?

A:

1778 □□□

warn
[wɔːrn]

v 경고하다

= **caution, alert, advise, notify, threaten**

+ **warning** **n** 경고

Q: Did the weather forecast warn us about the severe hailstorm expected later today? 일기 예보가 오늘 늦게 예상되는 심한 우박 폭풍에 대해 경고했나요?

A:

1779 □□□

waterproof
[ˈwɔːtərpruːf]

a 방수의

= **impervious, resistant, watertight, impermeable**

+ **waterproofing** **n** 방수 처리

Q: Is your phone case really waterproof as advertised?
당신의 휴대폰 케이스는 광고처럼 정말 방수인가요?

A:

1780 □□□

wavy
[ˈweɪvi]

a 물결 모양의, 흔들리는

= **undulating, rippled, curly, curvy**

+ **wave** **n** 파도

Q: Do you naturally have wavy hair or is it styled that way?
당신은 원래 곱슬머리인가요 아니면 그렇게 스타일링한 건가요?

A:

DAY 29 | DICTATION TEST

5회 반복 예문 QR

DICTATION TEST 예문 QR을 듣고 다음 빈칸에 올바른 단어를 쓰세요.

1761. How did the team celebrate their surprising ______________?

1762. What happens if someone ______________ the company's policies?

1763. Why has there been a rise in ______________ in that region lately?

1764. Was the movie too ______________ for young children to watch?

1765. Are most of your classes still held in a ______________ format?

1766. Which ______________ do you believe is most important in a leader?

1767. Is the mountain clearly ______________ from this viewpoint?

1768. What's your long-term ______________ for your career path?

1769. How many ______________ does the museum receive each year?

1770. Do you prefer ______________ aids when learning something new?

1771. Why is sleep so ______________ for maintaining good health?

1772. Do you still have a ______________ memory of your childhood?

1773. How did you discover your true ______________ in life?

1774. Is participation in this event completely ______________?

1775. Have you ever worked as a ______________ abroad?

1776. Are the workers satisfied with the current minimum ______________?

1777. Why did the child ______________ off alone in the park?

1778. Did the weather forecast ______________ us about the severe hailstorm expected later today?

1779. Is your phone case really ______________ as advertised?

1780. Do you naturally have ______________ hair or is it styled that way?

5회 반복 표제어 QR　5회 반복 예문 QR

DAY 30

30 days

AI 학습자료와 인강 youpass.co.kr

PREVIEW A 다음 단어의 뜻을 한국어로 써보세요.

□ wealth ______	□ wisdom ______
□ weapon ______	□ wisely ______
□ weed ______	□ withstand ______
□ weep ______	□ witness ______
□ weigh ______	□ wonder ______
□ whisper ______	□ worship ______
□ whistle ______	□ worth ______
□ whole ______	□ wound ______
□ widespread ______	□ wrap ______
□ wipe ______	□ yield ______

PREVIEW B 사진을 보고 알맞은 영어 단어를 **PREVIEW A**에서 찾아 써보세요.

______ ______ ______ ______

1781 □□□

wealth
[welθ]

n 부, 재산

= riches, prosperity, affluence, abundance, assets
+ wealthy **a** 부유한

Q: Should wealth be distributed more fairly in society?
사회에서 부가 더 공정하게 분배되어야 할까요?

A: ....

1782 □□□

weapon
[ˈwepən]

n 무기

= arms, armament, tool, instrument, means
+ chemical weapon 화학 무기 **biological weapon** 생물 무기

Q: Do you think artificial intelligence could ever be considered a powerful weapon in future warfare?
인공지능이 미래 전쟁에서 강력한 무기로 간주될 수 있다고 생각하시나요?

A: ....

1783 □□□

weed
[wiːd]

n 잡초 **v** 잡초를 뽑다

= unwanted plant, remove, clear, undesirable person
+ weed something[somebody] out (불필요하거나 부족한 대상 등을) 제거하다[뽑아 버리다]

Q: How often do you weed your garden during spring?
봄에 정원 잡초를 얼마나 자주 뽑나요?

A: ....

1784 □□□

weep
[wiːp]

v 울다

= cry, sob, shed tears, lament
+ weeping **n** 울음

Q: Why did she suddenly weep during the movie?
그녀는 왜 영화 중에 갑자기 울었나요?

A: ....

1785 □□□

weigh
[weɪ]

v 무게를 달다, 중요하게 여기다

= measure, gauge, consider, ponder, burden
+ weight **n** 무게 **weighty** **a** 무거운

Q: How much does your suitcase weigh?
당신의 여행 가방 무게는 얼마나 되나요?

A: ....

1786 □□□

whisper
[ˈwɪspər]

n 속삭임 **v** 속삭이다

= **murmur, rustle, hint, intimate, soft voice**

+ **whisper something to a girl** 소녀에게 무언가를 귀띔하다

Q: Did you hear him whisper something to her right before they left the room? 그들이 방을 나서기 직전에 그가 그녀에게 무언가를 속삭이는 것을 들었나요?

A: ....

1787 □□□

whistle
[ˈwɪsl]

n 휘파람, 호루라기 **v** 휘파람을 불다

= **blow, pipe, hiss, signal, tune**

+ **whistle-blower** **n** (기업 비리 등의) 내부 고발자

Q: Can you whistle a tune, or have you never learned?
곡조를 휘파람으로 불 수 있나요, 아니면 배워본 적이 없나요?

A: ....

1788 □□□

whole
[hoʊl]

a 전체의, 온전한 **n** 전체

= **entire, complete, total, intact, undivided**

+ **wholeness** **n** 전체성 **wholly** **adv** 전적으로

Q: Did you eat the whole cake by yourself?
케이크를 혼자 다 먹었나요?

A: ....

1789 □□□

widespread
[ˈwaɪdspred]

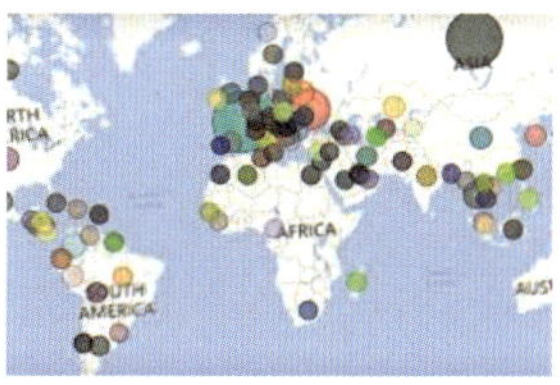

a 광범위한

= **prevalent, extensive, common, pervasive, rampant**

+ **widespread wings** 한껏 펼친 날개

Q: Is this problem widespread across the entire country?
이 문제가 전국적으로 널리 퍼져 있나요?

A: ....

1790 □□□

wipe
[waɪp]

v 닦다, 지우다

= **clean, rub, erase, remove, obliterate**

+ **wipe a dish[table]** 접시를[식탁을] 닦다

Q: Could you wipe the table after lunch, please?
점심 식사 후에 테이블 좀 닦아줄 수 있나요?

A: ....

1791 □□□

wisdom
[ˈwɪzdəm]

n 지혜

= insight, knowledge, sagacity, prudence, discernment

+ wise **a** 현명한

Q: What piece of wisdom has guided you the most in life?
삶에서 어떤 지혜가 당신을 가장 많이 이끌었나요?

A: ....

1792 □□□

wisely
[ˈwaɪzli]

adv 현명하게

= intelligently, prudently, shrewdly, sensibly

+ wise **a** 현명한

Q: Do you think the company spent its profits wisely on employee benefits? 회사가 이윤을 직원 복지에 현명하게 사용했다고 생각하시나요?

A: ....

1793 □□□

withstand
[wɪθˈstænd]

v 견디다, 저항하다

= resist, endure, bear, tolerate, stand up to

+ withstanding **n** 저항

Q: Can this bridge withstand strong winds and earthquakes?
이 다리가 강풍과 지진을 견딜 수 있나요?

A: ....

1794 □□□

witness
[ˈwɪtnəs]

n 증인, 목격자 **v** 목격하다

= observer, spectator, testify, perceive, see, evidence

+ witness box (법정의) 증인석

Q: Did anyone witness the accident near the intersection?
교차로 근처 사고를 목격한 사람이 있나요?

A: ....

1795 □□□

wonder
[ˈwʌndər]

n 경이, 놀라움 **v** 궁금해 하다

= marvel, awe, miracle, curiosity, ponder, question

+ wonderful **a** 놀라운 **wonderfully** **adv** 놀랍게도

Q: Do you ever wonder what life would be like on another planet?
다른 행성에서의 삶은 어떨지 궁금해 한 적 있나요?

A: ....

1796 □□□

worship
[ˈwɜːrʃɪp]

n 숭배, 예배 **v** 숭배하다

= **adore, revere, honor, venerate, devotion, adoration**
+ **worshiper** **n** 예배자

Q: Where do most locals go to worship on weekends?
대부분의 현지인들은 주말 마다 어디로 예배하러 가나요?

A: ....

1797 □□□

worth
[wɜːrθ]

n 가치, 값어치 **a** ~할 가치가 있는

= **value, merit, significance, cost, deserving of**
+ **worthwhile** **a** 가치 있는 **worthless** **a** 가치 없는

Q: Is it worth upgrading to the newest smartphone model?
최신 스마트폰 모델로 업그레이드할 가치가 있나요?

A: ....

1798 □□□

wound
[wuːnd] **n** [waʊnd] **v**

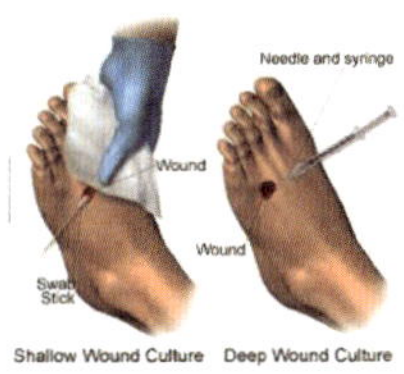

n 상처, 부상 **v** 상처를 입히다

= **injury, cut, lesion, harm, injure, hurt**
+ **wounded** **a** 상처 입은

Q: How serious was the wound after the accident?
사고 후 상처는 얼마나 심각했나요?

A: ....

1799 □□□

wrap
[ræp]

v 싸다, 감싸다 **n** 포장지

= **cover, enfold, enshroud, package, cloak**
+ **wrapping** **n** 자동차 래핑

Q: Can you help me wrap these fragile items for shipping?
이 깨지기 쉬운 물건들을 배송을 위해 포장하는 것을 도와줄 수 있나요?

A: ....

1800 □□□

yield
[jiːld]

v 산출하다, 양보하다, 굴복하다 **n** 수확량, 이익

= **produce, generate, surrender, give way, harvest, output**
+ **a high crop yield** 높은 작물 수확량

Q: Will the new solar panels yield enough electricity to power our entire house? 새로운 태양광 패널이 우리 집 전체에 전력을 공급하기에 충분한 전기를 생산할까요?

A: ....

DAY 01 DAY 02 DAY 03 DAY 04 DAY 05 DAY 06 DAY 07 DAY 08 DAY 09 DAY 10 DAY 11 DAY 12 DAY 13 DAY 14 DAY 15 DAY 16 DAY 17 DAY 18 DAY 19 DAY 20 DAY 21 DAY 22 DAY 23 DAY 24 DAY 25 DAY 26 DAY 27 DAY 28 DAY 29 DAY 30

DAY 30 | DICTATION TEST

5회 반복 예문 QR

DICTATION TEST 예문 QR을 듣고 다음 빈칸에 올바른 단어를 쓰세요.

1781. Should ________________ be distributed more fairly in society?
1782. Do you think artificial intelligence could ever be considered a powerful ________________ in future warfare?
1783. How often do you ________________ your garden during spring?
1784. Why did she suddenly ________________ during the movie?
1785. How much does your suitcase ________________?
1786. Did you hear him ________________ something to her right before they left the room?
1787. Can you ________________ a tune, or have you never learned?
1788. Did you eat the ________________ cake by yourself?
1789. Is this problem ________________ across the entire country?
1790. Could you ________________ the table after lunch, please?
1791. What piece of ________________ has guided you the most in life?
1792. Do you think the company spent its profits ________________ on employee benefits?
1793. Can this bridge ________________ strong winds and earthquakes?
1794. Did anyone ________________ the accident near the intersection?
1795. Do you ever ________________ what life would be like on another planet?
1796. Where do most locals go to ________________ on weekends?
1797. Is it ________________ upgrading to the newest smartphone model?
1798. How serious was the ________________ after the accident?
1799. Can you help me ________________ these fragile items for shipping?
1800. Will the new solar panels ________________ enough electricity to power our entire house?

대기중 영단어 1800 리스트

1. abandon
2. ability
3. aboard
4. abroad
5. absence
6. absolute
7. absorb
8. abstract
9. academic
10. accent
11. accept
12. access
13. accident
14. accompany
15. accomplish
16. account
17. accurate
18. accuse
19. achieve
20. acid
21. acquire
22. activate
23. active
24. adapt
25. addicted
26. addition
27. address
28. adequate
29. adjust
30. admire
31. admission
32. admit
33. adolescent
34. adopt
35. advance
36. advantage
37. advertise
38. advise
39. advocate
40. affect
41. afford
42. afterward
43. agent
44. aggressive
45. agriculture
46. aid
47. aim
48. aircraft
49. alike
50. aloud
51. alter
52. alternative
53. although
54. altitude
55. amaze
56. ambiguous
57. amount
58. amuse
59. amusement
60. analyze
61. ancestor
62. ancient
63. angle
64. anniversary
65. announce
66. announcer
67. annoy
68. annual
69. anonymous
70. anticipate
71. antique
72. anxiety
73. anxious
74. anytime
75. anyway
76. apart
77. apologize
78. apology
79. apparent
80. appeal
81. appear
82. appearance
83. applaud
84. apply
85. appoint
86. appreciate
87. approach
88. appropriate
89. approve
90. approximately
91. aptitude
92. architecture
93. argue
94. argument
95. arise
96. army
97. arouse
98. arrange
99. arrangement
100. arrest
101. arrogant
102. article
103. artificial
104. ashamed
105. asleep
106. aspect
107. aspire
108. assemble
109. assess
110. asset
111. assign
112. assist
113. associate
114. association
115. assume
116. astronaut
117. astronomer
118. athlete
119. atmosphere
120. atom
121. attach
122. attain
123. attempt
124. attend
125. attention
126. attitude
127. attract
128. attraction
129. attractive
130. attribute
131. audience
132. author
133. authority
134. automatic
135. automobile
136. available
137. avenue
138. average
139. avoid
140. await
141. awake
142. award
143. aware
144. awesome
145. awful
146. awkward
147. background
148. bacteria
149. badly
150. balance
151. bald
152. ban
153. bandage
154. banner
155. bar
156. barely
157. barrier
158. basis
159. bear
160. beat
161. beg
162. behave
163. behavior
164. belief
165. belong
166. bend
167. benefit
168. beside
169. besides
170. bet
171. bias
172. bill
173. billion
174. bind
175. biology
176. birth
177. bit
178. bitter
179. blame
180. blend
181. bless
182. block
183. bold
184. bond
185. boost
186. booth
187. border
188. bother
189. bow
190. brain
191. branch
192. breathe
193. breed
194. brief
195. brilliant
196. broad
197. broadcast
198. budget
199. bullet
200. bunch
201. burden
202. burst
203. bury
204. bush
205. business
206. cable
207. cage
208. calculate
209. campaign
210. canal
211. cancer
212. candidate
213. candle
214. capable
215. capital
216. capture
217. carbon
218. cardboard
219. career
220. carnival
221. carve
222. cast
223. castle
224. casual
225. caution
226. cautious
227. cease
228. ceiling
229. celebrate
230. cell
231. ceremony
232. certain
233. certainly
234. certificate
235. chain
236. challenge
237. champion
238. character
239. characteristic
240. charge
241. charity
242. charm
243. chart
244. chase
245. cheat
246. chef
247. chemical
248. chemistry
249. cherish
250. chest
251. chief
252. childhood
253. chop
254. chore
255. chronic
256. circuit
257. circulate
258. circumstance
259. circus
260. cite
261. citizen
262. civil
263. claim
264. clarify
265. classic
266. classical
267. classify
268. clerk
269. clever
270. cliff
271. climate
272. climbing
273. closet
274. clue
275. coal
276. coast
277. coincide
278. collaborate
279. collapse
280. colleague
281. collection
282. collective
283. college
284. combat
285. combine
286. comfort
287. comfortable
288. command
289. comment
290. commerce
291. commercial
292. commit
293. committee
294. common
295. commonly
296. communicate
297. communication
298. community
299. commute
300. companion
301. company

302. compare
303. comparison
304. compass
305. compete
306. competition
307. competitive
308. complain
309. complaint
310. complement
311. complete
312. completely
313. complex
314. complicate
315. complicated
316. compliment
317. compose
318. compromise
319. conceal
320. concentrate
321. concept
322. concern
323. concerned
324. conclude
325. conclusion
326. concrete
327. condition
328. conduct
329. conference
330. confess
331. confidence
332. confident
333. confine
334. confirm
335. conflict
336. conform
337. confront
338. confuse
339. congratulation
340. conquer
341. conscience
342. conscious
343. consent
344. consequence
345. conserve
346. consider
347. considerable
348. considerate
349. consist
350. consistent
351. constant
352. constantly
353. construct
354. construction
355. consult
356. consume
357. contact
358. contain
359. container
360. contemporary
361. content
362. context
363. continent
364. continue
365. continuous
366. contract
367. contrary
368. contrast
369. contribute
370. convenient
371. convention
372. conversation
373. convert
374. convey
375. convince
376. cooperate
377. cooperative
378. coordinate
379. corporation
380. correctly
381. costly
382. cotton
383. council
384. counsel
385. counselor
386. crack
387. craft
388. crash
389. crawl
390. crazy
391. creation
392. creature
393. credit
394. crime
395. criminal
396. crisis
397. critical
398. criticize
399. crop
400. crowd
401. crowded
402. crucial
403. cruel
404. crush
405. cultivate
406. cultural
407. cure
408. curiosity
409. curious
410. current
411. curve
412. custom
413. customer
414. cyber
415. cycle
416. damage
417. damp
418. dare
419. data
420. daytime
421. deadly
422. deal
423. dealer
424. debate
425. debt
426. decade
427. decay
428. deceive
429. decision
430. declare
431. decline
432. decorate
433. decoration
434. decrease
435. dedicate
436. dedication
437. defeat
438. defend
439. defense
440. define
441. definite
442. degree
443. delay
444. delicate
445. delight
446. deliver
447. delivery
448. demand
449. democracy
450. demonstrate
451. dense
452. deny
453. department
454. depend
455. depress
456. depressed
457. depth
458. derive
459. descend
460. describe
461. description
462. desert
463. deserve
464. desire
465. despair
466. desperate
467. despite
468. destination
469. destiny
470. destroy
471. destruction
472. detail
473. detect
474. detective
475. determine
476. develop
477. device
478. devise
479. devote
480. dew
481. diagnose
482. diet
483. dietary
484. differ
485. difference
486. difficulty
487. dig
488. digest
489. digestion
490. diligent
491. diminish
492. direction
493. disabled
494. disadvantage
495. disagree
496. disappear
497. disappoint
498. disappointed
499. disaster
500. discipline
501. discount
502. discourage
503. discrimination
504. discuss
505. discussion
506. disease
507. disgust
508. dislike
509. dismiss
510. display
511. dispose
512. distance
513. distant
514. distinct
515. distinguish
516. distract
517. distress
518. distribute
519. district
520. disturb
521. dive
522. diverse
523. divide
524. document
525. domain
526. domestic
527. dominant
528. donate
529. doubt
530. downtown
531. drag
532. dramatic
533. draw
534. drip
535. drown
536. due
537. durable
538. dust
539. duty
540. dynamic
541. dynasty
542. eager
543. earn
544. earthquake
545. ease
546. economic
547. economy
548. ecosystem
549. edit
550. editor
551. educate
552. education
553. effect
554. effective
555. efficient
556. effort
557. elaborate
558. elect
559. electric
560. electricity
561. electronic
562. element
563. eliminate
564. embarrass
565. embrace
566. emerge
567. emergence
568. emergency
569. emission
570. emotion
571. empathy
572. emphasize
573. empire
574. employ
575. enable
576. encounter
577. encourage
578. encouragement
579. endure
580. enforce
581. engage
582. engineer
583. enhance
584. enjoyable
585. enormous
586. enrich
587. enroll
588. ensure
589. entertain
590. enthusiasm
591. entire
592. entirely
593. entrance
594. envelope
595. environment
596. environmental
597. equal
598. equipment
599. equivalent
600. erase
601. escalate
602. escape
603. especially
604. essence
605. essential
606. establish

607. estimate
608. ethic
609. ethical
610. ethnic
611. evaluate
612. evaporate
613. eventually
614. evidence
615. evident
616. evil
617. evolve
618. exactly
619. exaggerate
620. examine
621. exceed
622. except
623. excess
624. exchange
625. excitement
626. exclude
627. exhaust
628. exhausted
629. exhibit
630. exhibition
631. exist
632. existence
633. exotic
634. expand
635. expect
636. expend
637. expense
638. experience
639. experiment
640. expert
641. explain
642. explode
643. explore
644. export
645. expose
646. express
647. expression
648. extend
649. extent
650. external
651. extinct
652. extra
653. extraordinary
654. extreme
655. fabric
656. facility
657. factor
658. fade
659. failure
660. faint
661. fair
662. faith
663. fake
664. fame
665. familiar
666. fancy
667. fantasy
668. fare
669. fascinate
670. fashionable
671. fasten
672. fate
673. fatigue
674. faucet
675. fault
676. favor
677. favorite
678. fear
679. feast
680. feather
681. feature
682. fee
683. feed
684. fellow
685. fiction
686. field
687. figure
688. filter
689. finance
690. financial
691. fine
692. firm
693. fit
694. flame
695. flash
696. flat
697. flavor
698. flesh
699. flexible
700. flight
701. float
702. flood
703. flourish
704. flow
705. fluid
706. fold
707. folk
708. following
709. forbid
710. force
711. forecast
712. foreign
713. foresee
714. forever
715. forget
716. forgive
717. formal
718. format
719. former
720. formula
721. fortunate
722. fortunately
723. fortune
724. found
725. fountain
726. fragile
727. frame
728. frankly
729. freedom
730. freezing
731. frequent
732. friendship
733. fright
734. frighten
735. frustrate
736. fuel
737. fulfill
738. function
739. fund
740. fundamental
741. furniture
742. further
743. furthermore
744. gap
745. garage
746. gender
747. general
748. generally
749. generate
750. generation
751. generous
752. genetic
753. genius
754. genuine
755. geography
756. gesture
757. glance
758. glory
759. glow
760. govern
761. government
762. grab
763. grade
764. gradual
765. gradually
766. graduate
767. graduation
768. grain
769. grammar
770. grant
771. grateful
772. grave
773. gravity
774. grip
775. grocery
776. growth
777. guarantee
778. guard
779. guest
780. guilty
781. habitat
782. haircut
783. handle
784. happen
785. hardly
786. harm
787. harvest
788. haste
789. hatch
790. heal
791. heaven
792. height
793. heritage
794. hesitate
795. hiccup
796. highlight
797. highly
798. hire
799. historic
800. historical
801. hollow
802. holy
803. honor
804. horizon
805. horizontal
806. horror
807. hospitality
808. host
809. hostility
810. household
811. humanity
812. humble
813. humiliate
814. hunger
815. hurricane
816. hybrid
817. hypothesis
818. ideal
819. identical
820. identify
821. identity
822. idiom
823. idle
824. ignore
825. illegal
826. illustrate
827. imaginary
828. imagination
829. imaginative
830. imagine
831. imitate
832. immediate
833. immediately
834. immigrate
835. immune
836. impact
837. impatient
838. imply
839. import
840. importance
841. impossible
842. impress
843. impressed
844. impression
845. impressive
846. improve
847. incident
848. incline
849. include
850. income
851. increase
852. incredible
853. indeed
854. independence
855. independent
856. index
857. indicate
858. indifferent
859. individual
860. indoor
861. industry
862. inevitable
863. infant
864. infect
865. infection
866. inferior
867. influence
868. inform
869. informal
870. information
871. ingredient
872. inhabit
873. inherent
874. inherit
875. initial
876. initiate
877. injure
878. injured
879. injury
880. injustice
881. inner
882. innocent
883. innovation
884. input
885. inquire
886. inquiry
887. insert
888. insight
889. insist
890. inspect
891. inspire
892. install
893. instance
894. instant
895. instead
896. instinct
897. institute
898. institution
899. instruct
900. instrument
901. insult
902. insurance
903. intake
904. intellectual
905. intelligence
906. intelligent
907. intend
908. intense
909. interaction
910. interest
911. interfere

912. interior
913. internal
914. international
915. interpret
916. interpreter
917. interrupt
918. interval
919. intonation
920. introduce
921. invade
922. invent
923. invest
924. investigate
925. invitation
926. involve
927. iron
928. irritate
929. isolate
930. issue
931. jail
932. jealous
933. joint
934. journey
935. judge
936. justice
937. justify
938. kindness
939. knit
940. knowledge
941. labor
942. laboratory
943. lack
944. ladder
945. landscape
946. lastly
947. latter
948. launch
949. lawyer
950. lay
951. layer
952. league
953. leak
954. lean
955. leap
956. lecture
957. legal
958. legend
959. lend
960. length
961. liberal
962. liberty
963. license
964. lid
965. lightning
966. likely
967. limit
968. linguistic
969. link
970. liquid
971. literal
972. literally
973. literate
974. literature
975. litter
976. load
977. loan
978. local
979. locate
980. location
981. locker
982. logic
983. logical
984. loose
985. loosen
986. loss
987. loyal
988. luxury
989. lyric
990. magnet
991. maintain
992. major
993. majority
994. manage
995. manipulate
996. manner
997. manual
998. manufacture
999. margin
1000. mass
1001. massive
1002. master
1003. masterpiece
1004. material
1005. mature
1006. maximum
1007. mayor
1008. meaning
1009. meanwhile
1010. measure
1011. mechanic
1012. mechanical
1013. medical
1014. meditate
1015. medium
1016. melt
1017. memorable
1018. memorial
1019. memory
1020. mend
1021. mental
1022. mention
1023. mentor
1024. merchant
1025. mercy
1026. merely
1027. merit
1028. merry
1029. mess
1030. messy
1031. metal
1032. metaphor
1033. method
1034. migrate
1035. military
1036. minimize
1037. minimum
1038. minor
1039. miserable
1040. mission
1041. mixture
1042. moderate
1043. modern
1044. modest
1045. modify
1046. monitor
1047. monster
1048. mood
1049. moonlight
1050. moral
1051. moreover
1052. mostly
1053. motion
1054. motivate
1055. motto
1056. mount
1057. movement
1058. mud
1059. multiple
1060. multiply
1061. murder
1062. muscle
1063. mutual
1064. mysterious
1065. myth
1066. narrator
1067. narrow
1068. native
1069. natural
1070. navigate
1071. navy
1072. nearby
1073. necessary
1074. necessity
1075. negative
1076. neglect
1077. negotiate
1078. neighborhood
1079. nerve
1080. nervous
1081. nest
1082. net
1083. neuron
1084. neutral
1085. nevertheless
1086. newborn
1087. noble
1088. norm
1089. normal
1090. normally
1091. northern
1092. notice
1093. novel
1094. nowadays
1095. nuclear
1096. numerous
1097. nutrient
1098. obey
1099. object
1100. objective
1101. observe
1102. obstacle
1103. obtain
1104. obvious
1105. occasion
1106. occupation
1107. occupy
1108. occur
1109. odd
1110. offend
1111. offer
1112. official
1113. omit
1114. operate
1115. operation
1116. operator
1117. opinion
1118. opponent
1119. opportunity
1120. oppose
1121. opposite
1122. optimist
1123. option
1124. order
1125. ordinary
1126. organ
1127. organic
1128. organization
1129. organize
1130. orient
1131. origin
1132. original
1133. originate
1134. otherwise
1135. outcome
1136. outline
1137. output
1138. outstanding
1139. overall
1140. overcome
1141. overlap
1142. overlook
1143. overseas
1144. overwhelm
1145. owe
1146. oxygen
1147. pale
1148. panic
1149. parade
1150. paragraph
1151. parallel
1152. paralyze
1153. pardon
1154. participate
1155. particle
1156. particular
1157. partner
1158. passage
1159. passenger
1160. passion
1161. passive
1162. paste
1163. path
1164. patient
1165. pattern
1166. pause
1167. pave
1168. peaceful
1169. pedestrian
1170. peer
1171. penalty
1172. per
1173. perceive
1174. perform
1175. performance
1176. perhaps
1177. period
1178. permanent
1179. permit
1180. persist
1181. personal
1182. personality
1183. personnel
1184. perspective
1185. persuade
1186. pesticide
1187. phase
1188. phenomenon
1189. philosophy
1190. photographer
1191. phrase
1192. physical
1193. physician
1194. physics
1195. pile
1196. pillow
1197. pioneer
1198. pipe
1199. pity
1200. plain
1201. planet
1202. pleasure
1203. plenty
1204. plot
1205. plural
1206. poet
1207. poetry
1208. poison
1209. polar
1210. pole
1211. policy
1212. polish
1213. political
1214. politics
1215. poll
1216. pollute

1217. pollution
1218. popularity
1219. population
1220. portion
1221. portrait
1222. pose
1223. position
1224. positive
1225. possess
1226. possible
1227. postpone
1228. posture
1229. potential
1230. poverty
1231. powder
1232. practical
1233. pray
1234. precious
1235. precise
1236. predator
1237. predict
1238. prefer
1239. pregnant
1240. prejudice
1241. prescribe
1242. present
1243. presentation
1244. preserve
1245. press
1246. pressure
1247. pretend
1248. prevent
1249. previous
1250. prey
1251. priceless
1252. pride
1253. priest
1254. primary
1255. prime
1256. primitive
1257. principal
1258. principle
1259. prior
1260. priority
1261. privacy
1262. private
1263. privilege
1264. probably
1265. procedure
1266. proceed
1267. process
1268. produce
1269. product
1270. productive
1271. profession
1272. professional
1273. professor
1274. profit
1275. profound
1276. progress
1277. prohibit
1278. promote
1279. pronounce
1280. pronunciation
1281. proof
1282. proper
1283. properly
1284. property
1285. proportion
1286. propose
1287. prospect
1288. protect
1289. protein
1290. protest
1291. prove
1292. proverb
1293. provide
1294. psychology
1295. public
1296. publication
1297. publish
1298. punctual
1299. punish
1300. pupil
1301. purchase
1302. pure
1303. purify
1304. purpose
1305. pursue
1306. qualify
1307. quality
1308. quantity
1309. quarrel
1310. quarter
1311. quit
1312. quote
1313. racial
1314. radical
1315. rainforest
1316. raise
1317. random
1318. range
1319. rank
1320. rapid
1321. rapidly
1322. rare
1323. rarely
1324. rate
1325. rather
1326. rational
1327. raw
1328. react
1329. realistic
1330. reality
1331. realize
1332. reap
1333. reason
1334. reasonable
1335. recall
1336. receipt
1337. recent
1338. recharge
1339. reckless
1340. recognize
1341. recommend
1342. recover
1343. recreate
1344. recruit
1345. recycle
1346. reduce
1347. refer
1348. reference
1349. refine
1350. reflect
1351. reform
1352. refresh
1353. refund
1354. refuse
1355. regard
1356. region
1357. register
1358. regret
1359. regular
1360. regulate
1361. reinforce
1362. reject
1363. relate
1364. related
1365. relationship
1366. relative
1367. release
1368. relevant
1369. relief
1370. relieve
1371. religion
1372. religious
1373. rely
1374. remain
1375. remark
1376. remarkable
1377. remember
1378. remind
1379. remote
1380. remove
1381. renew
1382. repair
1383. repeat
1384. repeatedly
1385. replace
1386. reply
1387. represent
1388. representative
1389. reproduce
1390. republic
1391. reputation
1392. request
1393. require
1394. rescue
1395. research
1396. resemble
1397. resent
1398. reserve
1399. resident
1400. resign
1401. resist
1402. resolution
1403. resolve
1404. resource
1405. respect
1406. respectable
1407. respectful
1408. respective
1409. respond
1410. response
1411. responsible
1412. restore
1413. restrict
1414. retire
1415. reveal
1416. reverse
1417. revise
1418. revive
1419. revolution
1420. reward
1421. rhythm
1422. rid
1423. riddle
1424. risk
1425. ritual
1426. rob
1427. root
1428. rotate
1429. route
1430. routine
1431. row
1432. royal
1433. rub
1434. rubber
1435. rude
1436. ruin
1437. rural
1438. rush
1439. rusty
1440. sacred
1441. sacrifice
1442. safety
1443. sail
1444. satellite
1445. satisfaction
1446. satisfied
1447. satisfy
1448. saving
1449. saw
1450. saying
1451. scale
1452. scatter
1453. schedule
1454. scholar
1455. scientific
1456. scold
1457. scratch
1458. scream
1459. screen
1460. script
1461. seal
1462. secretary
1463. section
1464. secure
1465. security
1466. seed
1467. seek
1468. seize
1469. seldom
1470. select
1471. selective
1472. selfish
1473. senior
1474. sense
1475. sensible
1476. sensitive
1477. separate
1478. sequence
1479. series
1480. servant
1481. serve
1482. session
1483. setting
1484. settle
1485. several
1486. severe
1487. sew
1488. shallow
1489. shame
1490. share
1491. shave
1492. shelter
1493. shift
1494. shock
1495. shoot
1496. shore
1497. shortage
1498. shot
1499. shut
1500. sigh
1501. sight
1502. sightseeing
1503. signal
1504. signature
1505. significant
1506. silence
1507. silly
1508. similar
1509. similarity
1510. simplify
1511. simultaneously
1512. since
1513. sincere
1514. sink
1515. site
1516. situation
1517. skillful
1518. slave
1519. slice
1520. slight
1521. slightly

1522. slip
1523. slope
1524. smoke
1525. smooth
1526. sneeze
1527. snore
1528. social
1529. soil
1530. soldier
1531. solid
1532. solution
1533. somehow
1534. somewhat
1535. somewhere
1536. sore
1537. sort
1538. soul
1539. source
1540. southern
1541. sow
1542. spare
1543. sparkle
1544. specialize
1545. species
1546. specific
1547. spill
1548. spin
1549. spine
1550. spirit
1551. splendid
1552. split
1553. spoil
1554. spontaneously
1555. spot
1556. spray
1557. spread
1558. square
1559. squeeze
1560. stable
1561. staff
1562. stain
1563. stamp
1564. standard
1565. stare
1566. state
1567. statement
1568. station
1569. statue
1570. status
1571. steady
1572. steal
1573. steel
1574. steep
1575. stem
1576. stereotype
1577. stick
1578. sticky
1579. stiff
1580. stimulate
1581. sting
1582. stir
1583. stock
1584. stomachache
1585. stove
1586. straighten
1587. stranger
1588. strategy
1589. stream
1590. strength
1591. stress
1592. stretch
1593. strict
1594. strike
1595. string
1596. strip
1597. stripe
1598. stroke
1599. structure
1600. struggle
1601. studio
1602. stuff
1603. subject
1604. subjective
1605. submit
1606. substance
1607. substitute
1608. suburb
1609. succeed
1610. success
1611. successful
1612. successive
1613. sudden
1614. suffer
1615. sufficient
1616. suggest
1617. suggestion
1618. suit
1619. suitable
1620. sum
1621. summarize
1622. summary
1623. superior
1624. supervise
1625. supper
1626. supply
1627. support
1628. suppose
1629. surface
1630. surgery
1631. surprisingly
1632. surround
1633. survey
1634. survive
1635. suspect
1636. suspend
1637. suspension
1638. sustainable
1639. swallow
1640. swear
1641. sweat
1642. sweep
1643. switch
1644. symbol
1645. sympathy
1646. symptom
1647. system
1648. tag
1649. tale
1650. talented
1651. tap
1652. target
1653. task
1654. tax
1655. tease
1656. technical
1657. technician
1658. technology
1659. temper
1660. temperature
1661. temporary
1662. tend
1663. tendency
1664. tender
1665. tense
1666. tension
1667. term
1668. terrible
1669. terribly
1670. terrific
1671. territory
1672. theme
1673. theory
1674. therapy
1675. therefore
1676. thirst
1677. thoughtful
1678. thread
1679. threat
1680. threaten
1681. thrilling
1682. throat
1683. tide
1684. tidy
1685. tight
1686. tissue
1687. tolerate
1688. tomb
1689. tone
1690. totally
1691. tough
1692. trace
1693. tragedy
1694. tragic
1695. trail
1696. trait
1697. transfer
1698. transform
1699. translate
1700. transmit
1701. transport
1702. transportation
1703. trap
1704. treasure
1705. treat
1706. treatment
1707. trend
1708. trial
1709. tribe
1710. trick
1711. trigger
1712. troop
1713. tropical
1714. truly
1715. trust
1716. tune
1717. twist
1718. typhoon
1719. typical
1720. ultimate
1721. unbelievable
1722. undergo
1723. underground
1724. underwater
1725. uneasy
1726. unexpected
1727. unfortunately
1728. unhealthy
1729. unify
1730. union
1731. unique
1732. unit
1733. unite
1734. universal
1735. universe
1736. university
1737. unreasonable
1738. unusual
1739. upset
1740. upward
1741. urban
1742. urge
1743. urgent
1744. utilize
1745. vacation
1746. valid
1747. valley
1748. valuable
1749. value
1750. variable
1751. variety
1752. various
1753. vary
1754. vast
1755. vehicle
1756. version
1757. vertical
1758. vet
1759. via
1760. victim
1761. victory
1762. violate
1763. violence
1764. violent
1765. virtual
1766. virtue
1767. visible
1768. vision
1769. visitor
1770. visual
1771. vital
1772. vivid
1773. vocation
1774. voluntary
1775. volunteer
1776. wage
1777. wander
1778. warn
1779. waterproof
1780. wavy
1781. wealth
1782. weapon
1783. weed
1784. weep
1785. weigh
1786. whisper
1787. whistle
1788. whole
1789. widespread
1790. wipe
1791. wisdom
1792. wisely
1793. withstand
1794. witness
1795. wonder
1796. worship
1797. worth
1798. wound
1799. wrap
1800. yield